THE GAME PRODUCER'S HANDBOOK

Dan Irish

THOMSON

COURSE TECHNOLOGY

Professional ■ Trade ■ Reference

ISBN: 1-59200-617-5

Library of Congress Catalog Card Number: 2004114487

Printed in the United States of America

05 06 07 08 09 BH 10 9 8 7 6 5 4 3 2 1

Publisher and General Manager of Course PTR:
Stacy L. Hiquet

Associate Director of Marketing:
Sarah O'Donnell

Marketing Manager:
Heather Hurley

Manager of Editorial Services:
Heather Talbot

Senior Acquisitions Editor:
Emi Smith

Senior Editor:
Mark Garvey

Marketing Coordinator:
Jordan Casey

Project Editor:
Estelle Manticas

Copy Editors:
Estelle Manticas, Karen Annett

Technical Reviewer:
Greg Uhler

PTR Editorial Services Coordinator:
Elizabeth Furbish

Interior Layout Tech:
Susan Honeywell

Cover Designer:
Mike Tanamachi

Indexer:
Kelly Talbot

Proofreader:
Gene Redding

Thomson Course Technology PTR, a division of
Thomson Course Technology
25 Thomson Place
Boston, MA 02210
http://www.courseptr.com

*This book is dedicated to every manager
who ever believed in me enough to hire me.
Each of you has contributed to
this book, my career, and to the products I've produced.*

FOREWORD

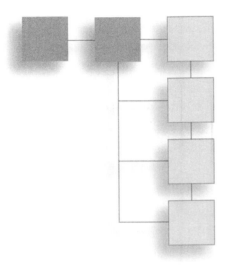

by Dave Perry

Back at the start of the video game business, there really was no need to have producers. It was usually a one-man show. One guy was the producer-designer-programmer-artist-business manager-animator-audio director-tester. You even had to make your own cup of tea and lick your own postage stamps!

Our industry, however, began on a relentless journey forward—not just expanding in size, but growing in quality and in reach. Around the world, gamers were demanding more immersive, more complex, and more exciting games. When they got what they wanted, they would reward the development team with massive sales (now rivaling the same kind of retail sales numbers that blockbuster feature movies generate).

Teams began to grow from one to two people, then two to four, then four to 10, and so on. Now teams comprise 30 to 60 people or even 100 to 200 people. That creates a lot of overhead and is several magnitudes more complex than when the industry was born.

Once any team grows beyond 10 people, our industry accepts that managing this team successfully requires the guidance of a producer. As that team of 10 people becomes 50, even the producer needs help! We've seen producers re-group, re-organize, earn respect, raise their value, and create more production roles. Production is now a department that is vital to the creation of any high-end video game.

Hollywood producers give a hint of where game industry production is going. They can pull together massive budgets (up to 10 times what we spend on the average game today) and—with about 400 people pulling together—an incredible experience, in the same amount of time that it takes to make a game.

Will it ever get that difficult for game-industry producers? I think even more so! Personally, I see a future where a merging of all types of media companies becomes commonplace. The job of producer will be critically valued, even more complex, and very highly rewarded for those who generate hits.

Colleges around the country are now offering courses and degrees in Video Game Production. You have a head start, as you now have a guide for students, beginners, and even seasoned professionals in your hands.

On that note, I congratulate Dan Irish on this first edition of *The Game Producer's Handbook*. I think it will be an invaluable resource for game producers for years to come and I thank him for the incredible amount of dedication and effort he has spent making this book available. It's my favorite work on this subject to date, and therefore I highly recommend it.

Thanks, Dan!

David Perry
President, Shiny Entertainment Inc.
http://www.dperry.com
http://www.shiny.com

This "DavidPerry - Recommended" logo is my personal stamp of approval, awarded only to extremely key projects, games, and books related to video game development. You can be certain that you will not see it often, and when you do, you should know that I highly recommend this product. —*David Perry*

ACKNOWLEDGMENTS

The author would like to thank the following individuals, without whose contribution this book would not have been possible.

Aaron Marks	Jason Della Rocca	Curtis Terry
Adam Carpenter	Kirsten Duvall	Ron Moravek
Adam Kahn	Lance Davis	Rusty Rueff
Alessandro Tento	Luke Moloney	Sheri Poclujko
Alex Garden	Mark Baxter	Stephane Morichere-Matte
Brad Anthony	Mark Cerney	Steve Schnur
Brooke Burgess	Michel Giasson	Stuart Roch
Craig Allsop	Michel Kripalani	Tabitha Hayes
Daniel Achterman	Mike Ryder	Tracey Rosenthal-Newsom
Dave Perry	Nick Waanders	Emi Smith
Geoff Thomas	Otto Ottoson	Estelle Manticas
Glenn Entis	Parker Davis	Sue Honeywell
Greg Uhler	Rich Goldman	Gene Redding
Jaap Suter	Clyde Grossman	Special thanks to Rich Robinson at VUG for sharing his version of the Risk Management worksheets and templates here.
Jack Wall	Trenton Lipscomb	
Jamie Fristom	Cort Buchholz	

ABOUT THE AUTHOR

DAN IRISH is formerly Executive Producer at Relic Entertainment, where he was responsible for *Homeworld2*, the sequel to the 1999 Game of the Year, *Homeworld*. Prior to working at Relic Entertainment, he was the producer responsible for the *Myst/Riven* franchise at Mattel Interactive and UbiSoft Entertainment, where he produced or started development of several *Myst*-related products, including *realMyst, Myst III: Exile,* and *Myst IV: Revelation.* Prior to working at Mattel Interactive, he held positions at Rocket Science Games, Spectrum HoloByte, and SegaSoft. He has also consulted on a number of interactive entertainment opportunities for such clients as DreamWorks Interactive, Evans & Sutherland's Digital Theater Division, Game Audio Network Guild, Auran Games, and Hanbitsoft.

Dan is also a published author with several books in print from Random House, Sybex, Pearson Publishing, and Thomson Course Technology.

CONTENTS

INTRODUCTION

Writing a book has a number of similarities to making a video game. There's never enough time or opportunity to include all the content that you want; there's always a way to make it more concise, fun, and interesting; there's a ton of people giving their opinions in how to make it better; and there's always a new deadline.

Who Should Read This Book?

This book is about how a video game producer needs to be a leader in the true sense—the person who helps game visionaries realize their vision. If you're a game visionary wanting to find someone to help execute and realize your vision, then read ahead and learn about what an excellent video game producer can do for you.

This book only scrapes the surface of what a career in the game industry holds. If you want a job where the same day is never lived twice—and where the days of being bored at work are gone forever—then read on. Few other jobs in few other industries can offer such a reward, and this book can help you realize that reward.

If you're a producer already in the game industry or other industry professional, you may find a few tips or tricks that you've not tried yet in this book. Or maybe you'll find one bit of advice that makes your next game better and the process of making it more efficient. You may also achieve a fuller understanding of the role of the game producer—an understanding that makes your job easier, better, and more rewarding. Despite being in the industry for more than 10 years, there's a lot that I still don't know. Every day is an opportunity to learn something new—maybe the same is true for you. But after the few hard lessons from the past I decided to put the little I know about the industry, along with the helpful tips from many others, into this book.

What's in This Book?

This book addresses the following topics:

- What a video game producer does and what types of producer roles exist.
- The common challenges faced by producers.
- How to facilitate the creation of excellent design documentation.
- The creation of proprietary game development tools, licensing of third-party software, and procedures for asset management and source control.
- Managing milestones and milestone creation.
- How a producer effectively conveys a winning video game vision.
- Financial aspects that govern a producer's decisions.
- How a video game producer's role relates to game design.
- How to produce an excellent soundtrack and why music is as important as the graphics.
- How to manage all of the materials needed to market your game.

How to Use the Appendices

Included at the back of this book are hypothetical examples of what some documents mentioned in the book might look like. Do realize that no one document is right for all projects and companies; each document should be personalized for the special circumstances of your project.

- Appendix A, "Sample Acceptance Letter," is an example of a publisher's acceptance letter that provides detailed feedback on a submitted milestone.
- Appendix B, "Engine Feature Checklist," offers a way to double-check that the technical design includes the features that are required for most games' engines.
- Appendix C, "Marketing Deliverables Checklist," is the checklist that all producers should review with the marketing department so that they are clear on when certain materials are needed for marketing to do their job.
- Appendix D, "Producer Tools," comprises several tools. Check the Course PTR Web site @ http://www.courseptr.com/downloads for periodic updates to these tools.
  - The Milestone Acceptance Test is a checklist that's used to make it easier for developers to submit complete milestones to publishers. The developer provides this checklist to the publisher for use when reviewing the milestone.
  - The Milestone Deliverable Checklist is used to ensure that all of the elements of the milestone are assigned to the responsible party and completed before the milestone is due.

- The Art Status Sheet is an example of a spreadsheet used to track the status of the art assets in a game.
- The Sound Content Sheet mirrors the purpose of the Art Status Sheet and allows the tracking of the sound content for a game.
- The Risk Management Plan provides a procedure to follow when assessing and managing risk.
- Appendix E, "What Goes into a Milestone Definition?" includes an example of a hypothetical milestone schedule showing the detail required to ensure clarity.

Where Are We Headed?

Today, the video game industry shares a uniquely similar background with rock and roll. The leading-edge, technology-driven, youthful force of rock and roll born in decades past have immortalized themselves in our new medium. The current youth generation embraces the video game medium—its art, content, and fun—while governments scrutinize and cast a wary eye on its artistic expression, interactive stories, dramatic combat, and stunning visuals.

For those of you who are—or who want to be—the Bob Dylan-style storytellers of the 21st century, Elvis Presleys of interactive entertainment, or even the John Lennons of compelling gameplay content, remember that just as in the recording industry, it takes a good producer to help a vision materialize into excellence. And if it is your company that helps to bring these products to market, hopefully your producers are the ones fostering those who have the ideas of tomorrow.

The game industry is still young. Founded just three decades ago, the evolution of the video game industry continues today, while the race to maturity is still far from over. The breadth of the appeal is constantly growing with each new game. By exploring ways to expand as well as to take compelling experiences to new depths, we get one step closer to that maturity.

Few other jobs, industries, or media formats offer an opportunity to constantly try something new, reach out to new people in new ways, and inspire the development of new art forms. While it is likely that we'll never fully explore the bounds of this opportunity, remember the timeless words of Goethe, "Whatever you can do, or dream you can, begin it."

Now you can "begin it" by turning the page.

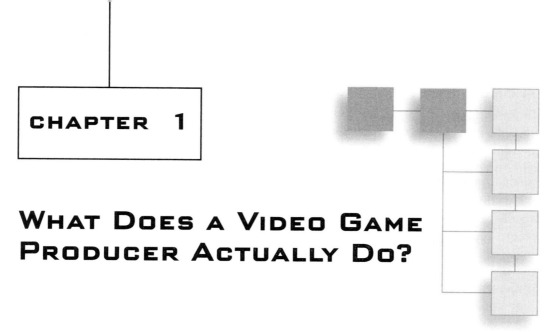

CHAPTER 1

WHAT DOES A VIDEO GAME PRODUCER ACTUALLY DO?

As you've purchased this book, you're probably eager to get straight to the point. I'll get straight to detailing just what a game producer actually does, because for many people (both inside and outside the video game industry), it is a mystery.

So just what does a video game producer actually do? As outlined by Dave Perry during his keynote speech at the 2004 Game Developer's Conference, a video game producer is the person

- Whose primary focus is on the delivery of the video game as a completed project.
- Who knows every person on the team by his or her first name.
- Who works late with the team and is available to provide guidance whenever necessary, any time, day or night.
- Who clearly communicates with anyone who can affect the game, positively or negatively, as it is the game producer's responsibility to bring everyone into the fold of game production.
- Who runs interference with anyone who can affect the game or otherwise sidetrack the product.
- Who does everything possible to sell, promote, and protect the game *and* the team.
- Who has the complete confidence that he or she can cross any obstacle and face any challenge.
- Who does whatever it takes to help the team deliver the game.

A Brief History of Producing

In traditional media and the entertainment business, a *producer* is one who assembles the cast of a play, brings an artist or talent to a studio, or organizes a publicly broadcasted event. The producer has an all-encompassing role; that is, he or she takes primary responsibility for the completion of the event, project, or program. Specifically, the role of a movie or television producer included casting, hiring a director, finding the script, handling contracts, distributing the finished product, financing, scheduling, location management, promotion, marketing, and PR (Public Relations). Similarly, the role of the record producer, an occupation that emerged with the popularity of the phonograph, involved finding talent, hiring the recording studio, securing the distribution and financing from a record publisher, promotion and PR events, as well as contracts and legal agreements for the artist, writers, and musicians.

In the 21st century, the role of producer has evolved, as new mediums of entertainment—most notably, interactive entertainment—have emerged. Today, the role of a video game producer may include all of the responsibilities of a television, movie, or record producer, plus a lot more. Indeed, interactive entertainment includes many aspects and challenges not faced by traditional movie, television, or record producers—for example, finding ways to include new rendering technology or the ideal set of game-development tools for specific product type; devising ways to ensure that the core compelling gameplay is clearly focused, communicated by the Design team, and included into the game's development; or ensuring that a highly addictive and compelling entertainment experience is outlined in the design documentation.

The Diverse Role of a Video Game Producer

If excellence is your goal as a video game producer, expect to experience many challenges. This section is designed to introduce the various types of diverse challenges you can expect to face as a video game producer, as well as some of the common responsibilities enjoyed by any producer, regardless of medium. They appear here in alphabetical order, not in order of importance. After reviewing this list, you should have a basic understanding of some of the challenges faced by producers and what their daily work consists of. As you'll see, a producer requires a wide variety of skills, experiences, and knowledge to meet the challenges they face on a daily basis. Although not every producer position is the same, nor does every producer face all these challenges, it is likely that during the course of your career as a producer, you'll find that every circumstance, skill, or trait listed here will prove valuable.

Actively Contribute

A producer contributes to the team effort, vision, and work required to complete the game. This means that the producer just does not sit in his or her office reworking the Microsoft Project schedule all day, but actively participates in team meetings, design meetings, problem solving, and design ideas, and makes decisions when required. The contribution of the producer should be seamlessly integrated into that of the team, providing the oil that keeps the team running smoothly.

Apply Good Decision-Making Skills

It may seem obvious that good decision making is a critical aspect of game producing. After all, who wants to make bad decisions? The problem is, you can't really know whether a decision is a good one or a bad one until after it's been made, hence the saying, "Hindsight is 20/20." *Good decision making* here refers more to the *process* of making decisions than the decisions themselves. Indeed, there may well be times when it is better to make a decision, even if it's wrong, than to endlessly delay on deciding or to flip-flop on the decision after it has been made.

Specifically, *good decision making* refers to the process of securing all relevant information, asking for recommendations and advice from other stakeholders, setting a deadline before which the decision must be made, and then making the decision and announcing it and the reasoning behind it to all who are involved. Even if a decision is wrong, following this process ensures that the team has an adequately clear direction during the course of developing the game and instills confidence in others about the producer. As an added bonus, if the reasoning behind the decision is sound, then the decision will be right the majority of the time. Of course, no one is a perfect decision maker, but not following a clear decision-making process only compounds the chance that a bad decision will be made for the wrong reasons—and worse, after much delay.

Attend Budget Meetings

At budget meetings, the producer must explain the status of the budget, accounting for how much money has been spent on the project and how much more needs to be spent on the game in order to complete it on time. This may often include an analysis of the profit-and-loss (P&L) statement for the project (or brand).

Be Forward-Thinking

Forward thinking means looking and reasoning ahead—one day, one week, or one month ahead—so that there is no opportunity for a problem to suddenly present itself as an obstacle to completion of the game. This includes investigating and finding ways to solve problems *before* they affect the game's development. Licensing the game-development tools and securing the rights to use third-party software in the game are excellent examples of the forward thinking that is required of a producer.

Other fundamental decisions related to the game's development include the minimum system specifications for the game, what video card it will support, or the number of platforms on which the game will be released. A producer must consider all the issues that can potentially affect a game's development and weigh them in a forward-thinking manner.

Build Consensus

Seeking to build a consensus whenever possible is generally one of the best ways to ensure a harmonious relationship within a team. Building confidence in the team by asking their opinions when forming a decision is one of the ways to build a consensus. Getting others to believe in your ideas as if they were their own is the principle behind building a consensus.

Sometimes a hard decision must be made, one that not everyone agrees with. But before getting to that point, do your best to build a consensus and take other's recommendations. Getting people to reach an agreement as a whole is generally a tough challenge.

Deliver Animation

While a video game is mostly about gameplay, a video game producer is often charged with delivering specific animations for the game to help convey the story, provide content for the marketing campaign or both. The demands created by being responsible for delivering both gameplay and animation simultaneously and in concert with the other requires an extreme amount of enthusiasm for the project. Creating a specially rendered movie trailer for marketing purposes is another good example of divergent tasks that a producer must balance against the other. In each case, whether the animation is used for marketing, in the game, or both, a producer must work closely with the art director and the animator to ensure that the animation is completed on time, is appropriate for the game, and uses conventional film techniques to show the progression of the story and how it relates to gameplay.

Develop a Pre-Production Plan

The producer must develop a *pre-production plan*, which is the foundation on which the game's overall development rests. In the pre-production plan, the producer works with the team leaders to establish the critical paths for completing the product and determines the recommended course of action for accomplishing their goals.

Pre-production is the time when the Game Development team prepares to make the game and lays the groundwork for that goal. Ideally, when the team begins production, all of the goals are clearly defined and the course is set.

Pre-production is also used to test and refine art export pipelines and game design documentation, as well as to establish the art asset listing for the game. Detailing the art, design, and feature requirements for the game and including them into a schedule is also part of this process.

tip

Often, I recommend completing a prototype or mini-game during pre-production that establishes itself as a test case for the real game that you're making. In addition to costing less than the final product, doing so enables team members to learn a tremendous amount about the process and to make adjustments as needed before undertaking development on a larger project.

Develop a Production Plan

Just as the producer must develop a pre-production plan, he or she must also develop a production plan, which is the actual documents or set of documents that comprise the plan for the game's development. Although a plan is often believed to remove uncertainty, in reality, the production plan is simply the best estimate of how the game is to be completed. The production plan consists of several smaller plans describing all the elements of the game and how they are going to be completed. This includes plans from each team involved in game creation, including designers, artists, and programmers. The production plan brings these different documents together, enabling interested parties to review the project as a whole, with an understanding of risks, the required budget, a feature list, the schedule, and art assets.

Specifically, a production plan consists of the following documents:

- **Essence statement or executive summary.** Simply put, this document outlines why the game is fun.
- **Creative design document.** This document outlines the creative and artistic vision for the game.
- **Technical design document.** This document outlines the required features of the game as described in the creative design document.
- **Risk-management plan.** This document outlines what the risks are and how to minimize them.
- **Schedule for development.** This can be a detailed schedule or just a monthly milestone schedule.
- **Budget and financial requirements.** This document outlines monthly cost allocations, capital expenditures, and the like.

Generate Game-Design Documentation

The producer must work with the Design team to clarify the game-design documentation and ensure that it is easily producible and cohesive. Game designers have an inherent predisposition to create overly complicated, complex, and disjointed designs, that may require a lot of development time to fix. Game designers are supposed to do this, but the producer's role is to help guide them back to the course of what is producible, possible, and still fun.

Handle Hardware Manufacturers

The producer is the key contact for hardware manufacturers such as Intel, NVIVIDA, ATI, Creative Labs, Microsoft, and console manufacturers like Sony, Nintendo and Microsoft's Xbox. The role of the producer in this context is to develop and maintain good relationships with the representatives of these hardware manufacturers, ensuring that the Game Development team has access to the latest hardware, drivers, technical support, and knowledge required to use the hardware to its fullest potential. This includes obtaining evaluation or pre-release versions of video cards and sound cards, as well as production versions, and ensuring compatibility with the widest range of hardware products, peripherals, and console add-ons, such as steering wheels, pedals, dance pads, or maracas (in the case of *Samba De Amigo*).

Handle Legal/Contractual Issues

A working knowledge of the law related to contracts and business litigation is often required of a producer. Although you're certainly going to have access to the advice of lawyers and other professionals, you need to understand the fundamental principles of contract law, civil litigation, intellectual property ownership, as well as the basic legal principles that go into contracts, such as exclusive and non-exclusive licenses. Although your first project as a producer may not require this knowledge, the longer you're a producer, the more likely it becomes that this knowledge will be very important.

Handle Licensing and Branding

Licensing includes developing and managing the relationship between the licensee and how the product's development evolves when created under license. *Branding* refers to the overall vision for a product (either within a licensed brand or an original brand) such that the product is consistent with the vision for the brand and supports the main strengths of the brand and the brand's development. A brand is a very important part of software marketing, as it includes the distinctive name identifying the product and the manufacturer. A producer must grasp the vision and concept behind both a license and the brand when managing the development of a video game using either or both.

Handle Middleware Issues

Middleware issues refers to the issues and challenges that face the Game Development team when they're using middleware tools, such as those provided by Criterion Software or Gamebryo. These middleware tools give game developers a standard set of tools and features to use in a limited variety of game genres. When the game design calls for a specific feature set or implementation beyond what the middleware can support, the producer must be able to understand and resolve the issues with the middleware. This can be done by contacting the middleware provider and asking for support or by licensing another third-party toolset to provide the required functionality for the game designers and world builders. Other times, it may not be that easy to solve, which is why the producer must devise a range of alternative solutions and help pick what's best for the game.

Handle Platform Transition

Platform transition refers to the period of time in the video game industry when an existing console platform is currently entrenched in the market and doing well but a new console is being readied for commercial release. During this period, game development for consoles becomes extremely challenging because the hardware for the new console plat form has often not been finalized, nor have video game developers been provided with development kits (specialized computer hardware for this new platform). The platform-transition period requires forward thinking on the part of a producer to facilitate the delivery of the hardware and flexibility in the game's design—not to mention the development schedule.

Handle Public Relations

Public relations involve meeting the press and presenting a pre-release version of the game for demonstration and evaluation. This requires time for a press tour, excellent speaking abilities, a well-honed message, and passionate enthusiasm for the project. Public relations are an ongoing responsibility of the producer—he must provide interviews, screenshots, and related material to ensure interest in the game in development. Excellent interpersonal skills are required when working with a representative of the Public Relations department at the publisher.

Handle Quality Assurance

Many producers, associate producers, and assistant producers are charged with the responsibility of overseeing the quality assurance and testing efforts for their games. In certain cases, this involves interfacing directly with hands-on testers who work with the Game Development team, or with a Quality Assurance department, with the liaison being through the lead tester or QA department managers. Working with the Quality Assurance department is challenging and stressful, yet is rewarding as the Game Development team fixes bugs and gets the product closer to completion. Database management is often required to input and track bugs properly.

Help Sales

The producer does everything he or she possibly can to help the sales of the video game. This includes meetings with the Sales department, buyers, and Marketing and PR departments, as well as working trade shows. The top-selling products require excellent support from their producers so that everyone involved in selling the product into the market will clearly understand the vision behind the game, and know why it is exciting and compelling. Clearly communicating that message to the sales channel, the industry, and the consumer is an extremely large part of a game's success.

Hire/Interview

The producer is largely responsible for hiring new members of the Game Development team. Of course, there are exceptions, but generally the producer is responsible for screening candidates and ensuring that they will work well with the rest of the team. Finding potential or new team members who will shine is a skill that every producer must develop if he or she is to be successful in the long term. The hiring and interview process usually includes programmer tests, designer questionnaires, in-person interviews, and phone screening. Some producers are responsible for salary negotiations, but all are responsible for ensuring that they hire the right people for the right job on the right team, and that everyone on that team will be able to work well with the new team member.

Interact with Upper (Executive) Management

A producer will often have the opportunity to work directly with upper management personnel and influence their decisions. Honing of this skill is very important because it affects everyone who works with you and, ultimately, your career as a producer. Understanding how executives evaluate opportunities, manage risks, and determine the right course of action is key.

Know Games

The producer must be one of the foremost authorities on video games. This means that the producer must apply his or her knowledge of games and understanding of why games are fun to the current project. Being able to discuss design principles with the Design team, articulate an artistic vision from a competing product, or critique a specific feature set in comparison to the overall market with the programmers are all examples of when a producer's knowledge of video games will be extremely useful.

Learn

Always look for new ways to improve methods, find efficiencies, improve best practices, and otherwise expand the learning opportunities for yourself as well as for the team. Referring to previous experience or knowledge as the ultimate resources limits the effectiveness of a producer. With emerging technology and development processes, producers should always be looking for ways to expand their learning capabilities and opportunities.

Manage Assets

Asset management is the process and method of managing the thousands of assets that must come together to complete a video game. This includes art assets such as models, textures, interface elements, menu screens, cinematic sequences, and special renders. On the design side, this includes world-building tools, multiplayer design, functionality specifications, use cases, story, script, core gameplay, and adherence to the game's essence statement. On the programming side, this can include tools, functionality, export pipelines, and documentation. Lastly, but certainly not least, asset management involves management of outside delivery of content such as voiceover recording, sound effects, music (ambient and linear), localization (including all the sound and text assets for several different languages), and the creation and delivery of marketing and PR materials for the game.

Manage Big Teams

Managing big teams is a massive challenge and presents its own unique set of challenges, such as the coordination of export pipelines, feature-set integration, and asset tracking. Indeed, merely communicating with your team becomes inherently more difficult when it is comprised of 60 to 100 people, as compared to a team of 30 or 40. The trick here is to break down the large team into several smaller teams and delegate responsibility for managing those smaller teams to other producers. Most importantly, focus on finding the people who work well together and put them in charge of key systems. They'll set the example in terms of productivity and efficiency for others.

Manage Foreign Localization

Foreign localization refers to the process of creating a game in one language and then localizing its content to apply in many worldwide markets. For example, most games are developed in English and then localized to German, Italian, or French. Generally, this means managing the process of including thousands of individual files that have an alternative language's voiceover, artwork, or menu screens in the game before it ships to retail stores. Creating product for worldwide markets is required for almost all successful video games. The localization process is often complicated and time consuming, and requires an excruciating attention to detail and a sound localization management process.

Manage Resources

Resource management refers to deciding when and where resources should be allocated. Obviously, every task cannot be done at the same time, so tasks should be prioritized, and then resources should be assigned to complete that task. This process of resource allocation often requires constant re-evaluation and adjustment in order to ensure that resources are properly allocated across a project that includes dozens of people and often spans several years.

Manage the Art Process

A producer must manage the process of creating artwork for the game. This includes tracking art assets as they are completed and identifying the art assets that are incomplete. Often, art-production resources will need to be reallocated to ensure that the art schedule stays on track. The role of the producer is to work with the Art team to manage this process and to plan for the appropriate risks.

Manage the Audio Process

This topic could be an entire job of itself. Producing audio involves managing the audio contractors who provide voiceover recordings, editing, sound effects, and music (both ambient and linear tracks), as well as mixing or recording in studio if that is required. Being able to produce audio and understand the impact of the sounds and music on the visual is as much an art as it is a science.

Manage Vendor Relationships

Managing vendor relationships is often overlooked and undervalued, but a producer often must contract with outside companies to provide key services that go into the game's development. Products or services provided by outside vendors include software support for 3D modeling applications (such as 3D Studio Max, Maya, and Lightwave), sound libraries, or even third-party software tools such as Incredibuild from Xoreax Software. Even computer manufacturers like Alienware have helped supply hardware used in the development of the games I've produced. Each of these vendor relationships is important.

Often, producers use vendors and contractors on multiple productions once they've developed a good working relationship. As the relationships are maintained, these vendors and contractors are easy to use on the next project, allowing you to skip the process of looking for a qualified vendor who can help make your game.

Manage Your Time

Time management is perhaps the most fundamental aspect of being a producer. Indeed, time management is the single biggest factor that affects whether a game is cancelled. Why? Because the one finite element in game development is time. It is impossible to make time go backward, but it is always possible to spend more money on a game, or to sacrifice the quality of a game. Time management is the process and method of allocating resources on a project to ensure that they have the most effective and efficient impact on the project within the timeline allocated for the project.

Pitch

Pitching is the ability to sell an idea or a concept—specifically, the game concept and development plan. When pitching a game, the producer must be the salesperson for that game to everyone who is listening, whether they be executive management, the publisher, or the press. A successful pitch requires a producer who is excited and passionate about his or her product and can effectively convey that excitement and passion to others so that they agree to buy the product. A game rarely gets off the ground without a good pitch.

Possess Industry Experience

Industry experience is important because it provides an accurate frame of reference for a producer. It should be noted that although there are some similarities, experience in the video game industry is unlike experience in the general entertainment industry. Having never lived the same day twice, an experienced producer in the video game industry is much more likely to be able to effectively problem-solve the common and uncommon challenges that every software project faces. The more years of experience a producer has, especially when coupled with projects on a variety of hardware platforms, the more valuable he or she will be. Experience on a variety of projects sizes is also valuable, as large projects have different problems than do small projects.

Provide Clarity and Focus

Clarity and *focus* refer here to the producer's understanding of the game and the compelling experience it provides to the user. With all the daunting tasks that lie in the path of a game's successful development, providing clarity on which are the most important is critical. Focus on the most important and high-risk tasks first. When the situation becomes daunting, with programming, art, and design requirements apparently on divergent paths, the producer's ability to provide clarity of the final goals of the project, and generate focus to that end, may save the game.

Provide Marketing Support

Providing support to the Marketing department is a challenging task for even the best producers. Demands for marketing assets, like screenshots, special renders, reviews of box cover artwork, magazine ad copy, and sell sheet reviews are just a few of the demands that the Marketing department places on the Game Development team. As a producer, the challenge is to find the best way to deliver these assets and information to marketing without affecting the team or sidetracking their development efforts to make a great game.

Schedule

Scheduling combines the skills discussed under "Time Management" and "Resource Management," and puts them into a plan that is presentable to others and easily understood. Often, updating the schedule can be a large part of a producer's role. Learning to master Microsoft's Excel, Project or even Access is an important part of managing the schedule.

Sow Discipline

Electronic Arts is one of the leaders in today's video game industry. Why? Because EA embraces a disciplined approach to software development and applies it to all areas of its business. Indeed, one of the most critical factors in the success of an organization is the discipline that it applies to its business and production methods. Positive discipline is an important part of an organization, because it ensures the business's long-term success.

As a producer, you can sow the seeds of discipline by doing the following:

1. Set goals for people and encourage them to succeed. Writing down these goals and offering rewards when they are achieved encourages your employees to do even better.

2. Obtain commitments from each team member to accomplish these goals. Obtaining commitments ensures that everyone understands your expectations and agrees to meet those expectations.

3. As work progresses, measure progress and benchmark results from one group against others who are tasked with similar roles. Note the progress of the team and its members, and identify when work can be done more efficiently or effectively.

4. Hold others accountable for their actions and their commitments, especially if they do not seek help when struggling with a task. Of course, several outside influences, external factors, complications, and challenges affect people's ability to complete work, but there are also many avenues to help them achieve their goals and overcome those challenges.

SMART Goals

SMART Goals is a slick acronym for goals that are

- **Specific.** Be as specific as possible when establishing your goals. Clarity is king in this regard. It's hard to motivate people to complete goals that are non-specific, and even harder to measure their results.

- **Measurable.** Measurable results are what matter. Finishing the project report by Friday or finalizing the functional specifications for the game's design by the end of the month are both measurable and concrete examples.

- **Acceptable.** Set your own goals. No one knows your capabilities better than you do. Determine what is acceptable for your own standards and then live up to or exceed them.

- **Realistic.** Don't plan for a lot of accomplishments if you know that only a few are really possible. Focus on a few big goals rather than many smaller ones.

- **Time bound.** Define when you want your goals to be completed as well as when you're going to have the time to work on them. If you write it down now, it is a lot easier to make it actually happen.

Take Ownership

When a producer *takes ownership*, it means that he or she has a personal sense of pride and accomplishment associated with his or her work and that of the team. *Ownership* refers not to taking credit for the work accomplished, but making it your goal to remove obstacles so that the work can be accomplished. A producer who doesn't take full ownership of his area or set of responsibilities is generally not very effective. Taking ownership of a project, game, or team must be balanced with an objective view of the game's development progress, goals, and marketplace conditions. A producer cannot take ownership for a project without regard for the external factors that affect a game.

Teach Others

Being able to teach others is another required skill. Because communication is a principal part of the job, producers must be able to communicate their knowledge, lessons, and experience to others on the team. Often, simply being able to explain the situation or circumstance or to answer questions from team members ensures that problems within the team are addressed before a noticeable impact on the team's productivity occurs. Being able to share the rationale behind a decision in a clear, concise way shows the team that decisions are not made arbitrarily. Other times, the producer may be called upon to integrate a new team member and teach him new procedures, methods, or best practices that will make his work more efficient. These types of situations require a producer to share his or her knowledge and to be able to teach to those who are willing to learn.

Understand Cinematic Production

Cinematic production includes the storyboarding, animatic creation, and actual rendering or filming of a game's cinematic sequences. These are the sequences that tie the story together with the gameplay for the user. A working knowledge of or a background in film direction, scene composition, lighting techniques, script, relevance to gameplay, and music scored to visual are important to success in this area.

Understand Development Systems

Development systems refers to the specialized computers required by game developers that allow development on proprietary platforms or game consoles such as the Xbox, Playstation 2, or Nintendo GameCube. Often, these hardware systems are difficult to procure; it is the responsibility of the producer to secure their delivery for the team. Only a limited amount of game development can be done on normal workstations without the use of a development system that emulates the actual hardware for which the game is designed and developed.

Work with the Programming Team

The producer must work with the Programming team to establish key goals early on in the development process and then ensure that the programmers have all the tools they need to succeed. Throughout the development process, a producer's job is to track progress, understand dependencies between workloads and features, establish critical milestones, and help solve (non-technical) problems for the programmers.

Software-Production Methods

All games are not alike, and neither are the methods used to create them. Indeed, there are several ways to develop a video game. This section discusses how some of the common software-production methods are applied. Along the way, you'll get an overview of how a video game comes together and how the process is managed. Further on in the book, I'll discuss the specifics of each portion of the game in more detail: what tools you as a producer can use to keep a project on track and how to apply them.

Code-Like-Hell, Fix-Like-Hell

The *code-like-hell, fix-like-hell* method of game software development, shown in Figure 1.1, is probably the most common and oldest model. Some advance planning is done, but rarely is it followed, updated, or referenced. Programmers code as quickly as they can to implement what they think the design calls for; it is then tested and fixed. This model is prone to failure because of the stressful situations that arise during the development. Programmers cannot work at a constantly frenetic pace, nor can designers and testers. As a result, this process breaks down over time. It leaves room for error, and those errors aren't fixed until after somebody finds them, at which point the code is further along than it was when the errors or bugs were introduced. This model is generally only suited for small projects with simple requirements because the code is difficult to maintain over a longer period (six or more months). This method is also referred to as the *extreme game development method* or the *XP method* and is shown in Figure 1.1.

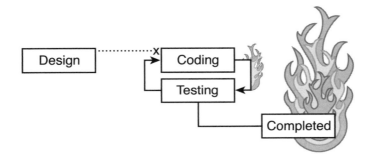

Figure 1.1
The code-like-hell, fix-like-hell approach.

Increments to Completion

Increments to completion is the software-production method that calls for the software to be developed in relatively compact, finite increments. Developing an adventure or first-person shooter (FPS) game using this process might work because once the world engine and tools exist, every piece of the game is simply an increment added to the original core. As the pieces come together from various parts of the team, they are checked against the high-level design document. The specifications of the design and the key requirements of the game are outlined in this high-level documentation, but low-level documentation is not completed until just before or just after the feature is implemented—usually when the designers and the programmers agree on what is possible with a feature and how it should be implemented.

One advantage of using the increments-to-completion model, shown in Figure 1.2, is that various features of the game can be developed in parallel or independently of the rest of the game's parts. This is often good in theory, but it is more challenging in practice to implement successfully without a high degree of coordination and easily modifiable code structures. Although the benefits of this model are not always outweighed by the detractions, a producer should consider that using this model often allows the team to demonstrate a playable game early on in the development process and continually progress as different systems, features, and artwork become available for integration into the game. Often, lessons learned from the first increments (such as a prototype phase) turn out to be quite helpful in the long run.

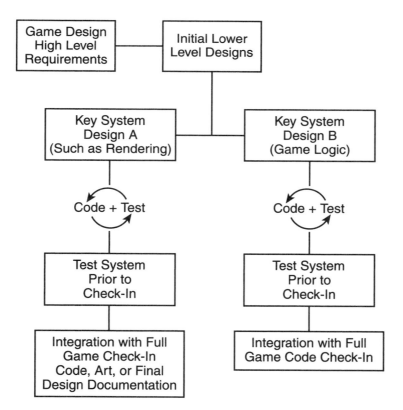

Figure 1.2
The increments-to-completion approach.

The Cascade

Cascade is used to describe an approach in which the entire team focuses on the next part or parts as one part of the game is completed (see Figure 1.3). Under this approach, parts of the game come together relatively quickly with little time for testing between feature creation and implementation. There is often a need to review and revise a previous part of the game because as more parts are added to it, the function, appearance, or intended usefulness of a particular feature may change. It is difficult to change major parts or systems of a game when using this model, and it requires that everything go correctly right from the start. For this reason, this method is not recommended for use in game development.

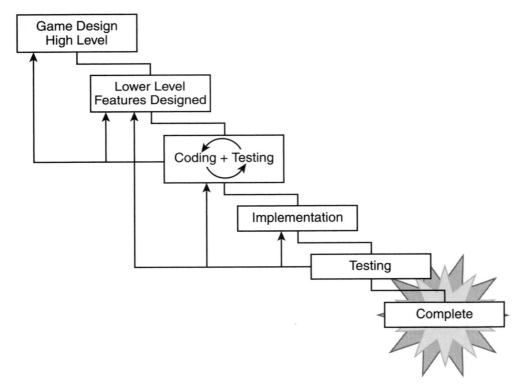

Figure 1.3
The cascade approach.

Iterate Until You Drop

The *iterate-until-you-drop* method is probably the most flexible software-production method in that its entire purpose is to help you, the producer, define the key areas of the game, begin developing them, and then finalize the game's design partway through the development process. This is often beneficial when a game developer is unsure what features will be included with competing products that are scheduled to be released around the same time. It allows the Game Development team to respond to changing market forces or demand, providing the flexibility to quickly implement working code such that the team, the publisher, and the game designers can iterate the fun factor of the game (meaning make the game more fun as they play it more and include more and more gameplay refinements with iteration). This is shown in Figure 1.4. As a generally useful process, iteratation is a process not to be undervalued. Especially when you consider the number of games that have been published in the history of software development that aren't fun.

This method is often useful and is sometimes recommended when the producer has the appropriate tools and understands the methodologies behind object-oriented code and software development. Sometimes, however, a situation's biggest strength can be its biggest drawback when it is not managed effectively. For example, most game designs fail to fully specify a complete list of the elements that make the game fun. Often times, the most fun part of the game isn't realized until the game comes together in some pre-release form. The iterate-until-you-drop method becomes exactly that: a never-ending treadmill of software development that can always be improved. Adapting to changing requirements is the critical benefit of this method. It is the producer's role to ensure that this method doesn't get out of control or become a justification for ever-expanding budgets and development timelines.

When using this method, keep in mind that using the proper tools and tactical methods is critical to completing the project without going over budget or investing many, many years in the same game.

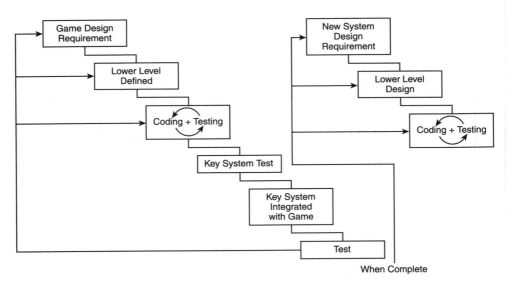

Figure 1.4
The iterate-until-you-drop approach.

Agile Project Management

In *Agile Project Management* (Pearson Publishing, 2004), author Jim Highsmith discusses an excellent method for combining the best of the iterate-until-you-drop approach with a few key principles that every producer should respect. I've provided the gist of Highsmith's ideas here because agile project management is a principle referenced throughout this book.

Agile project management, an excellent process for organized and disciplined teams, centers on the following key stages of software development:

- Envision
- Speculate
- Explore
- Adapt
- Finalize

n o t e

The name of each stage of the process references both the activities and the intended results of the stage. Highsmith avoids terms like initiate, plan, and direct because these terms are associated with a prediction of relative accuracy—of which video game software projects are probably the antithesis.

Envision

Envision refers to the game designer's vision or the essence statement of the game. Other things to consider during the Envision stage are scope, gaming-community support, and how the team will work together. During this stage, the key selling points of the game are determined, as is just what makes the game fun. This is when the question "What game are you making and who is it for?" is answered. In addition, this is the stage in which the question "Who are you going to use to make this game?" is answered. The Envision stage is where the game designer works with the producer to start spreading the enthusiasm for starting a new game-development project to management, and when key team members envision how they are going to work together.

Speculate

Speculation may conjure up images of reckless actions, gold panning, or playing the stock market. It's actual dictionary definition, however, reads as follows: "To mediate on a subject; reflect." A secondary definition is "To engage in a course of reasoning often based on inconclusive evidence." This describes precisely the actions required of a producer, a designer, an artist, or a programmer when beginning work on a game-development project. A producer should realize that when a plan is introduced, its purpose is to eliminate uncertainty in a highly uncertain process. When the uncertainly fails to evaporate, a producer should re-plan, although some fail to do so. Use of the term *speculate* accurately describes the reality of video game–software development, as well as the volatile market for video games.

The Speculate stage consists of determining the high-level requirements for the game; outlining the work required to complete the game; and creating a development plan (including a schedule with resource allocations), a feature list, risk-management plans, and a budget.

Explore

The Explore stage in agile project management refers to the process of finding and delivering features. Delivering the features required by the game design is the first and foremost objective of the Explore stage. You do this using effective time-management, resource-allocation, and risk-management strategies. Secondly, the team creates a collaborative project community with some elements of self-organization (so that the producer isn't burdened with questions such as who sits where). The producer simply acts as a facilitator during this process. Lastly, during the Explore phase, the producer must manage the team's interactions with management, Marketing, Quality Assurance, and any other stakeholders (like licensees).

Adapt

The term *adapt* refers to the necessary modifications or changes that are required to keep the project focused and on schedule. *Adapt* also refers to the incorporation of lessons learned and the application of those lessons to the project in midstream (generally, responding to change is more important than simply following a plan blindly), and to the life of the project, which means that an adaptation of the Envision stage is also possible as the team learns new information through its adaptations.

In this stage, the team's results are often viewable and open to criticism, both technical and creative. At this stage, the producer should analyze the project status as compared to the published plan. Often, this analysis should focus solely on the budgetary and fiscal impact of the game to date, with a comparison of the features required to play the game. The results of this analysis are included into the adaptation and re-planning stage for the next iteration.

Finalize

Finalize refers to the process of completing the project and doing all that is necessary to document and learn from the mistakes and lessons that this project taught the team and its producer. Often, the goal of a project ending eludes a Game Development team, as patches and constant upgrades or add-on packs are required, but most projects are worthy of celebration once they are completed.

Planning and Scheduling

Now that you have a basic understanding of the process involved in building a game, let's get onto planning and scheduling. There are two basic ways to schedule a project:

- The top-down approach
- The bottom-up approach

Taking the Top-Down Approach

The top-down plan is generally developed by a single person or a small group to provide an overview of what a project schedule *might* look like. Unfortunately, this plan often gets adopted as gospel and is rarely revised without considerable frustration and angst. A top-down plan generally does not involve the participation of those who are going to be called upon and tasked to do the things in the plan. Therefore, the top-down plan should only be considered a goal or a guideline. At best, it is a guess; at worst, it is totally wrong. This type of estimating tool fosters the understanding of what the game's scope and complexity may be. Be careful when creating top-down plans, guarding their release and clearly stating that they are to be revised when more information on the game is available, and when the input from the team is available.

Planning from the Bottom Up

When a producer plans from the bottom up, he or she gathers the relevant team members to work on developing a plan for building the game collaboratively and with a consensus of what is possible by when, and what resources it requires to reach that goal. All art assets, game features, and other project requirements are identified. This can generally only occur after a significant amount of pre-production planning has been conducted (the pre-production phase is discussed later in this chapter).

When planning from the bottom up, the first step is to identify short- or near-term goals. Work to establish these goals on a clear schedule, and then start checking off items on your feature or art-asset list, fitting the appropriate tasks into the schedule as your team concurs. By using this process and involving people from all disciplines necessary to develop the game, you'll share ownership in the schedule. People generally appreciate being asked for their opinions and input, and the scheduling process for video games is not an exception. Furthermore, it lessens the opportunity for a single team member, or a subset of the team, to fall behind schedule because they agreed to the schedule when it was created. (You'll be surprised at the extra effort people exert to protect their pride.) The alternative is much less desirable, especially when team members tell their producer, "I told you so" because the schedule was created without their input.

caution

The detailed, bottom-up plan is only as good as the game design. If you're working with a game design that is non-specific, ill-defined, or otherwise nebulous, be extremely cautious about committing to the plan you're creating.

Scheduling Constraints

When determining what type of schedule you want to follow when developing your game, you'll want to consider the two types of schedule-constraint models:

- Time-constrained model
- Resource-constrained model (including fiscal resources)

Both models provide an assimilation of several smaller plans developed by each of the team groups: designers, artists, and programmers. To establish your schedule, consider both of these models, as described next.

Each team lead (lead artist or art director, as well as the lead programmer and lead designer) looks to identify why and how his team can accomplish the goals of a project. To this end, he is responsible for creating the small portion of the production plan that relates to his area of responsibility. The lead programmer creates the programming schedule (with the help of the producer). The lead designer and lead artist create the respective Design and Art Production schedules. Then the producer combines these smaller schedules into one larger one and looks for dependencies, critical paths, and resource allocation requirements.

Time-Constrained Model

Reviewing the time-constrained scheduling model is the first step in determining a reasonable production plan. When working with the time-constrained model, focus on building a plan without accounting for the resource requirements. Simply determine the tasks, the features, the owners, and of course, the dependencies of each task. Take a guess at the duration for each task, and then try to link the dependant tasks together in a way that makes sense. The dependencies should be sorted such that the most fundamental and riskiest tasks come first in the schedule, followed by less-risky tasks. The point of this exercise is to determine whether it is even possible for a project of a given size and scope to fit within the timeframe a producer is considering.

Resource-Constrained Model

After you've created a time-constrained model for the production plan, convert it to a resource-constrained model. Focus your efforts (and that of the team leads) on assigning tasks appropriate to the skills of the available resources. Identify where and when the resource may complete the task, keeping in mind that you are still in the Speculate stage. Also identify key tasks for which no appropriate resource exists. That means you'll need to hire a new team member with the appropriate skills or recruit an existing team member to learn the required skills for this task. Clearly outline the work days, vacations, and weekends, and provide an allowance for sick days, meetings, and general administrative overhead (for all team leads).

This is where the scheduling gets challenging. Your next task is to include contingency buffers, such as working weekends and flexible days, in each part of the schedule and allocate your contingency equally across all areas of the production plan. Then look for ways in which to divide the production plan into major pieces, called *milestones*. This helps track the progress of the team and provides clear, measurable ways for management to review the status of the game's development.

note

The producer may have to re-create this constraint model several times during the game-development project as the game's development progresses. Realize, too, that the production plan you create is actually the assimilation of several smaller team plans, so focus on breaking down tasks into finite and measurable definitions.

When you switch to the resource-constrained model, you may realize that the game that's designed can't be produced due to various time and resource constraints. That means it's time to look for efficiencies or to start cutting features or subsets of the game's design.

Critical-Path Planning

The *critical path* is the series of tasks or events that make up the start and end of a project (see Figure 1.5). This series of tasks has no available schedule cushion or buffer. If you want to shorten the duration of a project, you must focus on the tasks that are on the critical path. Generally, only a relatively low number (less than 25 percent) of the total tasks of a game are on the critical path, but the items on the critical path generally *must* follow a specific order and sequence of events.

The critical path is the shortest route to completing the game, so it is important to properly plan for the tasks on it. Critical-path planning involves understanding and knowing the sequences of events and ensuring that all potential problems or hurdles associated with accomplishing the tasks on the critical path are addressed prior to reaching that task on the schedule.

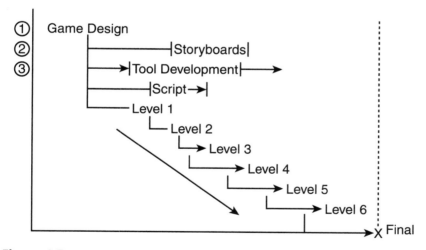

Figure 1.5
The critical path of this project is on the world and level creation, not the storyboards, tool development, or script.

Contingency Planning

Even the best plans go awry. That's why it's important to plan for contingencies before you launch into developing a game. Following are a few ways to plan for those unpredictable events that can throw a monkey wrench into any project.

Plan for Overtime

This is an industry standard in the video game industry; it's assumed that long hours will be required to keep the project on schedule. This has no fiscal impact on the developer or publisher of a video game because most employees are classified as professionals and are therefore exempt from overtime pay.

Hire Additional Personnel

Be careful when considering adding personnel to the team to ensure that it stays on schedule. Although at first glance it may seem that doing so is a great way to keep things on schedule, it often works in reverse. For one thing, additional people require additional management. Secondly, the addition of a new team member inevitably involves an introductory period during which the new hire becomes familiar with his or her role as well as the procedures and goals associated with the project. During this introduction, the new team member often slows others, preventing them from completing their work on schedule. Lastly, the addition of personnel always costs more money, not only in wages but also in equipment.

Work During Holidays and Vacations

Although some game-development and publishing companies have liberal policies regarding time off in lieu of other days worked, it is generally bad form to require the team to work holidays on a regular basis. Indeed, I do not recommend requiring team members to work on holidays or vacations as a contingency. Time off is important for employees for much-needed rest periods during times of high-intensity activity. Although I have occasionally persuaded employees during a busy period to work on a holiday or a vacation in exchange for a day off in the future, I suggest you to plan around holidays and urge your employees to take them. Just work with the team to ensure that vacations are on balance, and are scheduled at a mutually agreeable time for the employee, the team, and the project. In practice, this is not that hard; it just takes time, negotiation, and understanding.

Use a Formula

I'll discuss this later on in the chapter.

Don't Schedule Work for Team Leads

Don't schedule the team leads—that is, the lead programmer, the lead artist, and the lead designer—to do much work related to the actual production of the game; Allow them the time to delegate to their teams and to help manage the process; doing so ensures that the leads are free to jump into their team's work as required. Often, this is not entirely practical, because the team leads usually have many tasks that only they can complete. That said, if a producer works with each lead to establish a framework for minimizing their direct contributions and maximizing their indirect contributions, and refrains from scheduling a lead on any task that is on the critical path, it ensures that the project has ample flexibility to respond to changing parameters, requirements, or conditions.

note

The idea of not scheduling work for team leaders may give you pause. After all, the whole reason your team leaders became team leaders in the first place is because they produced excellent work. If the team leader for the Art team is actually your best modeler, wouldn't it make sense to put him on the job of *modeling*? Yes and no. If you put the lead artist in a managerial role rather than a production one, it enables that person to convey his or her skills to other team members. This cross-pollenization of skills can only help the project. As a compromise that enables you to, for example, enjoy the modeling skills your Art team leader possesses as well as to enable him or her to teach others, consider using the lead artist to set the standard for the 3D models and then have him oversee the rest of the 3D modelers to help them achieve the same standard.

Make Time for Testing After a Task is Completed

As a producer, you should plan for every programmer, designer, and artist to include some time in their daily schedule to test the completion of their—and others'—work. There are few bigger hassles than having team members turn in incomplete or erroneous code or art assets to a game; this breaks the game and prevents the team from playing it, not to mention affecting the team's ability to stay on schedule. Often, I assign a buddy to double-check a peer's assets before they are checked into the main source control being used by the game engine.

Set Aside a Contingency Reserve Fund

The producer should create a contingency fund for the inevitable day when the project faces a significant hurdle, or is threatened with going over budget or over time. It's a great feeling to be able to answer the heated question "How are you doing to pay for that?" with a very pleasant "Out of my contingency fund, of course!" I often show the contingency fund as a line item in my budget proposals and create it as soon as I start working on a game's budget.

Using a Formula to Calculate a Schedule

When a producer evaluates the list of the tasks required to complete a game, the first question he or she should ask is "How long will it take to reasonably complete this task?" The problem is that this is harder than you might think to calculate. The easiest way is to assume that one person is working at it full time until it is completed, but this is rarely the case because individuals often get sidetracked or required to perform other tasks during the work day (helping others, filling out insurance forms, attending meetings, completing report, writing e-mails, and so on). Believe it or not, a formula exists that can account for time off and help plan for other contingencies that inevitably interfere with the completion of any task. It's one that has been used in other industries, but that I've modified based on my experience with the game industry and call the "Extremely flexible project planning formula". Here's how it works:

Task Name:	Direct X Compatibility and Rendering
Best Case:	10 days
Worst Case:	25 days
Most Likely Case:	15 days
Formula:	2 (Best Case) + 3 (Worse Case) + Most Likely = X/6
Result:	2(10)+3(25)+15=110/6, or 18.33 days,
Practical Application:	18.33 provides a buffer of 3.33 days over the most-likely case scenario

Although this formula is not infallible, it does help to provide a buffer and to quantify a normally very difficult question. The best part is that a producer can go back to the task list, make adjustments, and re-estimate using this formula partway through the task or the project (as mentioned in the discussion about the agile project management theory's Adapt stage). You can also adapt the formula to reflect the specific circumstances of your team. For example, a team lead may not use this formula because he or she is able to concentrate only on actual game-production work 50 percent of the time, while the rest of the time is invested in administrative overhead. Therefore, you may wish to modify the formula to reflect this, showing that the team lead can only contribute to the project at 50 percent of the estimated 40 hours per week. Therefore, it may take a lead up to 36.66 days to complete this same task (assuming all other things are equal).

Software-Factory Efficiencies

A *software factory* is an organization that uses a set of processes and methods that work like a factory does—with each set of tools or technologies being specialized, but remaining interchangeable and reusable depending on the needs of a specific project. The software factory is built around the core understanding that the code, tools, and documentation from certain features and game engine systems are to be reused. In this way, they are in constant need of updating, but are to remain useful and independent components.

note

The concept of the software factory is simply summarized here for your easy reference and understanding. Read Chapter 11 of *Game Architecture and Design,* by Andrew Rollings and Dave Morris for complete details relating to the software factory.

There are many advantages to using a software factory, including the following:

- The average length of a project is shortened if the team already has a set of familiar tools.
- Cross-platform releases are inherently easier because the team is already familiar with how common libraries are used for different platforms.
- Often, the code that is written using these tools is more stable and reliable because it uses components that are tried and tested. Indeed, although doing so can be difficult, using the software-factory approach makes it is possible for code to be reuseable, maintainable, and well-documented.
- The software-factory method enables the dissemination of information about core systems of the factory. This is helpful in the event a team member leaves; the project does not grind to a halt or become seriously jeopardized because the departing team member is taking valuable knowledge with him or her.
- It is often easier for the producer to estimate and track progress on a project that is using the software-factory approach because he is familiar with how similar system were implemented on previous projects using the same factory methods.

That said, there are a few disadvantages to using this approach that should not be understated. For one, setting up a software factory can be as expensive and time-consuming as making a game itself. That's because the factory requires tools such as libraries, world-building tools, sound-placement tools, level editors, engine architecture, object placement and preview tools, and key-rendering libraries.

Other disadvantages include the following:

- The first project undertaken using this method often takes longer because the factory is still being set up. Wrappers libraries (small tools used by the team to ensure the hardware specific functionality of the game on a particular hardware platform) must be developed for each platform, allowing the code and libraries to be used on multiple platforms.

- Although the code is generally more generic in a software-factory environment, it is more difficult to develop and account for all the possibilities and potential uses of a particular routine. As such, this code often takes longer to develop in the initial stages.

- If you add new people to the team, there will be a learning curve for them when it comes to using the software-factory methods and libraries, as these can be quite specialized.

- Generally speaking, more administration and forward thinking is required when creating a software factory.

Stages of Game Development

Now that you have a sense of the various issues surrounding game creation, let's look at a hypothetical game project from beginning to end and identify the major stages of the process. Of course, each publisher has its own specific procedure for creating games, but nearly all boil down to the phases outlined here, which I've tried to simplify somewhat.

Concept

The *concept* phase is when the game concept is written down. It's when brainstorming occurs, and when ideas are generated.

Prototype

During the prototype phase, a prototype of the game is developed so that users can start to experience the fun as described in the concept documentation. The prototype phase typically lasts 2–4 months, depending on the tools available to the team to create a prototype.

Pitch

During this phase, game developers pitch their game to management or, if the developers don't currently work for a game publisher, to a publisher's representatives. The pitch explains why the game is a great concept, why it is ready and right for the video game market, whether it is producible, and how it will be developed.

Green Light

This phase begins after the pitch is approved for production, and involves gathering a team to begin working on the game. This phase may involve interviewing and contacting several video game–development companies to assemble the right team for the game. Often, a game cannot enter pre-production until business and legal issues around the project are resolved, such as who owns the technology and the creative intellectual property such as the main character and story.

Pre-Production

Pre-production is when the Game Development team works on defining the production pipelines, identifying the needs and uses of the tools they'll need to make the game, and outlining and fleshing out the details behind the game's design.

Production

Production is when the game building actually begins. 3D models are created, worlds are built, sound is recorded, textures are applied, cinematics are filmed, game logic is authored, and all the other pieces of the game are made and put together. This is often a long process—at least 12 months, and often much longer.

Quality Assurance

The *quality-assurance* or *testing* phase often occurs at the final stage of production, about 3–4 months before the game is scheduled to go to manufacturing. During this stage, the game is tested for bugs, errors, deficiencies, or incompatibilities.

Final Gold Master

The Final Gold Master phase is when the master CD is burned and sent to the manufacturing facility for duplication. In the case of a console game there's the "Submit to Hardware Manufacturer" process, which requires attention to detail and potential revisions to meet their approval guidelines. Each hardware manufacturer has their own rigorous testing guidelines and each product must meet or exceed their own QA requirements of functionality and playability.

In the case of online games on either console or PC, teams must continue to work together even after the Final Gold Master phase to fix bugs and prepare patches for release prior to the game being available in retail stores.

Video Game Development Process Models

There are two basic models for a video game's development. The standard model and the Forward loading risk management model. The advantages and disadvantages of each are discussed in detail in Chapter 8. However, in order to provide some context of how this model works and its practical application, I've included the standard model here for consideration and familiarization.

The standard development model shows the common approach to video game development of the past few years. By following this model, the game development team has the most risk in the project at precisely the time in which the project is the most expensive on a daily or weekly basis. While this is often unavoidable, when it is possible to avoid the convergence of risk and expense, a producer should do so.

Since this is the common method, it is widely accepted that there are few alternatives to this model. However, a new model was proposed by Mark Cerny at the DICE conference in 2002. Avoid the standard model whenever possible, focusing on defining the fun in your game before the costs start increasing. By managing risk a producer excels at their job and ensures that the financial investment in the project is responsibly managed.

The Final Word

Now that you've had a chance to skim the surface of all that a producer is called upon to do in the pursuit of excellence and success, turn to the next chapter to understand the specialties of each role and how they differ by company, project and specialty area.

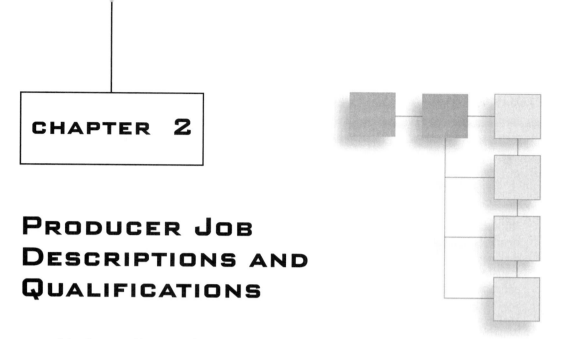

CHAPTER 2

PRODUCER JOB DESCRIPTIONS AND QUALIFICATIONS

This chapter discusses the various producer roles. Producer roles can be found at game publishers as well as independent game developers or studios. Producers may also be responsible for working with an internal or with external teams (or with both, in some cases). There are many variations on the role of a producer, and this chapter will solidify the roles and job descriptions into a few understandable categories. However, keep in mind that these are not absolutes. Each company has different methodologies, procedures, guidelines, and qualification requirements. Electronic Arts has a different production management structure than does Microsoft or Activision. A producer at Electronic Arts might actually be in more of a design or creative role than at Activision or Microsoft. Program Manager at Microsoft may be a much more technical role than a producer at Electronic Arts.

As you read through each role description and qualification outline, the key point to take away is that producers have areas of specialty, just as programmers can focus on graphics over gameplay or artists can focus on modeling and texturing instead of animation. A more creative producer—one who can lead and take a hands-on approach to designing a producible game—is a totally different role than a third-party producer who goes searching for the next hot title from a third-party software developer. While there are similarities in the roles, the skills and qualification for each specialty are different. It is certainly possible to adapt to a new and challenging role, but you should focus on the specialty that fits your core competencies, strengths, and talents.

Producer Role: Assistant Producer

Let's start at the very beginning with the role of an assistant producer (AP). While this is often the most challenging and frustrating role—and reaches into the lower end of the compensation scale—the assistant producer role can be quite rewarding. First, let's look at some of the general qualifications required for an AP at different types of companies.

note

> This section discusses the roles of an assistant producer. The role of associate producer is often not clearly differentiated from assistant producer. One way to categorize associate producers is that they have the capability to manage one or more independent SKUs without daily input from their managers. But an associate producer would generally not be a manager for a single product or an entire product line. As an example, associate producers are often responsible for the Game Boy version or the port of the original game to that platform, or are responsible for one of the other SKUs—but not the lead SKU (like the Xbox and PC SKU). The role varies from company to company. When in doubt, check recent job postings to make sure you understand the requirements for candidates for this role.

Assistant Producer at a Publisher

The assistant roducer role at an entertainment software publisher can vary widely between companies, projects, and production teams. Who they work for is one of the main considerations of an assistant producer. Often, the type of manager (producer) who supervises their work can make a tremendous difference in the scope of responsibilities for their job, as well as in their satisfaction in that role. Assistant producers with trusting managers are often charged with a lot of responsibility. The first goal of an assistant producer should be to establish confidence in their abilities with their producer.

Assistant producers at a publisher can be involved in the following areas of the business:

- Internal game development, working with internal teams.
- External game development, including third-party product development with a focus on game design and design review, and on quality assurance management.

Read on for a closer look at what an assistant producer does in each of these areas of the entertainment software publishing business.

Internal Game Development: Working with Internal Game Development Teams

An assistant producer who works with the full (internal) Production team in the development of video game products talks daily to the Production team, much as an AP at an independent developer does. The AP and the producer act together to implement agreed-upon goals and methodologies. Additionally, this AP position is responsible for developing and delivering the final game design for specific game areas from which the whole team works to build the game. Responsibility for sub-projects, such as audio implementation or motion-capture data delivery, may be key elements of this role. A successful individual often takes a high-level concept, understands agreed-upon team goals, and implements that concept. Experience working with other products (especially a console product) is always a big plus in this role.

Successful candidates for this role often emerge from the Quality Assurance department, or were interns in a production assistant role. Once an AP gains the experience of just one product cycle (from concept to commercial release), he is much more valuable to the company than when he started in the role.

External Game Development: Working with Third-Party Product Development

The role of an assistant producer in third-party product development varies greatly, depending on the genre of product, the producer, and the company. Third-party product development focuses on relationships with individuals at other outside companies, so an assistant producer in this role needs to be professional, responsive, and prepared when dealing with outside vendors and people who are under contract to develop the game for the assistant producer's employer, the publisher.

note

Third-party product development is the term used to describe working with outside, independent game development teams and companies. These companies generally have no direct relationship with the hardware manufacturer, such as Sony, Nintendo, or Microsoft.

This type of assistant producer could work with both internal and external development teams, and could be required to juggle both types of roles.

Assistant Producer Job Requirements

An assistant producer is regularly responsible for the project management and quality assurance coordination of games and entertainment services (online game components). The assistant producer also manages all deployment projects for the group, as well as game build and game design evaluation of each title in development. Specific emphasis on or passion for a particular type of game is a tremendous asset to a person in this role.

Having a passion for their product or genre means driving, and taking full responsibility for, the QA process, including providing the QA team with instruction, managing time versus resources against a budget, and approving overtime in concert with the QA manager. The role is primarily responsible for establishing and coordinating effective build procedures (getting new builds for testing from the independent developers and cycling them through QA and providing the feedback required to improve the product).

Assistant producers in this category are often responsible for managing schedules for localized (foreign language) versions and ports (to other platforms or media). This requires interfacing with and supporting developers, licensors, and other departments within the software publisher, especially Marketing.

The assistant producer is often responsible for reviewing and contributing to design documentation, using discretionary judgment on key game design features, their effectiveness and compelling nature, as well as management reports of the online usage.

Naturally, the AP in this category must assist the producer in the daily project management, scheduling, and decision-making processes of the game.

Following are some typical requirements for this role:

- One to two year's video game industry-related experience or equivalent in education and training.
- Sometimes, two years in a lead tester role is advantageous. This means that as the lead tester, you were responsible for leading a QA team.
- An outstanding demonstrated passion and knowledge of video games is always a plus.
- A passion for the product genre and product is always required in an AP role.
- Being willing to travel occasionally in support of your projects is often a requirement.
- Knowledge of gaming technology is always a bonus.

Also desirable are strong time-management skills. Prove your ability to meet deadlines on multiple projects by finishing smaller projects on schedule or by working with QA to enhance the efficiency of the feedback process. Learning how to manage small projects is the first step along the way to being put in charge of larger ones.

Effective verbal and written communication skills are absolutely required, as the role of an AP is to problem-solve and bring potential crises to the producer before they become actual crises. The ability to define problems, recommend solutions, and establish resourceful conclusions are excellent foundations to have when starting off as an AP.

An Assistant Producer at a Developer

This section discusses some of the responsibilities of an assistant producer at a developer. The assistant producer is responsible for assisting the producer in all aspects of their role. The assistant producer's role is to ensure that all details of the project are handled, while maintaining a commitment to leading industry standards.

The AP is primarily responsible for managing the team and tracking each team member's progress according to the schedule. The AP may also be directly and indirectly involved with the game designers, working closely with them to ensure that the game features are implemented as designed and are tested and revised so as to conform to the design documentation and milestone-acceptance criteria.

Job Requirements

Following are some of the job requirements of the assistant producer in this category:

Maintain Project Schedules

The AP helps create and maintain project schedules. By knowing what each team member is working on and what features are going into the game at all times, the AP provides the first line of defense against a project falling behind schedule.

Maintain Project Management Documents

The AP is responsible for maintaining most project and game management documents. This may include production documents, such as the art asset list and features lists. Working closely with the game design team is required to ensure the project documents reflect the requirements of the design documents.

Takes Meeting Notes

The AP is also responsible for taking and distributing meeting notes. This is a principal part of the role, as so many things are happening during development. It is imperative that an excellent and referable record is kept of when production and design decisions are made, so that they can be referenced at a moment's notice.

Interacts with the QA Team

An AP is the principal liaison with the QA team, providing QA with builds and bug-fixing assignments and support. By maintaining bug list for team, the AP is the single point of contact for all fixed and open bugs that are identified in a software project prior to commercial release.

Assists with Communications

With excellent communications skills, a passion for the game they're working on, as well as an excellent understanding of the gameplay, APs assist with external communications, especially for fans and fan Web sites. Coordinating information released to fans—including behind-the-scenes looks, interviews, and screenshots—are all responsibilities of the AP role at a developer.

Assists Producer

Lastly, the AP must assist the producer in fulfilling all of his or her responsibilities —that's pretty much a catch-all category for anything else that the producer needs to have done.

Other Job Responsibilities

Other job responsibilities are usually less frequent demands on an AP's time. I don't want to characterize them as *less important*, as they still need to be done. These types of duties include evaluating gameplay and the fun-factor of the product with a critical eye toward improving the specifics of the game's design or implementation. This often includes the coordination of internal focus groups for a critical analysis of how the game is being implemented and designed.

Another necessary task is to compile detailed release notes, or *regression lists*, for all builds sent to publishers for evaluation. These notes that accompany each build describe what has changed and what's new in this version.

Another secondary responsibility is online fan community maintenance, such as message board participation and providing assets to the Web development team for an update of the product's online presence. The AP is the key contact for the online "mod" community and fan group support for the product. By creating and maintaining an online "mod" group for the product, the AP ensures that there are plenty of fans ready to participate in the creation of new content, such as multiplayer maps, new missions, or alternative characters.

The AP also helps coordinate any online beta testing with the publisher and the publisher's QA team. This often includes e-mail updates, message board posting, and IRC chats with the fans prior to an online beta test.

The AP may also help in the creation of any post-ship tools, support, and content.

A Top Ten List for Assistant Producers

Advice from Geoff Thomas, Relic Entertainment

Assistant producers are exposed to every aspect of game development. On any given day, the AP will be sitting in on design meetings, providing feedback on art direction, tracking progress on feature implementation, risk-managing project schedules, and all the while absorbing as much information as he/she can handle. The position is unique in that you have full interaction with the development team (in the trenches, so to speak) while at the same time working with the publisher, the press, the fan community, and external contractors. To excel at this position is to know how to multi-task!

Here's a top ten list of what it takes to succeed in the assistant producer role.

1. Know your game. This is a no-brainer. APs are involved with as many areas of production as they can handle, so they need to know as much about their game as possible. Having this knowledge will enable you to take part in decision-making and help you to steer the game in the right direction. Being able to provide cross-team insight into how (and why) systems work is an invaluable skill that the producer and leads will come to draw on again and again.

2. Know your industry. It's not enough to simply understand how your studio works or what the vision of your project is. Keep on top of industry news, trends, and competitive titles.

3. Be process-oriented. Producers and assistant producers alike spend most of their day in interrupt mode. Establishing (and sticking to!) processes that define how you handle your work will not only translate into a less stressful day, it will make you much more productive.

4. Be proactive. At all times you'll need to stay on top of requests, problems, and dependencies (tasks which aren't complete yet and that hold up other tasks from being completed). Even at the best of times, people on your team will be too busy with their own work to keep on top of what everyone else is up to. When they turn to you for help, be ready.

5. Keep morale high. This is one of the most important areas of the AP position. Keeping the team excited about the project and making sure the focus stays positive is critical to successful development. Shield the guys in the trenches while making sure that the publisher is happy with and confident about the title.

6. Be a facilitator. The AP's primary focus is to, well, assist! This means being available to help not just the producer, but all of the project leads, the publisher, the QA team, fan sites, publications—anything that can't afford to sit on the back burner.

7. Never stop learning. What makes this position so fantastic is that each time you gain competence in an area of your job, a new responsibility comes your way. It's the perfect path to becoming a producer because as you gain experience, you end up taking more and more off of the producer's shoulders.

(continued on next page)

A Top Ten List for Assistant Producers (continued)

8. Pay attention to detail. Assistant producers simply cannot afford to be sloppy in this area. The devil is in the details, and little things love to snowball into huge problems.

9. Never consider any job too small. There's a lot about game development that's glamorous and fun. There's a lot more that's mundane and—let's face it—boring. When your project leads are too busy to work on the little stuff, you have to be prepared to jump in. Let them worry about the graphics engine instead of who on their team needs a new video card.

10. Never be afraid to ask questions. It's always better to ask about what you don't under-stand than to pretend you do. As much as you know, there's more that you don't. Your team will be happy to share what they know with you, and you'll be better able to plan your project if you glean whatever knowledge you can from them.

The Producer's Role

There are two types of producers. The first type is the producer who works at the develop-er; this is the person who is in daily contact with the development team and is responsible for its performance. The second type is the producer at the publisher, who is responsible for third-party product development (external development). This person is responsible for evangelizing the product within the company and to the media.

As I discussed earlier, the producer is the person who is most focused on and responsible for delivering a finished product on schedule. This rule applies to almost every company in the gaming industry. While there may be different variations on the role of producer, the key is that the role is senior enough so that the person in it can take full responsibili-ty for managing the project as a business. Secondly, the producer in any specialty or com-pany focuses his efforts on and is capable of producing the game title that he is charged with. The producer is able to take full responsibility for his product on multiple SKUs, and can supervise others and make informed and intelligent decisions related to the design and development of the game.

Let's take a look at some of the key responsibilities of someone in this role at a software publisher.

A Producer at a Publisher

This section offers a brief look at the job description of a producer at a publisher. Keep in mind that this is a broad description and that the specifics of the role vary depending on company. Doing whatever it takes to get the job done and the product complete is gener-ally the main focus for producers in this role.

Again, this role parallels the requirements and structure outlined in the assistant producer description. Generally, producers at software publishers work in two types of projects: 1) the internally developed product developed by an internal team and 2) the external project undertaken by an external development team.

First, I'll discuss producing an internal product through an internal development team at a publisher, which is very similar to the job of a producer at a developer, except that often you have to do the work of both roles—the producer on the development team and the producer who is focused on external development.

Internal Development: A Producer's Job Description

The producer is ultimately responsible for every aspect of the game. It is the producer's job to make sure that the project is completed on time and on budget, while maintaining a commitment to industry standards.

The producer is responsible for facilitating all decisions of the product development team. Conflict resolution and proactive problem solving are the key aspects of this job. Often problems arise that cannot be easily resolved. Therefore, it is the producer's job to make the decision that moves the project forward on schedule.

note

Producers generally report directly to the executive producer, who is responsible for many titles within a single brand or business.

The producer is directly responsible for the assistant producer and the project leads (the lead artist, lead programmer, lead designer, and art director).

Primary Responsibilities

The role of producer is much more encompassing than this overview may lead you to believe. Daily supervision of direct reports and review of weekly task lists takes up a large part of the job—generally, 20 percent of your time every week. Working directly with an assistant producer to ensure that the project schedule is updated on a weekly basis is another critical focus.

note

When working with an assistant producer, producers should take time to understand what an assistant producer wants to do long term. Then discuss how they can best assist that person in accomplishing their goals and career education. Hire APs who can help accomplish the project by looking at problems in ways that are different from your way. While they won't always be right, adding diversity to a team provides the opportunity to expand your consideration and problem solving abilities. Generally speaking, hiring people who you suspect are smarter than you—and who deliver results in improved ways—can only help the project and your career as a producer.

Evaluating whether resources are properly allocated to the project is a constant responsibility. The producer is ultimately responsible for maintenance of the project schedule, even though the assistant producer generally does the work. The producer should understand and know about all changes to the schedule and what their impact will be; knowing this information helps the producer ensure that the project is on time, on budget, and of AAA quality. The producer is primarily responsible for providing up-to-date schedules for the team and executives on a weekly basis.

The producer often makes decisions regarding who should be working on what features and why. Properly allocating resources for the tasks is an important aspect of the producer's job.

The producer maintains the team vision. This cannot be understated. If the team does not know where the product is going, or if there's a conflict between the lead designer and the art director, it is the producer's responsibility to maintain a cohesive and consistent vision that resolves the conflict. This includes maintaining harmony between team members, even to the lowest level of the project.

Outside contractors are often hired to create the sound and music for a game. Sometimes outside talent, such as voice actors, animation studios, and other professionals are hired to complete voiceover work or finish cut scenes and other animation. Management of outside contractors is also the responsibility of the producer. The producer is required to be able to handle and resolve conflict with outside talent who deliver content or assets for the game that do not meet specifications or quality standards.

The producer must facilitate communication and decision-making at all levels of the team and the executive management. By providing a regular update to the executive management covering any problems and their proposed solutions, as well as any unresolved problems, the producer demonstrates an element of control and understanding that usually strengthens the confidence of executive management.

A producer's ability to proactively identify potential problems and solutions is a constant and ongoing responsibility. Do whatever is necessary so that problems do not surprise you, or at least have a contingency for almost every problem. This means that you should never be caught unprepared for the worst. But, of course, you must expect the best and convey that assumption to the team.

Finally, ensuring that the team is fully staffed and fully supplied with necessary equipment to do their job is the last piece in the intricate puzzle of being an internal team game producer.

Secondary Responsibilities

It is difficult to discuss some responsibilities as being secondary to the role of the producer, as at the end of the day, *everything* on the project is the responsibility of the producer. However, some secondary responsibilities might include working with the business development team to evaluate new game development opportunities. Other responsibilities that fall into this category might include documenting best practices and completing post mortems for each product so that other development teams may learn from your experience—including mistakes and successes.

Other secondary responsibilities may include design reviews of other projects in development for which you're not directly responsible. Sharing ideas, experiences, and procedures that work well on your project with other producers constitutes a valuable contribution to the company.

The Producer and Designers

An often unavoidable part of being a producer is working with the design team to resolve conflicts in their design. Conflicts can arise when what is technically feasible or what meets the overall game scope feasibility standards comes into conflict with what the designers are considering in their written design. For this reason, producers should have a distinct understanding of the design issues related to the specific genre of the game that they are producing. A producer who is committed to excellence understands design issues without being a designer or wanting to do the designer's job.

Sometimes, producers at publishers are called upon to fulfill dual roles and as both producers and designers. While companies such as Electronic Arts have a practice of doing this on many of their successfully developed, internally produced franchises, this practice has some drawbacks for video games based on original concepts, intellectual property licenses or other types of creatively challenging titles. Roles and responsibilities that are clearly delineated to the job description help ensure that the "design by committee" process that producers are used to doesn't hold up the game's development.

At the end of the day, a producer is a producer and not a designer. Such a distinction clarifies responsibilities and allows people to focus their talents on what they do best.

A Few Specifics

Here are some of the additional duties and responsibilities that producers for an internally developed game (working at a publisher) may face.

- Defining the monthly milestones with leads from the team. *Milestones* are measurements of where the project is at certain points in time. A review of a milestone from an internal perspective helps the management of the publisher determine which products are poised for success and which ones should be cancelled. Internal teams that devise and rely upon a milestone schedule are generally more disciplined, resulting in higher-quality products and on-time delivery schedules.

- Ensuring that the team leads are managing each of their groups to meet the monthly milestones requirements. This involves daily and weekly management to ensure that each member of the team is performing to expectations. Often, weekly lead meetings are the time when problems are resolved and action plans are formed.

- Keeping up-to-date, realistic schedules. Updated schedules with realistic assumptions are critical to ensuring a successful product launch. The primary responsibility of the producer in this regard is to review and interface with the team leads and work with the assistant producer to update the schedule to reflect actual work completed and remaining work to do.

- Managing the development of new tools and procedures that enhance efficiency within the development team. Finding efficiencies in the tools and pipelines is part of the core responsibility of an effective producer. Looking for and efficiently managing resources includes developing new procedures, such as export pipelines or work flow enhancements. For example, licensing a new art tool that might help the artists create and apply textures to models in the game is the type of efficiency that a producer should always be looking for.

- Providing feedback and doing annual performance reviews for the team. Giving annual reviews is an important part of being an excellent manager. Providing constructive feedback to team members, as well as acknowledging key performers within the team, is critical to being an effective leader.

- Managing external contacts, such as original equipment manufacturer (OEM) deals and the media. The producer is the key contact for external contacts, such as OEMs (such as NVIDIA or ATI), who want to ensure that the game is compatible with their system and that their hardware includes the features that game developers need. Keeping and managing media contacts is another demanding part of a producer's role. The media involvement in a game usually occurs during the final stages of a product, when time is at a premium.

- Facilitating communication links to Marketing and the QA lead. This is critical in the final stages of any game's development. Clear communications are the basis of any successful relationship. A producer must be clear, concise and excellent in all communications, written and verbal.

- Overseeing management of bug tracking and interfacing with the Quality Assurance department. While the producer is not the direct and daily contact during most of the testing and quality assurance process, he or she is responsible for finding the right method for inputting, tracking, and resolving bugs.

- Preparing and presenting progress reports and weekly updates for the executive producer. This update process should be respected even during times of intense development and schedule pressure. The process of preparing a weekly update report should be used to update your manager with the details of the project, as well as facilitate discussion of any challenges their potential solutions.

- Handling any problems that arise and reporting unresolved issues to the executive producer. This is often referred to as *escalation*. Escalating a problem or challenge allows you to return to solving the problems that you know you can solve and allows your manager to help by solving the problems that you cannot.

External Development: The Producer's Job Description

When working in a third-party product development management role, your job as producer is to manage the relationship between the publisher and the external developer. It is also your job to manage the development contract in place governing the relationship. It may seem as if the producer only has a cursory or limited impact on the product's development, but in reality, the producer's role is crucial, required, and often can make the biggest impact in terms of how commercially successful the game is.

The producer is the primary representative of the project to the outside world for the publisher. The producer is chiefly responsible for budgeting, scheduling, staffing, sourcing, and tracking development. Producers generally negotiate contract terms within the guidelines provided by the publisher's management. They are also responsible for ensuring that the developer's team deliverables are met in a timely manner. They report progress to the publisher's management, as well as to other departments within the publisher, such as Marketing, Sales, and QA.

The producer is also responsible for project relations and ensuring clearly defined deliverables and goals for all departments the work on the game, including Marketing, Public Relations, Quality Assurance, OEM (Original Equipment Manufacturers), and Licensing. A producer position may have an associate or assistant producer who reports to them.

Overall Responsibilities

There are some similarities in the challenges faced by both internal and external producers. Read on to uncover the unique aspects of both roles as well as some recommendations in how to overcome the unique challenges of each.

- Make daily updates to the schedule and budget. This information is generally provided by the developer, and the external producer usually interprets what he understands to be risks.

- Serve as primary contact for the development team at the publisher. Communicate with the publisher generally via telephone and e-mail several times per day.
- Manage the development budget while working with the brand manager to ensure that the key messages and features of the game are understood.
- An external producer actively works to eliminate any obstacle that interrupts or interferes with the development team's progress or ability to do great work.
- Coordinate the efforts of the development team so that those efforts support the marketing initiatives and brand manager of the project as much as possible.

General Requirements

Although college degrees are preferred, they are not required. Many producers can be successful without a college degree, as long as they are committed to excellence.

As a producer, you should have on your resume a minimum of two major titles on PC or current console platforms and a track record of on-time delivery as an assistant or associate producer. Primarily responsibility for the completion of at least two projects means that you were able to take full responsibility for completing that project. At least two year's of experience is usually the minimum required before being considered for a producer role.

Following are other skills and knowledge producers should have:

- Excellent communication skills, in order to work closely and effectively with many internal and external groups.
- Knowledge of PC hardware, operating systems, and standard APIs; familiarity with PS2, Xbox, and GameCube hardware, development tools, and console manufacturer product submission procedures.
- Good comprehension of all aspects of multimedia, film, the dynamic narrative, and game production—specifically graphics, design, programming, audio and video production, QA, and localization.
- Comprehensive knowledge of game genres and ability to spot good products and concepts prior to full development. A background in competitive products, demographics, market preferences, and biases of game players are useful in this role.
- Familiar with standard project accounting procedures, including budgets, Profit and Loss (P&L) statements, and *pro forma* financial analysis.
- Experience as a producer on a AAA title.
- Great enthusiasm for playing video games.
- Aggressiveness in finding new ways to problem-solve and work through resolutions. Is able to hold others accountable for their work product.

- The ability and confidence to proactively approach the product, anticipating and solving problems before they detrimentally affect the project.
- Organizational skills and attention to detail. The producer is the pillar of strength for the team, and must know the status of all aspects of the project at all times. Making a game requires the simultaneous management of hundreds or thousands of details, bringing them all together in a resolution that results in an excellent software product over a period of several years. A producer generally cannot succeed without this trait.

This description should dispel some of the myths about the role of being a producer at either a game developer or a publisher. The point is that you can't be an excellent producer without loving your job. Now, let's take a look at the senior role in production management, the executive producer role.

Role Definition and Success at Electronic Arts

Interview with Rusty Rueff, Electronic Arts

Rusty Rueff, Vice President of Human Resources at Electronic Arts had a few things to say when asked about the producer's role in the success of products published by EA.

Q: What is the difference in job functionality between an assistant producer and associate producer? What differentiates the role, responsibilities, and the employees in these roles at Electronic Arts?

A: An assistant producer typically has clear area for which they are responsible. For example, providing screen shots to their marketing partners for publishing on an advance Web site. Or tracking licensing arrangements for a subset of players in a sports game.

An associate producer has a more broad set of responsibilities. For instance, they may be responsible for multiple elements in the production of a game level. Associate producers may have one or more assistant producers reporting to them.

Q: What benchmarking techniques does EA endorse or use across its studios to ensure that each producer is functioning at an acceptable level? Is there a way to provide them assistance if they are not meeting the common benchmark?

A: A set of performance objectives is set each quarter for each producer. They report their progress against these individual objectives.

At the product level, producers have deliverables (for example a design element, or level map) that are tracked in the overall project management schedule. This provides another tool to track progress of the producers.

(continued on next page)

Role Definition and Success at Electronic Arts (continued)

At a general level, there are role definitions and performance standards set out for assistant, associate, and producer levels. These definitions help their managers benchmark appropriate performance expectations.

Q: What difference in job functionality between a senior producer and an executive producer? What are the principle leadership characteristics EA requires of executive producers?

A: Senior producers carry responsibilities for such things as an entire level of the game, relationships with Sales and Marketing, or coordination with production artists. Senior producers often are responsible for an SKU or a particular game as designed to be played on a particular platform.

Executive producers are overall product team leaders. They carry responsibilities for the game concept, its design, and usually, the development (art, audio, engineering, and so on) of a game. In addition, they often carry responsibilities for all the products in a given franchise (for instance, all baseball games within the *MVP* franchise or all racing games within the *Need for Speed* franchise).

Executive producers must be product leaders—meaning they understand the consumer audience and the creative definition of a game targeted at them. They are often team leaders, meaning that they maintain the focus and productivity of the large number of people in a product team. In addition, executive producers are expected to contribute to the success of the overall studio in which they work. An EP manages people, processes, and technology to balance the scope, resources, and time necessary to deliver a highly rated, successful game.

Q: In a producer's interaction with the executive staff, what are the ways in which a producer can achieve a higher degree of success?

A: In any product development organization, senior executives must decide how to allocate resources across a number of potentially successful products. The ability to present a game concept in a compelling way is critical to the success of an executive producer. As the game development progresses, the ability to convey the progress of that game and its potential sales success is critical for the executive producer. These presentations typically involve extensive, often multi-week preparation by teams of individuals.

Q: How are disputes or disagreements between executives and producers at EA resolved? Can you give an example of a situation in which a producer worked to resolve a conflict?

A: A good example involves proposing new products. One racing game was presented but the concept was neither green-lighted nor funding given. However, critical feedback on the game concept was given. Six months later, the executive producer returned to represent the product and give a demo that had been built out of salvaged resources. This time, executives were impressed enough to take the product into a funded pre-production status.

Producer Roles: Executive Producer

While the term *executive producer* is often tossed around to describe a variety of activities associated with creative direction or overall management of a project, in this book, I will examine how this role is structured at some of the leading companies in the game industry and discuss how this role can add the most value to the management of a project or set of projects.

Executive producers manage the brand as a "business" unit. What this means is that the executive producer is responsible for managing the business profit and loss statement (P&L) for the brand, and for achieving fiscal corporate goals. This might mean cutting projects in favor of green-lighting others. It also means looking at the big picture of the brand and how investing in it is going to be rewarding for the company.

The executive producer role is very similar in required qualifications and inherent challenges whether it is performed at a developer or at a publisher. Because of this, the role at both types of company has been consolidated here, with specific notes identifying the variations in roles where appropriate.

What Makes an Executive Producer?

As a senior development executive, the executive producer must be versed in both the business and creative elements of running an entertainment software franchise. As an executive, an understanding and foresight of critical business issues related to the brand are critical skills for this role.

The executive producer is required to offer creative input and direction to help guide the brand to a successful place in a highly competitive market. Executive producers often assemble and manage third-party producers who oversee several off-site (third-party) game developers. Most publishers have development contracts that require external developers to work under stringent quality and delivery standards and the executive producer is responsible for enforcing those standards as well.

An executive producer leads the global business effort and vision for a brand. Powerful presentations skills to senior management and the media are required. Naturally, an executive producer must be persuasive and instill confidence. Having sufficient industry-specific experiences to rely upon to help them distinguish between products of high potential impact and those that have failed is critical to establishing that confidence.

Finally, EPs must be able to clarify the vision for the brand, conveying that vision to other department executives and internal leaders. Complete confidence in determining how best to exploit the brand on hardware and software platforms (such Xbox, Playstation 2,

PC, GameCube, or online) to the intended user base and key demographic is another critical skill. This means that the executive producer should possess a complete understanding and vision for how each product in a brand will live up to its maximum potential on each platform.

Following is a list of more qualities an employer expects of any candidate for the executive producer job:

- Leadership abilities, such as being able to work independently and to identify and resolve issues with a positive outcome.

- Strong ability to evaluate product, coupled with a refined intuition into what makes a game fun.

- An understanding of and ability to integrate marketing concepts with product development's creative initiative behind the product.

- A willingness to take and manage risks and tolerates failure as a step toward growth.

- Integrity and the ability to inspire trust and confidence.

Generally, the executive producer has several direct reports (people who report to him), including producers, associate and assistant producers, team leads (lead programmer, lead designer, lead artist, and so on), and even, sometimes, a creative director. However, the reporting structure generally depends on the company and the project. Reporting structures are usually fairly flexible.

What Makes an Executive Producer at a Developer?

Generally, executive producers at a developer are responsible for multiple projects and multiple teams. What usually distinguishes them is their focus on the execution of the development of a game. Generally, an executive producer at a developer is an officer of the company who can focus on the strategic goals of the company and their development plans, while still maintaining a responsibility for the execution and completion of those goals.

The EP may interface with the publisher at a level higher than the normal producer relationship, focusing on future projects and the direction of the relationship with that publisher.

Other Production Management Roles

In addition to the producer roles described above, there are other product management roles at software companies. This section provides an insight into the variations of those roles and how they work. Sometimes they require a technical skill, expertise or background.

Product Planner

The term *product planner* comes from Microsoft and is specific to Microsoft's organization. This position and role was moved laterally from other product groups to the gaming group at Microsoft. Following is a description of the role.

Product Planner Job Description

A product planner's role is to help develop and define the future of a game or a franchise, or even the future of product peripherals. Working with a publisher who is also a hardware manufacturer can be quite challenging.

The product planner focuses on planning for the varied array of video game console products, or even on peripherals like controllers, remote control units, headsets, and future products. This role is similar to that of an executive producer, but with less involvement in the direct product development.

Primary Responsibilities

To quote a recent Microsoft job posting, "The primary responsibility for this role includes developing and driving customer and market requirements in the product planning process." This is a complicated way of saying the product planner must evaluate the market and determine what it needs, then conceive a way to develop that product. Generally, this market-driven approach works in well-established genres or with hardware products where it is possible to predict the demands and requirements of the market. The creative endeavor of creating a game based upon purely original content is extremely challenging to plan, as it is nearly impossible to schedule "creativity" to occur within a specified timeframe. I discuss market-driven decisions and product driven markets later in this book.

The product planner role is focused on conceiving and developing the product idea, then taking it to the Product Development, Marketing, Sales, and Business Development teams to establish its feasibility and longevity. The product planner then works with the development teams to focus the efforts the research and the market analysis that gathers customer input.

Throughout the product development stages, the product planner is focused on features, schedule, and trade-off decisions. An example would be the trade off of including more features but delaying the release of the product for several months or years. Managing the product through each phase of development and balancing each of these compromises is what a product planner does—this is very similar to the role of a producer. This is generally done by aggregating, analyzing, and communicating customer feedback, or market research. Once this is complete, the product planner develops a market-wide competitive understanding (such as a feature comparision list, anticipated ship dates of competitive products, as well as early feedback from testing) and analysis that drives the implementation of a successful product development plan, including projected costs.

Once the development plan is outlined, indentifying the key points in the schedule as well as the overall development budget, the product planner can further develop the business models as well as identify new ways to generate revenue from this product. A product planner must be able to communicate recommendations and influence change within the development process and structure (without mandating it), especially into extremely dynamic environments that may have many variables.

Teamwork is critical, and the product planner must foster the ability to drive results across functional areas of the company. This means the product planner must have an understanding of the goals of the company and how other departments are charged with meeting those goals. Specific goals may be revenue targets, market share acquisition, or technology deployment (as in the case of an Xbox live). As the produt planner must cooridinate and facilitate avenues for constructive input from Program Management, Design, Development, Marketing, Business Development, and Sales departments.

This requirement of coordination of input from various departments is further complicated by the need to develop and manage research that efficiently and effectively captures consumer needs. This research information must be communicated effectively to the product development teams.

Strategic thinking and critical analysis skills are imperative for a product planner. Excellent written and verbal communication, coupled with the ability to achieve objectives and deliver results on multiple projects is another must.

Experience in the games business is generally preferred for a product planner candidate. Qualifications generally include a minimum of four to six year's experience in marketing, product planning, strategic marketing, or business development. Microsoft often requires a BS/BA degree—and sometimes an MBA—for the product planner position.

Program Manager

Microsoft also has a program manager role, which is responsible for the more technical aspects of being a producer. Program managers are charged with the specific implementation and management of feature implementation and less concerned with the responsibilities that go with managing a budget and a schedule. In short, the program managers work to ensure that the game is fun. As this is the case, an outstanding program manager is driven to create, deploy, and support the development of individual game products of games on either the PC or Xbox platforms.

This role seeks to strengthen the developer support services (such as DirectX support, or Xbox SDK support) provided by Microsoft to its development team for the Xbox and Windows games. The program manager is generally the strategic point of contact between Operations, Marketing, and Development; the PM must also interface with internal and external partners. The product manager is involved in the entire lifecycle of a product or service, from its specification and development through deployment and ongoing upgrades.

Primary Responsibilities

One of the principle tasks for the product manager is to communicate as the voice of the game team to other departments. The role is well suited to those with experience in digital media as well as new social online applications (like online chat features, avatars or even online worlds found in MMORPG products) and video games. By following the new trends in digital entertainment, the product manager allows his team to benefit from that understanding. But the PM is a leadership role that requires experience in management of the product on a daily basis.

Coordinating the development process with a strong emphasis on project management is generally what Product Managers do. By working with each team to plan the project execution and milestones, the product manager helps guide the team as to what is producible and what is not. Planning and managing schedules and coordinating milestones are daily responsibilities. The product manager is responsible for communicating project status to other departments, such as Marketing and PR—especially bug counts and updates to the anticipated ship dates.

Some more technically oriented product managers may contribute to the specification writing process, and may interface with other software groups in the division to manage dependencies (deciding the order of tasks in the software's development).

Qualifications for the position generally include at least four years' program or project management experience developing retail software products. Experience in the full cycle of retail products is required. Noone can do this job without excellent verbal and written communication skills or strong organizational skills. Naturally, an excellent knowledge of software development processes and engineering practices is helpful and highly desirable.

The ability to prioritize and make strategic tradeoffs must be a demonstrated strength of a PM candidate. The ability to develop great products within the product vision and strategy takes negotiation skills and an ability to deal well with ambiguity and change.

Finally, the ability to work around unknowns and to eliminate dependencies is what the team relies upon the product manager to do. Product Managers with a strong creative flare and an ability to convey that vision are the most successful.

Development Director

For this book, we've referenced the job description for development director from Electronic Arts, as they've demonstrated a success in the division of their production management roles, bringing credibility to their organizational style. Other companies may have the same job title, but the role description varies from company to company. The development director job description is quoted below from Electronic Arts' Web site:

"As a partner with the producer, the Development Director provides overall leadership and influence at a franchise-wide level. The Development Director will either manage a game franchise or manage one or more components of a complex, large, and strategic project."

Primary Responsibilities and Qualifications

Here's a list of some of the other requirements of this role, as published by Electronic Arts.

- Strong focus on managing performance through coaching, mentoring, and training.
- Strong communicator using active listening skills such as clarifying, understanding, and confirming.
- Able to build a strong effective team; effective at selecting strong people or coaching employees through performance issues.
- Able to address challenging motivational situations and coach in areas of personal strength.
- Able to think outside the box in a challenging and ambiguous environment; being resourceful and creating constructive and innovative solutions.
- Able to effectively partner with peers outside of team to establish alliances and aid in strategic planning.
- Defines initial project scope and delivery schedules; manages day-to-day project schedules and motivates team towards a common project goal.
- Can translate business goals into action.
- Has strong resources planning experience; effective at identifying opportunities to share and reuse between internal and external or central teams.

- Able to initiate or implement development process improvements to achieve efficiencies.

- Acts as a change agent for process improvements.

- Proactively identifies risks associated with meeting project milestones; ensures necessary steps are taken to resolve issues which may impede progress or compromise project's objectives.

- Strong ability to set objectives as well as prioritize and organize task/people assignments.

- Responsible for budget and planning process; manages overall SKU budget, forecasting, and administration for defined project scope.

- Can contribute towards building a realistic business case that anticipates short- and long-term business demands.

- Proactively anticipates and adjusts for problems and roadblocks, partnering with the producer to find equitable and efficient solutions.

The partnership with the producer means that the producer is still responsible for implementing and producing the creative vision for the product, but the development director acts as a check-and-balance system so that the most important issues have the proper resources allocated to him. This allows the producer to focus on fulfilling the vision for the product—he knows that the responsibility for securing the right resources to complete the project is being covered by the development director.

Production Assistants and Interns

Serving as a production assistant or intern is often the way to get started in a production role. If you're just out of school, or want to get some hands-on experience in understanding what producers do, these are the roles to start in. While the production assistant or intern is often given the mundane jobs related to administrative work, testing or product evaluation, meeting preparation, and note taking, this type of involvement in the production process allows a clear perspective on the entire product development process. Being a PA or intern is an easy and low-risk way to understand the business without making a long-term commitment to a role.

A Good PA Makes a Difference

I've found that the right production assistant can make a huge difference. The role of a production assistant is to assist the producer or a group of producers in streamlining the efficiencies of their roles. A smart production assistant who believes in the group in which he's working should look for ways that he can assist the group, rather than just waiting to be told what to do. Production Assistants can fulfill much of the administrative and mundane tasks of the producer.

For example, a production assistant can be given the responsibility of double-checking the lines of dialog in a script against the lines of dialog accounted for in the localization database. A production assistant who can clarify any discrepancies he finds frees up the producer to focus on solving other, more complex issues for the project.

Any excellent production assistant can be promoted through the ranks to assistant producer and eventually producer, given enough experience, guidance, and good judgment.

Production Team Management

Now that you've reviewed some of the producer roles in the game industry, let's see how the talent in these roles might be used to make the maximum impact on a team, a project, and a company. This section explores some ideas on how to get the best work from those who work with you, work for you, or manage you.

Hire Smarter

Generally, the smarter a person, the most usefulness they have to the producer role. Don't be afraid to hire someone who seems smarter or more competent that you in certain areas —such people can help get your work completed and goals accomplished.

While it is sometimes true that very smart people have underdeveloped social skills, communication is a skill that can be taught and learned, while inherent intelligence, deductive powers, and perceptiveness are generally gifts that stay with a person from birth to death.

Practice Respect and Consideration

Treating others with respect and consideration seems like a basic concept, but it often is overlooked. I know, as I've overlooked it myself, dishing out orders on what needs to be done by when and by whom. A better approach is to respect everyone's contribution and ask for volunteers once a task list has been developed. Gradually work through the task list until all of the tasks have a volunteer assigned to them.

Consideration comes in many forms. The monetary consideration one receives from doing a job is often secondary. The primary consideration for many in the game industry is the fact that their contribution to something larger is appreciated and valued. Make sure to show your team this consideration and they'll reflect it back to you. Give others the opportunity to shine and they will. By expecting the best from others, you create a belief in them that they're successful. Often, that's just the jump-start people need to really make a significant contribution without fear of failure.

Create Opportunities

Most people are generally concerned with themselves, and those that actually go out of their way to create opportunities for those that work with them really distinguish themselves. The best way to do this is to volunteer your project or your team for the challenges that are faced at the executive level, or for a new opportunity that's never been faced before at the company.

For example, on one project on which I was a producer there was a requirement for a live-video shoot, one in which Hollywood talent would be used. The challenge (and therefore an opportunity) that I faced as a producer was coordinating all of the prop creation, wardrobe, and other pre-production issues that go into a video shoot. The opportunity that was created was for an associate producer to take responsibility for those aspects of the production and keep it within budget. I provided the AP a clear, concise, budget and helped her identify all of the pre-production elements, then provided her with a timeline for accomplishing these objectives. The PA had never accomplished such an involved aspect of video game production prior to this project, but it was a great opportunity for her to learn to how to take full responsibility for an entire sub-project and complete it on time and within budget. She was thankful for this opportunity and it helped her earn the confidence she needed to fulfill the rest of her responsibilities later on in her career.

Why Being a Video Game Producer Is So Fulfilling

Why is being a video game producer a wonderfully fulfilling role? Here are a few reasons why.

Seeing the Finished Product

One of the main accomplishments of being a producer is being able to hold out a game box and think: *I helped make this*. Then you can enjoy watching people get excited when you give them a copy of the game. Naturally, it becomes even more exciting if your product is selling on the order of magnitude of the last *Grand Theft Auto* title. There is a value to being able to show your work as a finished product to others. Many jobs do not offer such a circumstance or reward. They are never-ending jobs that have little visible accomplishment.

Having an Impact on Others

A producer has the opportunity to impact many people— from co-workers and peers in other departments to the team he works with to external developers, licensees, and the press. And last, but certainly not least, the producer has an opportunity to impact the lives of the consumers who buy the game—it is gratifying to know you have allowed people to experience something that they may have only previously imagined.

Gaining Event-Driven Experiences

There are two types of event-driven experience that can be rewarding to a producer. There's the story, and then the actual gameplay. The gameplay creation is when a producer helps create the tools and the environment for people to play the game while they create the events through online multiplayer gaming environments as fans do for most RTS games like *Command & Conquer* or *Homeworld*. The other type of rewarding event-driven experiences are those events that go into making a video game. There's a nearly endless list of events that can be rewarding to a producer, including casting, filming, designing, integrating technology, creating a story, creating the animation, visualizing the game concept, creating a gameplay prototype, recording the music for the soundtrack, testing, and seeing the game on the shelf.

Realizing Film and Thematic Composition

As video games are form of entertainment, there are elements of film and thematic composition in each product. This can be rewarding for the producer, who helps shape and realize that concept and its presentation to the fullest extent possible. This is often the heart of the experience for the end user, so take pride in its creation.

Engaging in a Multi-discipline Experience

Being a producer provides many opportunities for engagement in the areas of the project in which are most interesting and where your contribution is most valued. If you're a producer, you have an opportunity to use your talents of organization and direction as well as any talents in the areas of game design, storytelling, writing, music, and thematic development.

Helping to Develop the Music

Music is a highly emotional component to any entertainment medium, especially an interactive entertainment software product. As a producer, you have an opportunity to foster the development of an original piece (or pieces) of music that work with your product. What this means is that composition may last forever.

Working with Smart People

Working in the entertainment software industry provides many opportunities to work with smart people. Clever people challenge each other to achieve the best, and find solutions to difficult problems.

Telling Stories in a New Way

The story-driven experience has its roots in the most ancient form of communication, storytelling. But with an interactive medium, linear storytelling is no longer required. It provides an entirely new way to interact with a story. And more importantly, the story and drama on which the game is based is generally a reward when it is completed and implemented in an interactive medium. Video game producers have a real opportunity to help tell stories to society in an imaginative new way.

Using New Technology

During the development of a video game, a producer is constantly searching for new methods, processes, and technology to integrate into the game. As a producer, being responsible for helping to research, understand, and decide how to implement a new technology is an educational and productive experience generally exclusive to engineers and R and D staff. As a producer, the role you play in deciding which of the newest technology is integrated into a game is very rewarding, when you can see the results on screen.

The Final Word

After reviewing the descriptions and challenges of the various producer roles, you'll see that it is no easy task. Turn to the next chapter to learn about the specialties of producers and how to focus your talents where they'll make the biggest impact and hit hard toward making a great game.

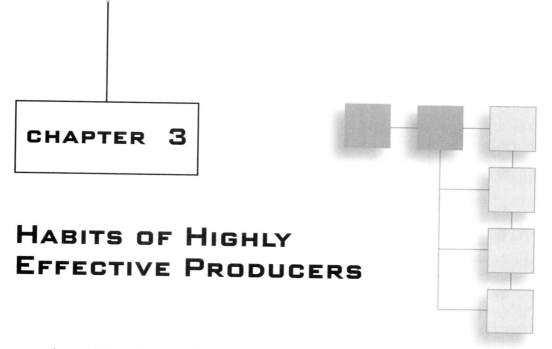

HABITS OF HIGHLY EFFECTIVE PRODUCERS

The guidelines that Stephen Covey wrote in the *Seven Habits of Highly Effective People* can be applied to the role of a producer. A large part of the role of a producer is being available for the team. This section discusses what to do for the team and the project to make the most of your investment.

Traits of a Successful Producer

During the course of my career, and after reviewing many reference sources on leadership, management, and software-production management, I've noticed that successful producers possess certain key traits. I've outlined these traits here in alphabetical order.

Accepts and Expects Criticism

A producer's job is not to be friends with everyone, but to guide his or her team through the game-development process to a successful conclusion. Of course, such a role encourages criticism, so expect—and welcome—it. In any heap of criticism you'll find nuggets of gold; these nuggets can make you rich in understanding. If you accept criticism that's constructive and use the feedback to improve your practices, methods, or approach to problem solving, you're on the road to success. If you receive criticism that you don't feel is worthwhile or valuable, then discard it and move on.

Achieves Results

The achievement of results is generally regarded above all else as demonstration of ability. Find yourself committed to an achievement, and you shall arrive. The achievement of results speaks to the volumes of small accomplishments that must occur in order to create a successful video game. Form your daily habits around achievement of results, however small, one day at a time.

Curtails Ego

A producer with a large ego fails to recognize others for their contributions. This can be most detrimental, making the producer's job more difficult and less enjoyable. Indeed, a big ego can turn good people away from working with you. After all, who wants to work with an egomaniacal project leader? The less you care what others think about you, the more likely they will appreciate your abilities as a producer. Remember, actions speak volumes more than words, so be sure that your actions are consistent with your belief that your ego is in check.

Demonstrates Integrity

Since the ancient Greeks bestowed their wisdom of the ages to the rest of civilization, the value of a good name has been paramount to all who are successful. *Integrity* with respect to the role of the producer refers to being able to resolve political differences in an objective and positive way without taking sides, but remaining professionally committed to the project. Ensure that others believe in you and your integrity. It will last much longer than the game or the project; indeed, it will follow you throughout the rest of your career.

Demonstrates Professionalism

Being professional in all circumstances is critical to maintaining an objective leadership position. "Never let them see you sweat" and "Don't take things personally" are two mantras you should adopt. The example that the producer provides to the team, management, and the industry at large forms the basis of the outsider's belief about the game—its viability and whether it's in good hands. Professionalism is one of the cornerstones of producing effectively.

Displays Contagious Enthusiasm

Your role as a producer is to establish yourself as the person most willing to give for the team and the team's goals. Your enthusiasm for the goal, the project, the game, the team, the company, and your role in it must be contagious. As a source for inspiration and encouragement to others, the producer must shine brightly with contagious enthusiasm. Who wants to follow a leader who doesn't believe in or like where he or she is going?

Doesn't Fear Failure

Everyone fails at some point. This is a natural part of life. Often, however, people avoid opportunities because those opportunities increase the likelihood of a failure in the future. The fact is, however, that from each failure comes a lesson—and from the lesson an opportunity to grow stronger and succeed in the future. A producer cannot be afraid to fail, because each failure yields its own opportunity for growth and understanding as well as success. Do not become complacent; instead, venture forth into the challenges that video game–software development offers without fear!

Doesn't Rush to Criticize

Although it is often easy to see the mistakes of others, sometimes the best approach is to ask clarifying questions about a person's work or approach to the work before criticizing the outcome. Often, you may discover that a team member thought he or she was delivering as expected and simply needs you to clarify your expectations.

Of course, the most important rule when you feel criticism is warranted is to provide others with the same respect you'd expect from them. Allow and guide them to benefit not just from the specific correction that is required to their work, but from the process as a whole. Such an approach can only increase the degree of respect and esteem the team member holds for you, the producer—thereby ensuring a harmonious working relationship as well as a more dedicated team member.

tip

Refrain from personally attacking anyone, regardless of his work performance. You can always work to remove someone from the team if he or she cannot accept honest, constructive criticism.

Empowers Others

Leaders are built through their ability to lead and inspire others. If you, as a producer, are enabling others to do their best work, then they'll respect you for empowering them to deliver their best. Live with the fact that most people won't be able to do some key tasks as well as you do at first, but then realize that as they learn, chances are they'll develop new efficiencies, skills, and procedures to accomplish those same tasks, but in less time and with more quality. Give others a chance to achieve their dreams, and they may just surprise you with the results. By giving up tasks, roles, and responsibilities to others, it frees them to learn and frees you to lead.

Follows Through

Follow through is perhaps the most important skill and trait a producer can have. A lot of people take follow through for granted. Recognizing a commitment and ensuring that it's carried out is the primary responsibility of the producer. The ability of a producer to follow through on his or her commitment is paramount to building team confidence. If a producer cannot follow through on his or her commitments, there is virtually no way for that person to succeed in the long term.

Has a Positive Attitude

A positive attitude is one of the most important attributes a producer can have. Why? The Game Development team faces many problems every day, from mundane frustrations to near catastrophes, and it's the producer's job to help solve problems. If a producer has a positive attitude when dealing with all of the problems associated with software development, he or she can effectively solve those problems. After all, have you ever witnessed an effective problem solver who complained constantly and had a bad attitude? When you undertake your role with a positive attitude, it improves productivity and the quality of the work performed. Besides, it's much easier to work with happy, positive people than with those who have a bad attitude. If you want your team members to have a positive attitude, then you need to start with one yourself.

Inspires Others

The ability to inspire others is a powerful trait. As a producer, others look to you for wisdom, perspective, strength, attention, and proof that you care about the game, the team, and the company. Your honesty in the face of challenges and mistakes is also an important example for others. Often, when a leader admits a mistake, apologizes, recovers, and continues toward the goal, the team enjoys a profound experience in seeing that you're human after all!

Is Decisive

Often, video game–development projects are plagued by indecision. The ability to be decisive, whether the decision is right or wrong, is valuable. The team reacts to the producer's actions and decisions; by delaying in making a decision, the producer lessens the amount of time the team has to implement the decisions. This prevents the next set of decisions from being made in a timely manner, causing a cascade of delays. Try to make decisions early, communicate them clearly, and provide insight into your decision-making process. Waiting to make a decision until all risks are mitigated usually means that any competitive edge has been lost in the delay.

Is Discreet

Discretion—specifically, the ability to respect confidentiality—is one of the traits required of an excellent producer. In any leadership role, there is an inherent opportunity for the leader to know privileged information. Respecting others' requests for confidentiality can only help you do your job and build respect in the long term. If others know that they can trust you with their secrets, then you'll have the information you need to do your job well and to head off problems before they occur.

Is Passionate

A producer must be able to passionately lead a team. This means that the producer must believe in the game concept, direction, and vision. Effectively conveying his or her passion for the product to the team is a very important part of being a producer. The producer must maintain his or her emotional connection to the game concept and vision throughout the development process, up to and including the completion of the product. The dominating and powerful belief in the product must be contagious in order for the producer's passion to be effective.

Is Reliable

Reliability is another critical trait for a producer. As an example to the team, the producer must show that he or she can be counted on in all circumstances. Delivering the same results, with a commitment to quality, is required of almost every producer. Working late with the team to meet a critical deadline, ensuring that all of your responsibilities are completed in a timely manner, and ensuring that contingency plans are in place are just a few examples of being a reliable and excellent producer.

Laughs

Successful leaders look to find humor in facing the daily challenges of life. Indeed, humor is often the lubricant for tense situations, of which you'll experience many during the development of a game. Humor helps leaders remain cool under pressure, and helps keep the challenges in perspective. Case in point: President Reagan, after surviving an assassination attempt in which he was seriously wounded, quipped to the doctors upon arrival to the emergency room, "I hope you are all Republicans."

Be careful, however, not to employ sarcasm in your humor or to use humor to indirectly criticize someone on the team; doing so may be unsettling and unproductive. Benevolence in humor is always the best course for ensuring that others appreciate your point of view. As the old saying goes, "Laughter is the best medicine." It is often true that the best and healthiest organizations know how to laugh at themselves.

Leads by Example

In basic terms, *leadership* is getting others to do what they don't want to do to achieve the results that you want. Leadership also encompasses the ability to convey a degree of confidence to those who are working with you that the leaders of the project are going to make the right choices. Whether you're the executive producer or simply an assistant producer or associate producer, you'll need good leadership abilities.

The best way to lead is by example. That is, if you're asking the team to work accomplish a specific objective or implement a certain gameplay feature by a specific time, make sure that as the producer your work is completed on schedule and that you've met the commitments promised to the team in return for their accomplishing this task. Ensuring that you've made the decisions so that work can progress is another case of leading by example. Don't delay on a making a decision and then expect the team to make up for your delay. As a producer, you do more than what you ask of others. By being a role model, you set the work ethic standard. Practicing what you expect of others, offering your support, demonstrating that you care, and being there to make it happen shows that you're a passionate, committed member of the team.

tip

Andrew Carnegie once said, "No man will make a great leader who wants to do it all himself, or to get all the credit for doing it." This mantra holds true in the video-game industry as well. Whenever possible, give the credit to those you're leading. In the end, it makes you a more effective leader. Empower those you work with by giving them full responsibility for their portion of the game. The results generally are surprisingly positive.

Meets Commitments

A *commitment* is a personal promise to perform a duty or task. When you make a commitment, you make a statement about yourself and about your values. Your willingness to fulfill the commitments you make to others—to do exactly what you said you were going to do—is a key indication of how much you value that commitment, and of the strength of your word.

Commitments are made both by people and by organizations, and an organization's value depends on its ability to meet a commitment. Often, an organization's ability to fulfill its commitments depends on each person in the organization meeting his or her own individual commitments. As such, the organization's commitment is only as strong as the weakest link within the chain of commitments. As a result, your ability to meet your commitments increases your value to the team and to the company.

note

As a producer, you have the added responsibility of making commitments on behalf of the entire team. If you make it a habit to fulfill your own commitments, you'll find that others will prefer to work on your team, and that they'll be motivated to do everything possible to meet their commitments to you. As a result, in the long term, you'll enjoy greater flexibility and freedom, and the ability to manage as you desire.

Perseveres

Perseverance is an ageless trait that has propelled countless leaders to greatness. Being determined to complete a goal that might elude others because it is perceived to be too difficult is what sets a producer apart as an effective leader. At every job, on every game, every producer I know has considered quitting his job at one time or another when the going got tough. They didn't, and each time, the end result was the attainment of their ultimate goal: the development of a great game.

Shares a Vision

Sharing a vision entails creating and believing in a greater purpose that everyone on the team can relate to. By providing this vision—and in the end—a purpose, the producer can establish a positive outcome of the team's efforts. You have a much better chance of completing a long journey inspired by a vision of success than one that is just a forced march. Great accomplishments start with great visions.

Shows Business Savvy

Every producer has some element of business responsibility, and *business savvy* is a generally a required skill. Programmers, artists, and designers do not want to have to worry about the business elements of a project. They want someone who is as good at business to manage the project while they are creating art, code, or design. A good producer allows each member of the team to focus on his or her discipline without worrying about the business aspects of a project. A producer who is business savvy clears a path on which the team and the project can succeed. Negotiating deals for software tools, cooperative or complimentary products, or required third-party software licenses are just a few examples of where business savvy helps the team accomplish its goal. Other elements may include voiceover talent negotiations, hiring the right contractor, or negotiating with partner or licensee. If a producer does not demonstrate some business savvy, then it is unlikely he or she will be able to achieve a promotion in the role of the producer.

Shows Respect

The old saying "Respect is not given but earned" is never truer than when used to describe what is required for a producer to succeed. Demonstrating respect for other's ideas, initiative, passion, and advice is of paramount importance for producers. The producer earns respect by demonstrating initiative, follow through, and a commitment to excellence. At the very least, if you simply do what you say you're going to do, then you'll be able to earn at least a little respect.

Takes Initiative

Initiative is the power or ability to begin and to energetically follow a plan, task, or enterprise with determination. The initiative of the producer sets an example for the entire team. The end result of the team's collective work is widely affected by the initiative demonstrated by the producer. The producer must take the initiative to solve problems before they affect the game's development. It is almost impossible for a producer to demonstrate too much initiative.

Takes Risks

John F. Kennedy once said, "There are risks and costs to a program of action. But they are far less than the long-range risks and costs of comfortable inaction." Indeed, the acceptance and willingness to take risk is what liberated millions of people from the bonds of war in the 1940s. Simply put, the extraordinary does not come to those who do not take risks. Practice taking small risks first, and then build your own method of managing risks. Over time, you'll grow to take larger and larger risks and be ready to face the failures and rewards as they come.

Organization and Successful Processes

The basic habits of highly effective producers start at the project and daily management level. This section discusses a few of the ways (by no means is this an all-inclusive list) you can be a more effective producer. If you turn these principles into habits, you will have laid a solid foundation for becoming an excellent producer.

Do Daily Delta Reporting

The tool I've found to be of foremost use to a producer is the Daily Delta Report. This term comes from the mathematical reference to the word *Delta*, meaning *a finite increment in a variable*. This process is used by some of the industry's top game developers to ensure that they're tracking and managing the development of their games efficiently.

A Daily Delta Report is a list of all of the changes in task or feature completion or states. This means that each member of the team sends a quick e-mail at the end of the day listing the work that was completed only, not everything that was worked on during the day. These individual three- to five-line emails are sent to the assistant producer or the producer who then group each person's email details by their contribution area (art, design, production, and programming) into a single report, published the following morning. The Daily Delta Report provides a clear outline of the daily accomplishments of game development progress from each team member—the finite increment in an easily reviewed fashion.

The producer or assistant producer compiles the myriad of e-mails from the team into a single comprehensive report of all the team member's accomplishments and distributes the report at the beginning of the following day. It is an easy process which allows the producer to understand and follow what each team member is doing without being intrusive on a daily basis. When everyone the entire team has this report, this means that everyone has the same information that the producer does about what was worked on and for how long. It promotes communication and problem resolution, as on large teams it is sometimes difficult to know what everyone else is working on. If you're an artist working on animating a character and the programmers are working on a key feature of the animation engine, reading this report allows the opportunity you to collaborate in a timely basis and discuss the requirements of the animation engine.

Collaboration and clarity is promoted by Daily Delta reporting. It's less intrusive and takes less time than an assistant producer going around an interrupting everyone to get their statuses. If every accomplishment, or delta, is archived, there's a clear record of what the entire team did on each day of the project (assuming that these emails are saved into their own folder). This makes understanding and rectifying mistakes easier and makes possible progress for benchmarking purposes.

Ask Clarifying Questions

The foremost aspect of the producer role is to clearly understand at what stage the project is in and what it will take to complete the project on time. There's virtually no way to do this without asking questions of others. But there's a way to do that that's more effective than constantly asking "Hey, when is the DirectX integration going to be done?"

When asking a clarifying question, you should pose it in a non-confrontational, non-accusatory manner. "What remains to be done to complete this feature and how I might help overcome some of the challenges you're facing?" Is a much different question than "You said that you'd have this feature complete by now—why is it more than three days late?" By asking clarifying questions you make it clear to the person whom you're asking that understanding him is your first priority.

Clarifying questions can also prevent an emotional outburst from an overstressed team member and help identify other problems before they become more acute and disruptive to the whole team. For example, I've often just taken a team member to lunch and asked them about how their work is going, what they are enjoying or not enjoying and why. It is not surprising that learning this type of information can help you understand a specific part of your project, but it can also help you understand a specific team member's challenges. By listening first, you establish a level of rapport and trust with the team members, and establish yourself as someone who can help solve problems.

This approach also prevents the natural human tendency to cover up for mistakes and hide faults. Often, the team member does not want an immediate solution from the producer so much as to know that his concerns are being heard. An immediate response from the producer is not mandatory as it is sometimes better to just think about the answer before responding.

Table 3.1 lists some examples of clarifying questions to use in a variety of situations.

Table 3.1   Clarifying Questions for Common Situations

Situation	Clarifying Question
Team member wants a raise (outside of the normal performance review process).	I'd like to understand why a raise outside of the normal performance review process is warranted? Please help me understand type of (financial) recognition you are expecting? How do you think that your pay rate measures against others in the industry and the company?
A team member Is unhappy with his raise after a performance review.	Do you feel free to speak to me candidly about what elements of your performance review were unsatisfactory, unclear or unfair? Do you have a clear idea about what performance improvements would make next year's review an outstanding one? What elements of your performance review weighed most negatively on your overall rating?
I'd like to help you outline a plan to achieve the performance review rating you want for next year.	When can we sit down and outline and plan and a goal list?
When a team member is behind schedule.	What challenges remain to completing this work? Is there anything that I can do to help improve the efficiency of completing this task? Are there any tools that you're lacking?

Situation	Clarifying Question
When a team member is behind schedule.	Which elements of this task did I not account for in the schedule when it was established? Can we discuss the plan for completing this task by a new deadline?
When a team member is upset with the behavior or performance of another team member.	Can you please tell me how you feel or how his behavior upset you? Why do you think that he acts this way? What factors do you believe contributed to this behavior? Do you believe that he meant his actions against you personally?
When someone is upset at the decision of an executive or higher level manager.	How did you feel when you learned of this decision? What are your suggestions for how I should respond to the impact of this decision?
When someone is habitually late to work.	What is inhibiting your ability to get to work on time? Did you realize that your lateness affects others? Can you take a moment to understand how your not being here on time affects everyone else who is here on schedule?
When work quality is insufficient.	What steps do you think are necessary to get your work product quality to a higher level? Do you understand why this work product can't really be used in our game without affecting many other elements? What can we do to help increase the product quality of your future work? Do you need more time? Better tools? Or a better understanding of the requirements at the beginning of the work?
When there's a disagreement over the creative direction of the product.	Can you help me understand exactly where you're coming from and why you feel this way? What other concerns do you have with this direction? What do you suggest we do to minimize this issue and solve it effectively?
Wants a day off (with little or no advance warning)	Did you realize that your absence is going to affect the team's ability to complete our work on schedule? How did we not know about this potential situation before now? What can I do in the future to make sure we plan for these types of occurrences?

Anticipate the Needs of Others

Anticipating the needs of others means being flexible and adaptable about responding to the direction of the product with a focus on what each team member is going to need to succeed in their role. For some team members, this means the right tools and plug-ins for Maya, 3D Studio Max, Lightwave, or whichever 3D software package the team is using. Anticipating the needs of programmers might require that you help outline which tools are going to be licensed from a third party and which ones need to be developed internally.

Another way to anticipate the programmers' and the artists' collective needs is to help formulate the plan for the assignment of critical path tasks and features to ensure that the items on the critical path of the project schedule are completed on schedule.

Naturally, it is difficult to anticipate the needs of others without a clear and open communication process, so ensure that a fundamental communication network is available for constant collaboration among the team members.

To effectively anticipate the needs of others, stay away from the "Dilbert" management style and company structure. An authoritarian management style undermines a producer's ability to understand and anticipate the needs of other. More importantly, team members find it easier to fall into the role of complaining without taking any steps to improve the situation.

Always Call People Back and Answer E-Mails

While this may seem like a simplistic principle, returning people's calls (whether it is today, tomorrow, or next week) is a valuable trait. It ensures that people will call you to discuss news, and that you're afforded every opportunity to understand and anticipate external problems or opportunities that may affect your product. Being responsive is one of the traits that is highly respected and appreciated by others—you're not wasting their time making them wait for a callback or stalling on making a decision until some later date.

The rule that I try to live by is that everyone gets a return phone call by the end of the day—or at least on the way home. The exception to this rule is when I'm traveling and it is not practical to return the call until later.

It is often easier and more convenient to send a caller an e-mail to let him know that you received their voicemail and that you're working on the situation. I often send a response e-mail saying "Thanks for your call today. I need to gather the right information before I call you back to discuss this further. I should be able to get in touch with you by [date]." This is a great way to be responsive without being evasive or committal.

Returning people's calls is a way to distinguish your performance and approach from those who may consider it acceptable to not respond unless it is to their advantage. I've been able to get my calls returned by people I needed to speak to because they knew that I would always call *them* back. Respect breeds respect, and in this industry respect is an important and valuable commodity that often takes years to develop.

Always Follow Up in Writing

One of the most important parts of effective communication is confirming that the other party clearly understands your position and what you're saying. One of the ways that I've found to be effective is to follow up important phone or in-person conversations with an e-mail. Politely restating your understanding of the conversation and identifying the next steps to be taken is an important tool in ensuring your project stays on schedule. There's nothing worse than, after having a conversation with the IT department and expecting a problem to be solved by a certain date, you later find that the IT guy has been waiting for two weeks for you to confirm the specifications of the hardware and the cost that you've budgeted.

To prevent such situations from arising, I follow up with the individuals involved in a conversation with an e-mail stating:

- The issues that I remember being discussed.
- The proposed and agreed-upon resolutions.
- Who is responsible for completing the agreed-upon tasks.
- The date or time by which the tasks are to be done.

This simple procedure has undoubtedly prevented numerous mistakes and misunderstandings (especially on my part) from affecting the team or the rest of the company.

Confirming your understanding in writing. Be especially sure to clarify critical and sensitive situations such as those concerning performance, compensation, critical path schedule items, and public relations events.

It has often been said that the first rule of corporate America is to "cover your ass" or "CYA." The "always follow up in writing" trait is not to be construed as motivated solely by CYA. In fact, CYA emails are generally very transparent and are easily distinguished from those motivated by an individual concerned with the project's success and that of other team members. Don't get the CYA rule confused with responsible and clear communications.

Understand the Contract

For external development teams and third-party producers, understanding any existing contracts is a fundamental and necessary skill. While the authoring of an external development or license agreement is not usually the sole responsibility of the producer, understanding the key principles, milestones, conflict resolutions and goals for the project as outlined in the development agreement is an excellent way to ensure that you're effective in your role.

Once you understand the key principles behind the agreement, it become easier to administer and drive toward completing the goals outlined therein. I've witnessed development teams reach the point of total frustration because the contract was so vague and the goals so ill-defined that it would have been nearly impossible to meet the objectives in it when it was signed.

If you inherit a project with a poorly defined contract or one that's hard to understand, read through it and create a checklist of key dates and goals. Then ensure that you understand the way to resolve conflicts or disagreements within the framework of the contract. They are almost always evitable, so the sooner that you understand them the better.

Follow the Contract

Once an understanding of the contract has been achieved, there's the second step of using documentation to support your case and ensure that you're following the procedures and definitions in the agreement.

Make sure that for each milestone review or license-review stage, you have a checklist clearly specifying all of the details in the milestone review and how they relate to the agreement. Provide a place for acceptance of the milestone, with a signature line or other indication that what's been provided is acceptable and meets the terms of the agreement.

While it may seem disadvantageous to the product's development process to follow the strict letter of the agreement, I've rarely seen a producer take the heat for a project that remained on schedule because he stuck to the milestones outlined in an agreement rather than modifying the product to be the best or the coolest, or to include features or content that was not specified in the agreement in the first place.

If you don't agree with the terms outlined in the agreement, then work with your management to update the contract to reflect a reality that makes sense for the product and its marketability. Propose a solution for improving the circumstances and restrictions of the original agreement. But until that agreement is executed and in place, you probably shouldn't proceed on a course of action which deviates from the spirit or letter of any agreement regardless of external force or outside market factors.

Project Skills: Scheduling and Rescheduling Constantly

While some producers may consider the constant need to schedule and reschedule a big hassle, if an efficient process exists to handle this process, it is much less of a hassle and more of an administrative issue. Often, this "hassle" surrounds the use of Microsoft's Project software. Scheduling and rescheduling is a necessary procedure for producers to follow. Requirements, features, designs, available resources, and time all change during the course of a project, and there are not any solutions around having to constantly re-evaluate and consider all of the variables and their impact.

MS Project is a complex and detailed software scheduling tool. Its value lies in when it is used, how it is administered and updated, and the depth of expertise of its user. The expectations are from its use often are not paralleled with the depth of expertise of the user and it can be frustrating to use in such cases.

Generally, I recommend MS Project for the Envision and Speculation phases of the project. MS Excel is often more easily adapted to tracking progress and identifying the remaining work, while MS Project is valuable in high lighting key dependencies within the task structure of a project.

I often reschedule a project as many as 12 times per year, returning to the Envision and Speculation phases for each of the remaining milestones and applying what I've learned from the completed milestones to the remainder of the project. Be prepared to continually revise estimates and adjust expectations, while identifying new dependencies.

Postmortem Reports

One of the most valuable procedures in the video game industry is the publishing of postmortem reports. Publishing the findings outlined in these reports—either online at http://www.gamasutra.com or in print in Game Developer magazine—is a primary way the video game industry has differentiated itself from other facets of the entertainment industry. These reports highlight what went wrong and contrast that against what went right on a recently completed project. This allows others to learn from the mistakes and successes of other teams.

One of the practices that I've found to be valuable is to provide a way for team members to prepare a postmortem report on the project and submit it for review by management. I've even taken it one step further, in asking for short postmortem reports at the end of each milestone. Documenting successes and failures ensures that the failures are identified, communicated, and recorded, while the successes are recognized. This is the first step toward repeating the successes and minimizing the chances of repeating the failures.

Allowing team members to express their disappointment and do some self-analysis ensures that the communication lines remain open. The next project is one step closer to being a self-organizing team and being more adept at finding the best solutions for any challenge.

Always Tell the Team the Truth

The lead programmer for one of my recent projects suggested I include this point, after having worked with several producers who hard a hard time telling the truth. Producers may get used to negotiating with outside third parties, when it is often disadvantageous to discuss the entire truth behind an issue; when dealing with the team, however, it is imperative that your word be the 100 percent truth.

No matter how small the discrepancy in your story, it will be perceived as a lie, and you may get a reputation for abusing your position by attempting to manipulate others for a particular advantage. For such an infraction, a producer can lose almost all respect that he has worked long and hard to earn. Don't let this happen to you—provide complete honesty in all your dealings.

The Commitment to Excellence

As described in the dictionary, "Excellence is the quality of possessing good qualities in an eminent degree." Being committed to excellence is the mantra for those producers who desire to have their team succeed in creating an excellent product. This doesn't mean that your game will be a top-seller or will get unanimously great reviews. But if you're committed to excellence, the game has a much higher likelihood of reaching those goals than if you don't. Being committed to excellence is the foundation that successful products are built on.

Being committed to excellence means that as a producer and a leader, you set the example for others to follow in terms of standards of acceptable work product, professional behavior and creative problem solving abilities. This commitment shines through in everything that you do, from writing clear e-mails (with no spelling mistakes or typos) to writing and presenting quality reports to giving informative presentations to holding successful public relations events. When you're asked if you're going to be able to complete something on-time, you're answer should be a resounding yes—and you should deliver. Don't agree to finish any task unless you know is can be completed excellently.

A superior product can only emerge from a team that is committed to excellence in everything they do. Try to share your commitment to excellence and passion for the product to everyone on the team, from the most junior to the most senior member, thereby empowering them to be make the commitment to excellence reflect in their final work product.

Achieving Excellence

Achieving excellence means using your gifts and talents to become one of the best in your field. But excellence does not necessarily mean being number one, though sometimes winning awards is a byproduct of excellence. A commitment to excellence means simply that you are always trying to improve and build upon your talents, however possible.

For example, excellence in being a producer may mean having the best music, the most compelling game design, a fully integrated story, a slick user interface, or the best level design and implementation. Or it could mean achievement of a technical goal, such as texture compression, or poly rendering achievements that bring a new vitality to the interactive experience.

In order to achieve excellence, first you have to be committed to finding it whenever possible. Make it a state of mind that permeates every part of your work.

What Is Required for Excellence?

The following subsections discuss some of the traits necessary to achieve excellence

Passion

Real passion for a project is similar to being committed to running a marathon to the finish line. The race may be long, hot and sweaty, but the goal of finishing the race keeps pushing the runner forward. Those who are exuberant about their goals act to accomplish them.

Courage

Pursuit of a goal, a dream or a collective vision requires courage. It means not being afraid of failure and moving ahead in spite of your doubts and fears about the outcome.

Higher Standards

The key to excellence is setting high standards by example. Always ask yourself, "Is this the best I can do?" and "Am I settling for less than I can be?" You must set the bar high and continually raise it if you want to achieve excellence in your work. Demand more of yourself than anyone else will demand from you.

Working Hard and Smart

The great football coach from Alabama, Bear Bryant, once said, "It's not the will to win that counts as much as the will to prepare to win." If everyone wants to win, then they need to put in the effort and time to prepare to win. But very few people want excellence enough to invest the exhausting effort and preparation required to be the best.

How Does a Commitment to Excellence Apply to Producers?

One way for a producer to apply a commitment to excellence across a large team is to take clear and personal responsibility for a certain portion of the game. Following this rule, I took responsibility for the creation of the soundtrack for *Myst III: Exile*. By taking that personal responsibility and conveying my commitment to excellence to all involved, from the composer to the orchestra to the development team, I helped set the standard for what the overall experience would be for the user. This commitment to excellence was realized when we recorded the soundtrack with a live orchestra in Seattle in late 2000. It started with an audition of several top composers, a clear design direction, and an eminent set of standards that we were trying to achieve.

One time, I was on a team working long and hard hours to complete a milestone on schedule. Additionally, I was supervising the production and editing of a trailer for the game. Somehow the editor included footage captured from the game that clearly displayed a rendering error. While it wouldn't have been apparent to the average viewer, it was noticeable to the team. The opinion was unanimous that we should replace the footage with something better and more compelling. So it was back to the editing room. We found an even better piece of footage that improved the overall composition of the trailer. It was released a few days later and was well-received. The commitment to excellence paid off and I'm glad that was instilled in the team.

Why This Principle Is Important to Producing a Hit

This principle is important for producing a hit for many reasons. First, there are so many factors that require success in order for a video game to reach a hit status—meaning commercially successful product—that it is often a daunting set of challenges.

A producer who is committed to excellence some things working against them.

- Market timing.
- The focus of marketing efforts.
- The reliance upon the applicability of critical technology.
- The adopting of the technology in the marketplace (especially 3D hardware chipsets),
- The sales force's ability to place product in the market at the right time
- Operational issues, such as manufacturing slots and schedules.

I could go on and on listing the many challenges faced between the game's original concept and actually getting it to the user. But, if the product is not excellently made, these factors may be overcome and yet the game is still not a commercial success. Products take time and money—your time and the publisher's (or someone else's) money. You'll never get that investment of money and time back if it is wasted on a product that's mediocre.

As a producer, you are charged with supervising the investment of millions of dollars, as well as hundreds and perhaps thousands of man-months in making a game, it should be an excellent product when it reaches the marketplace. If it is not, what was all of the hassle for it in the first place? Remember the old adage: "Excellence always endures.... It remains long after cost is forgotten."

How to Get Known for Excellence

Reaching excellence in any area of life means setting the highest standards. One of the greatest benefits to making a commitment to excellence is that people remember and regard excellence highly. By establishing yourself as one committed to excellence, it generally opens up doors, new opportunities and people who want to work with you again. This network and reputation is one of the most valuable parts of your career.

Ensure that your team knows that you're committed to excellence. Demonstrate this with your actions and reinforce it with your statements. Discuss how the team was committed to excellence when meeting with journalists. Above all, get the word out that this is a product completed by a team committed to excellence. You'll be doing yourself and your team a huge favor that pays dividends.

Rules That Apply to All Producers

This section discusses some of the rules that apply to all producers, why they are important to understand and apply to your work as a producer.

Knowing What You Don't Know

"The hallmark of wisdom is knowing what you don't know." - Socrates

There's no way that a producer can know everything that needs to be done, when it needs to be done, and how it affects the game's development. But the challenge is to try to understand everything that you can about the game's development while relying on others to know everything about their area of responsibility and to report the noteworthy challenges to you.

Understand that a producer may want to or try to know everything related to the game, but it is usually not possible. Also know that you don't have to give the right answers or propose solutions immediately when confronted with challenges. Know that you won't have all of the answers all of the time.

- Knowing what you don't know requires consistently applying a few principles in your daily routine.
- Know that you may not be the best game designer, programmer, or art director in the industry.

- Know that others are often times better qualified to make certain decisions and recommendations.
- Know that you don't know everything that the leads from each department do.
- Know that you don't face the same challenges that each of the team members do in actually creating the parts of the game that form the sum of the whole.
- Know that, while you may have ideas on how to market the game and make it appeal to a broad audience, you may not know the best way to spend the media budget.

The Immutable Law of Resources, Quality, and Time

All games are comprised of three basic elements: resources (meaning talent, financial resources to hire the best talent and tools), quality (the quality of the game and its design specifications, and naturally, the time (money) it costs to bring that all together. If you change one factor, the others must change as well. So if, as a producer, you need to decrease the time it will take to complete a project, then you need to increase the resources required and/or decrease the quality of the game to make sure it can be completed within the time constraint. Or if you want to change the specifications for the game—say, by increasing the quality to make the game more competitive—then the project (generally) will require more time and resources (which equates to money).

One of the biggest traps to fall into as a producer is to believe that making the team work long hours of overtime is more productive. When overtime is the norm, it becomes no more productive than what is typically accomplished in an eight or nine hour day. Burnout is a common occurrence among development teams that are forced into long periods of required overtime to meet an impossible deadline.

How to Quantify the Unquantifiable

There are always a lot of variables that go into making a video game, and it is best that you start trying to understand and quantify these variables early. Often the task is so daunting, so large, and so ill-defined that you may think, "Oh, let's just start and then we can make firmer plans once we know what is possible." This course of action is not recommended.

With most developers in the game industry, there's always a resistance to the imposition of a more defined team structure, process, procedure or methodology. "Restrictions tend to stifle creativity" is the general consensus. But while ineffective procedures may slow down productivity, effective procedures increase productivity and efficiency.

Begin with a functional specification and a use case of the creative design. A functional specification is a description of how the game functions. A use case is a list, table, or report detailing all of the potential uses that a user would see if the creative design were implemented as specified. Then those two elements are divided into features and task, art assets, and tool requirements. When that long list has been written, you've quantified the previously unquantifiable work required for the game.

You'll be glad you took the steps to quantify the unquantifiable before beginning the epic adventure of embarking on a game's development.

Chapter 9 discusses the process of creating a game's development schedule. I also recommend reading Erik Bethe's *Game Development and Production*, by Wordware Publishing, as well *Agile Project Management* by Jim Highsmith (published by Pearson Education).

The Game Developer's Conference

The last section in this chapter is a recommendation that all producers attend the annual Game Developer's Conference (GDC) at least once in their career—preferably, attend every year.

The annual GDC is held in March. The URL for the conference Web site is http://www.gdconf.com/.

The GDC is an official trade conference "by game developers for developers" of all forms of entertainment media, including computer games, console games, mobile entertainment, arcade entertainment and location based entertainment and naturally, online gaming.

The GDC has thousands of attendees each year. When that many experienced game developers get together, it forms sort of a nucleus of creative energy and motivation. There are excellent professional networking and business opportunities for the individual. With the annual gathering of game development professionals, many of whom are leading the $23 billion video game industry, this tremendous source of knowledge and benchmarks cannot be overstated. The forum provides global access for programmers, artists, producers, game designers, audio professionals to exchange ideas, helping to shape the future of the industry.

There are lectures, panels, tutorials and round-table discussions, including a variety of topics of common interest to the industry. All are headed by leading industry experts. There's also access to demonstrations of the latest and greatest game development tools, platforms and development services.

The Final Word

Being effective as a producer is about the talent coupled with leadership. While it is challenging to be able to handle the administrative tasks of scheduling, budgeting, and being fiscally responsible, the talent makes the biggest impact in the effective habits that a producer adopts. Those habits ensure that the decisions are made on the right timeframe and the talent of others is afforded the opportunity to be recognized.

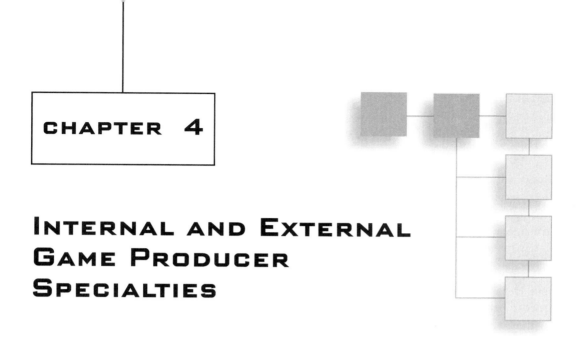

CHAPTER 4

INTERNAL AND EXTERNAL GAME PRODUCER SPECIALTIES

This chapter discusses the various specialties that producers throughout the industry offer to their teams and their company. The theme is to play to the strengths of the individual along with emphasis on finding the fun in your job and in your game in development. There are numerous specialties of a producer, paralleling the specialties in other disciplines in game development. Here are some ideas on how to get the best out of yourself as a producer.

Specialties of a Game Producer

In the video game industry, there are various types of producers who specialize or demonstrate strength in one area over another. This chapter explores the different specialties of producers and how each type can use his or her strengths for success. But remember that at some point, every producer must call upon some element of the special knowledge listed here.

If you have a mind for business but only mild opinions and interests in game design, there's still a role for you in this industry. If you have more of an interest in design and art production than for scheduling, you can find a position where you can use those skills as well. Almost every job has unenjoyable aspects, but the role of the producer is one of the most versatile roles in the industry, so you're bound to find the job appealing in some areas. Explore your talents and learn to focus them when and where they have the most impact.

Legal and Business Facilitator

A producer who is focused on the legal and business aspects of the game is generally in a higher-level leadership role, but as an assistant producer, you may be fortunate enough to have a chance to learn these skills and principles from an EP.

The producer who is the legal and business facilitator needs to understand the subjects discussed in the next subsections, and must be able to negotiate well. Negotiations involve complex topics such as right reversals, sublicense ability, distribution agreements, ancillary rights, delivery dates, and a host of other topics that require a legal understanding.

More than 99% of all projects have some legal agreement necessary for their completion, so it is important that producers to not perpetuate ignorance of the law. Reliance on attorneys is part of working in entertainment software, but more knowledge can help the process be more efficient. Most attorneys do not have time for educating producers. Furthermore, attorneys generally do the easiest work first.

If a producer can do as much of the legal legwork as possible, making the job easier for the attorney to quickly review the legal points and ensure they have been sufficiently addressed, this allows the game's development to get underway sooner.

A producer for a publisher may also be involved peripherally with the negotiations for a licensee, such a movie studio or celebrity athlete like Tony Hawk or an actor like Vin Diesel.

Business Contract Law

Since business litigation concepts govern most business agreements, let's take a short tour through the complex world of contract law. Outlined below are the various parts of a contract that have particular relevance to software development.

note

The information listed in this book should not be substituted for the competent legal advice of an attorney.

Contracts are written to clearly outline the business promises between two parties. These promises are ones that a court of law will enforce. In order for a contract to be legally binding, the parties must exchange a promise for adequate consideration (money) and benefits. The money offered must be fair for the work performed.

n o t e

Common law is the legal principle that the law evolves with the times. Judges can interpret the law and what other courts have found to be consistent with the law over time. This principle means that different courts can interpret laws differently, depending on the facts surrounding the specifics of a situation. Society may have changed since the law was written and this principle allows the courts to interpret and apply the law with some common sense.

Statutory law (written for a particular jurisdiction) may require that some contracts be put in writing and executed with particular formalities.

This section discusses the various parts of a contract and why they are relevant to video game development. It is not meant to be a complete and full discussion of every element of an agreement, just a brief overview of what goes into an agreement. This type of material constitutes an entire course for first-year students in law school.

This section also outlines the principles and parts of a contract so that when you're speaking with an attorney, your manager, or an executive, you will have a cursory understanding of the key elements involved in completing an agreement, whether it be a license, development, or work for hire agreement.

c a u t i o n

Do not enter into an agreement without a lawyer. While it may seem fine to outline a letter of intent and then to start negotiating a contract's deal points and specifics, there is a whole host of considerations that lawyers have which you as a producer, do not.

Following are brief overviews of common contract law topics.

Assignments

The Assignments section of an agreement generally deals with whether or not the contract can be assigned to a third party without breaching the contract. Contracts with a developer cannot be assigned (in whole) by the developer to some other third party without consent of the publisher. A publisher doesn't want a different team completing the work specified in the agreement. And, since industry consolidation is commonplace these days, these restrictions prohibit the developer from selling out to a third-party that may compete with the publisher. The publisher hired the developer for their talent to complete a specific amount of work and deliver a marketable product, and that's what they expect.

However, generally the obligations of a publisher can be assigned to a third party, giving the publisher the flexibility to assign the agreement to a new publisher or a new party controlling or purchasing their business, as is the case in today's environment of corporate mergers and acquisitions of publicly traded companies. This is relevant to the game's development, as a producer may suddenly find that the overall strategy of the publisher has changed when they've assigned the agreement to another company who's purchased their business.

Breach

Breach is when a specific promise outlined in the agreement fails to be fulfilled on schedule or otherwise according to the terms of the agreement. Breach commonly results when either party fails to submit something in a timely manner, such as when the publisher fails to meet a milestone payment within the time provided for in the agreement.

Choice of Law Clauses

These clauses specify the choice of law that will be used to interpret the agreement in the event that a dispute arises that proceeds to litigation. If you are in Washington and you're negotiating an agreement with a company in California, and the choice of law is California, then the agreement will be interpreted (and litigated) in California. Your attorney may not be licensed to practice in California, and in that case you'd have to hire a lawyer who is before proceeding to trial.

Conditions

Conditions are the specific conditions under which the parties agree to perform the work and provide the compensation specified in the agreement. Conditions are very specific and measurable. An example might be "Milestone acceptance is conditional upon conformance with the design specifications and testing." That means that the milestone acceptance is conditional upon a review and test of it by the publisher. The publisher can reject the submission if it does not materially conform to the specifications outlined in the agreement.

Consideration

An advance royalty payment is paid as an "advance" on the royalties expected to be paid to the developer. The advance payment is paid only when work is completed, submitted, and accepted by the publisher.

A *license fee* is different in that it may be structured over several payments as well (the fee to use a movie license or specific technology, for example).

The party receiving the royalty or license payment earns the advance as the work is accepted, but the royalties aren't actually "earned" until the product is sold and money is collected by the publisher so that the amount of money owed by the publisher to the developer exceeds the royalty payments that were previous advanced to the developer.

Covenants Not to Compete

Naturally, if a developer is contracted to work on one product in a specific genre, the publisher or licensee wants to focus efforts on making that game the best it can be. So if a developer is building an RTS for Microsoft, it is unlikely that the contract would allow that same developer to work on an RTS for Vivendi Universal, as the product might compete with the product from Microsoft.

Damages and Remedies

Damages and remedies are provisions in an agreement that specifies what will happen if the contract is breached or is otherwise unfulfilled. These clauses are specific and allow for very precise set of circumstances. For example, if a developer is sold to a competing company before the work on its existing contracts is completed, one of the damages and remedies may be for the developer to refund all the amounts advanced under the agreement to the publisher. This could amount to several million dollars, so be careful when considering damage and remedy clauses.

Duration and Termination of Contract

Most contracts have a *duration*, meaning that they last for a specific amount of time. Other contracts are in perpetuity. Be sure to clearly specify how to terminate the agreement and what steps must be taken in order to terminate the agreement prior to the end of its duration. The duration of a development agreement may end when the work specified in the agreement is complete. However, the responsibility to pay royalties on the product may extend indefinitely, depending on how successful the product is.

Implied Contracts

As a producer, you make it clear that any statement that you make to any outside third party is not an implied agreement or a contract in any way, unless and until an officer of the company has signed the agreement. Often when you're dealing with contracts on a daily basis, it is easy to understand and propose terms that you may know to be generally acceptable. But it is important that you do not obligate your company to fulfill the terms until an executed agreement is in place to govern that business relationship. All contracts that I've seen used language specifying that the agreement constitutes the entire understanding between the parties and oral modifications are prohibited; only written modifications have any force or effect.

Intellectual Property Ownership

Intellectual Property (IP) Ownership is one of the most complex issues that you'll be required to understand as a producer. Who owns the IP is important to understand when working on a game that uses an IP license. Be sure that the contract clearly determines who owns the intellectual property related to the creative aspect of the game as well as the technology that's used to create the game. In many cases, these are principal issues that determine the direction of a relationship or a business contract and—in the case of a disagreement—whether litigation is worthwhile or not.

When dealing with license agreements (licenses to specific intellectual property) be sure to clearly understand how the property can be used and what degree of freedom the producer has. Managing a project that uses a third-party intellectual property could be a routine as a third-party licensed tool like Miles Sound System from RAD Game Tools or as significant as a *Star Trek*, *Tony Hawk*, or *Spiderman* movie license.

Independent Contractors

Whether you work at a developer or at a publisher, chances are that at some point you're going to need to use independent contractors. Therefore, it is important that you work with your counsel to prepare a clear, concise, and specific independent-contractor agreement. That agreement should specify the work to be performed, the acceptance criteria for the work, who owns the work (rarely do independent contractors own their work), and the time in which the service is to be provided and completed. Make sure you follow the Internal Revenue Service's (or your local taxing authority) independent contractor rules to ensure that the relationship maintains the independent contractor relationship and does not become classified as an employee.

Microsoft learned this the hard way when they were sued by a group of independent contractors and temporary employees, who were deemed to be full time employees and subject to the normal benefits offered full-time employees. The Ninth Circuit Court of Appeals held that the workers could not be excluded from Microsoft's benefit plans because they were common law employees, not ICs. The case hinged on the fact that Microsoft's own published plans contained ambiguous definitions of just which employees were covered. (The case is Vizcaino v. Microsoft Corp., 97 F.3d 1187 [9th Cir. 1996])

Independent contractors are usually used to complete specific tasks for a specific duration of time and can work at home. A few examples of where you can use independent contractors to help out your product include

- Storyboarding
- Sketches
- Pre-production artwork
- Sound and music composition and integration
- Script writing
- PR or demo work

Check with your own Legal department before hiring an independent contractor.

Letter of Intent

The Letter of Intent, better known as the LOI, is a brief outline of terms used by producers to begin a review of the discussion points (such as budget, timeline, and technology use) related to completing an agreement. Attorneys generally recommend using a "nonbinding" LOI, meaning that the company is not bound by any of the terms in the letter—it just specifies the terms for clarity and discussion purposes. The practical application is that the LOI can be turned over to your attorney to have him finalize the agreement with the other party's counsel. Even though most attorneys don't recommend using LOIs, I've found them useful and an efficient way to get a project rolling.

License

A license is the right to use another person or company's intellectual property for inclusion in your own product. Such licenses clearly specify how the license can and can't be used. Generally, in the gaming industry, license is given only for game consoles and computers, meaning you cannot take the property and use it on any other medium, such as a movie or TV program. Those rights may already be licensed to another party. Alternatively, if you're licensing a technology or a tool like DivX or InstallShield, those are generally specific use licenses good for only one or two products and perhaps their derivatives (like an expansion pack, sequel, foreign language version, or even a port of the game to a different platform).

Nondisclosure

Nondisclosure provisions are very common in the entertainment industry, especially in video games. A nondisclosure agreement or provision says that you cannot disclose to any third party the information contained in the agreement or the work covered by the agreement unless the information is disclosed to the public. This type of provision to guards against disclosure of the product you're working on and the technology used to create it and any other proprietary information.

Milestones

The milestone definition is the part of the contract that you, as a producer, are going to be most responsible for. The milestone definitions specify the work that needs to be completed by certain dates and what state the game should be in. These definitions need to be clear, measurable, and concise. Writing clear and effective milestones is discussed in detail later in the chapter.

Offer and Acceptance

Offer and acceptance are key principles of contract law. An offer is made by one party, and the acceptance of that offer by the other party constitutes an agreement. Make sure that whenever discussing terms with another party, you make clear that your agreement with the proposed terms does not constitute an acceptance of the offer. A producer should always take an offer and proposed deal points back to his management and present them for one final review before confirming acceptance.

Option Exercise

Option exercise refers to the right that is provided in some contracts for one party to exercise their option on a product. This could be a case in which the developer has an option to develop other properties within the same intellectual property franchise but the publisher has the option of first refusal on such a proposal (this is often called the *right of first refusal*). Other such options might be for the publisher to reuse the technology created for a product in a different product, provided some compensation is granted for the option granting that right.

Place of Performance

This term refers to where the work is to be performed, and generally refers to specific development efforts. If you're a developer and you're going to subcontract some of your work out to a team in Eastern Europe or China, then you should disclose that in this section of the contract. The publisher may be expecting you to develop all of the content and complete all of the work at the place of performance designated in the agreement.

Third-Party Software Inclusion

Generally, a developer will need to use third-party software licenses and technology to complete a product. Miles Sound System, Bink Video, DivX, Quicktime, InstallShield, Unreal, and Gamebryo are all examples of third-party technology that is used to help developers complete their work. Make sure that the contract calls for disclosure of all third-party software licenses so that each party knows the terms of the third-party license agreement with respect to the product.

Time of Performance

Time is usually of the essence when creating a development agreement, so be sure to clearly specify when the performance of the work will start and when it is expected to finish.

Warranties

Warranties are promises that each party makes to the other party regarding the performance of their duties under the agreement. Obviously, a game developer must warranty that they have all of the rights necessary to develop and license a game to a publisher, and that the work will be commercially viable. These promises are generally left for the lawyers to decide and define.

Business Knowledge Requirements

There are several components of the business aspects of video game production that every producer should be aware of. Following is a cursory overview of the elements related to a business agreement and a product's development. This is by no means an inclusive list, as every product has a different set of deal points and business objectives.

Components of an LOI

Listed below are the key components of a Letter of Intent. As a producer working for either a publisher or a developer, these are terms that you should be familiar with prior to the finalization of the contract that you'll be charged with administering. While it is often true that all of these terms are negotiated prior to a producer's involvement in the game production cycle, being aware of them sooner rather than later is makes it easier to proactively problem-solve and prepare yourself for the challenges that game development offers.

- **Product.** Product is the product name that the deal comprises. If you don't know the name, refer to the product as "the product currently known as" and then state the working title of the game. It can always be changed later.
- **Platforms.** Platforms denote which platform rights the contract addresses. It could be a multiple-platform, simultaneous release on the PC, GameCube, Playstation2, and Xbox. Be sure to clarify which platforms this deal covers.
- **IP Ownership.** As discussed previously, clarify up front who owns the intellectual property rights related to both the creative concept and the technology.
- **Royalty Rate.** The royalty rate is the percentage of net revenue that is paid to the developer from the money actually received by the publisher. It varies widely, but generally amounts to between 10 percent and 25 percent, depending on the product and the market factors. The royalty rate is usually inversely related to the total amount advanced for the product.

- **Advances**. *Advances* is the term used to refer to advance payments against royalties earned. Basically, the publisher advances money to the developer or licensee, based in part on what the royalty rate is, how much the product is expected to sell, and how much it costs to complete the product. This amount is usually what the developer invests in making the game.

- **Cross-collateralization**. Specify early on in the negotiating process whether the royalties (and the advances) for each product's stock keeping unit, or SKU, are going to be cross-collateralized. This means that the PC version of the game won't pay royalties until the PS2 and Xbox version have earned more than the advance royalty payments. The short explanation is that the advance royalty payments from all SKUs are lumped together into one big sum. The overall game (all SKUs) need to earn more than that advance before a developer is paid any money beyond the advance royalty payments.

- **Milestones and Gold Date**. This specifies the estimated completion date of the product. The gold master is completed and accepted by the publisher on this date. Then it is sent to manufacturing to be replicated and shipped out to stores. Generally, this date is just a goal or a guess on when the product is going to be completed, but if arrived at through solid product planning, a developer should be able to achieve this date within a few weeks or months.

Writing Clear Milestones

Creating milestones can be like playing a game of darts. Creating an accurate milestone list is difficult and requires in-depth analysis and calculation. Even then, the results are not guaranteed.

Milestones for a project are included in a contract in the form of an attached schedule. The developer submits a deliverable to the publisher for each date specified. The publisher determines whether the deliverable meets the requirements of the milestone in the contract (the publisher normally has a maximum of ten days to review a milestone, after which time the milestone is deemed accepted if there is no written response to the developer), and if so sends the developer a payment.

Milestones must be assigned before development begins, and they are legally binding. However, it can be difficult to determine at the start of a project exactly what tasks will need to be done nine months or even 18 months later. Also, developers and publishers can have different ideas about how a product's development will progress. Poorly written milestones can lead to misunderstandings and conflict between the developer and publisher, since they're legally tied to money.

Let's say a hypothetical contract contains a milestone: "Write terrain-rendering engine." When the milestone schedule was written, the developer and publisher agreed that it was a good milestone that fit the schedule well. When the time came to write the terrain-rendering engine, a programmer at the developer wrote a very nice engine that could render textured terrain of varying heights. However, when he presented his work to the publisher, they asked him where the dynamic terrain Height Importing tool was and why the terrain only supported one texture at a time. He responded that those were separate tasks and were not part of the milestone. Both publisher and developer, in this case, are victims of a vague milestone.

A vague milestone is any milestone that could be interpreted differently by the developer and the publisher. The developer might believe that a deliverable meets the standards of the milestone and the publisher might believe that it doesn't. This will cause resentment if the publisher withholds payment or issues payment for a deliverable they do not feel is acceptable. The contract is almost no help in these cases, as the only legally binding document is open for interpretation.

A vague milestone is also a milestone that does not provide any information about the true progress of the project. Here are three examples of this second type of vague milestone:

- Have a playable level up and running
- Complete interactive demo
- Convert the graphics engine to 32-bit

"Have a playable level up and running"—what does that mean, exactly? The problem here is the ambiguous *playable level*. This can mean anything from having a text character moving on a flat plane with a single sound effect playing to three fully textured 3D characters with all animation frames moving on a rotating, dynamically lit, 10-screen by 10-screen area—with display of ten working objects, full mouse and hotkey control, and a host of other required features.

This milestone should give precise parameters of what is expected to be "running" in the milestone. To truly be planned and completed correctly, this milestone should be broken down into its various components. Otherwise, the developer's "progress" is not measurable.

The "Complete interactive demo" milestone has the same problem as the "playable level" milestone. What does a "demo" entail, and in what way does it need to be interactive? How can it be complete if the publisher doesn't know what is being reviewed for completeness? Always be very careful when using the word *complete*. In this case, it could mean complete in terms of speed, art quality, art quantity, or base functionality. Any word with so many interpretations is trouble in a milestone definition.

To correct this milestone, fully define what comprises the demo, what portion of the game will be interactive, and what *interactivity* actually entails. With proper definition, anyone should be able to determine whether or not the milestone is complete (and thus "acceptable").

The "Convert the graphics engine to 32-bit" milestone sounds okay on the surface—and it is the best milestone description of the three—but it should be broken down into its relevant subsections. What portion of the original code needs to be converted, and what conversion method will be used? Will it be a complete re-write, or a bare-bones fix to simply make it work in 32-bit? What specific 32-bit features will be supported, and what ramifications will this have on game design and art creation? Will a new tool be required to deal with art or converting art in order to allow the artists to support this new graphics engine? This milestone should really be broken down into appropriate subsections to help the programmers analyze what tasks will be required.

An Adventure Game Gone Wrong

The early milestones of the hypothetical "adventure game of the century" schedule included designing the game. Milestone conditions in the contract described things like "Design for X-factor World and included levels complete." Since the components of the desired design were not outlined, the producer was not happy with some of the early designs. The developer had meticulously laid out architectural diagrams and long, wordy game element descriptions. However, there was no script written for the characters in the age, no drawings to indicate visual style, and no summary of what exactly the players needed to do to solve each game element. Basically, there was a misunderstanding about how much detail was required for various components of the design.

Therefore the producer re-wrote the milestone definition and included it in an amendment to the development agreement between the publisher and the developer:

Puzzle Design For Mountain and Electric Worlds

This includes a written overview of the historical perspective of the level: what its purpose is in the game universe, what its basic rules are, who wrote it, why, and when. This deliverable describes the game elements that a player must solve at the same level of detail as would be found in a strategy guide for the game. This detail included identifying the game elements and describing each. It includes enough information so that readers know all the pieces of the big picture, not including walkthroughs or complete designs. No brainstorming notes are submitted, only recommended game element concepts. Concept sketches that give a feel for the overall theme of the level are included, as well as brief descriptions of important environmental effects of the level.

Here are some guidelines for writing clear milestones.

- Break every task down into its base components and write them in the milestone schedule. If the milestone calls for a "design" of an area, write exactly what a *design* entails, such as game element descriptions, NPC profiles, and concept art.

- Avoid imprecise words such as *some* and *most*. These are easy to fall back on in the early stages of design, when the exact details of a project are unknown.

- It should be obvious from a glance whether a deliverable meets a milestone or not. There is no such thing as a 70 percent complete milestone. That's like saying a person is 70 percent alive. The milestone is either completely finished or completely unfinished.

- There can never be too much detail. You must analyze the milestones and make sure there is enough information to fully identify the components of each milestone.

- If you do not have enough information to write an unambiguous milestone, mark it TBD and detail it when you have more information. Remember that milestones are legally binding, and if you write a vague milestone with the intention of clarifying it later, you may find yourself in world of conflict nine months later when it is staring you in the face.

- Base milestones on a complete game design document and on a complete technical design document. Make sure you review both documents and verify that everything is addressed within the milestones. Reference the design document in the wording of the milestone description where appropriate. If there are 50 monsters to be designed in the product, then those 50 named monsters should be specified as to preliminary and final versions in the milestones.

- Include a statement in one of the contract schedules that provides for changes to the design/technical document after good faith negotiations and agreement by both publisher and developer. This is important to state, so that the developer cannot make material changes to the game design without consulting the publisher. This prevents game designers from writing and submitting overly ambitious game designs.

- Milestone items that are iterative in nature (for example, design docs, interface concepts, voice scripts, and so on) should usually have more than one milestone attached to them, such as first draft and final draft, at a minimum.

- Programming milestones should be based on explicit engine features or measurable progress towards those features.

- If there are technical specifications that you do not understand, ask for assistance to evaluate and interpret milestone information.

- Understand the publisher requirements for the project. Any dependencies required by the publisher must be included in the developer milestones. For example, plan deliverables for trade shows sizzle/playable demos, screen shots, behind-the-scenes information for magazine or online articles, sketch art, and finished game art assets for Web site creation, final text assets for localization, and so on. Each producer should sit down with marketing/PR and also with localization to discuss respective plans and schedules as they relate to having required materials tie into specific milestones. These requirements obviously will need to be delivered to the developer for incorporation into the milestone schedule.

- Other key areas, such as full mock ups of final art screens, sample characters, interface, level views, and so on must be delivered either at the time the design document is delivered or very soon thereafter.

- The developer must deliver the *first playable* milestone as soon as possible. This cannot be emphasized enough. This first playable, or prototype, milestone should request that the developer deliver final quality assets and technology.

- Do not let the developer leave key technical hurdles, such as multiplayer programming, until the last minute—even if using GameSpy or some other third-party software for the final version. The multi-player version of the game should be up and playable early and before the single player version is complete.

- Plan milestones approximately one month apart. If milestones are too close together, the developer is spending too much time creating and discussing deliverables and not making the game. If they are too far apart, the publisher is too far out of the loop and unable to react quickly to problems. Milestones can be farther apart in the early design or engine development stages, and should usually be closer together as the product reaches the critical milestones of Alpha, Beta and Final.

- The time between Alpha, Beta, and Final should be at least one month each. However, as a general rule for games, there should be a two to three month gap from Alpha to Beta, and at least a two month gap from Beta to Final. For large RPGs, the gap should be at least three months from Beta to Final.

- Don't forget to include specific milestones that need to be delivered to and approved by any licensor that you're working with.

Why the Producer Is Key to Realizing a Vision

As you can see after reviewing this section, there's a lot of consideration that goes into the business and legal side of video game development. This is the crucial first step in realizing a vision from a creative design. If you, as a producer, don't lay a good foundation with excellent business and legal provisions in the agreement, the process will be more difficult later on and you'll find your time invested in solving problems that were preventable rather than focusing on problems that could make the product better and sell more.

The Creatively Inclined Producer

This section discusses how a creative visionary for a game can manage in a producer's role. There are quite a few examples of industry leaders who've succeeded in this role, such as Peter Molyneux of Lionhead Studios, Wil Wright of Maxis, Warren Spector of Ion Storm, and Alex Garden of Relic Entertainment. But it is not easy, and there are certain risks. Consider that there are advantages and disadvantages to this division of labor. Let's look deeper into this approach to understand the advantages and disadvantages.

First, the advantages: The producer who holds the creative vision for the product generally has a distinct and contagious passion for their role. This can be a powerful asset to a team and its motivation to complete a project. Secondly, if the producer is the creative visionary for the product, hopefully he can convey design decisions that balance the production concerns without much disagreement or dissent. Third, a producer in this role may have great support and guidance from other associate or assistant producers that can balance his focus on the creative with an application of the practical production concerns.

However, there are several disadvantages to relying on a producer to execute both components of the producer role effectively, such as balancing creative and emotional decisions with that of objective concerns is an inherently difficult challenge. The producer may be less effective when his emotional connection to a creative decision comes in conflict with the requirements for the game shipping on time and on budget. There's also an inherent possibility that the producer will discount other creative ideas and input as being of less value than his own. This does not promote team unity or artistic respect. And lastly, once the producer is in the role of creative visionary, there is some question as to whom is principally responsible for the business and legal aspects of the game's production and how they are being balanced and addressed.

Rely on a Good Producer

In order for the creative visionary (often the lead designer, but perhaps the producer) to be 100 percent effective and focused on the creative vision for the product, it is often necessary for him or her to delegate responsibilities and objective decision-making powers regarding production to another producer. Being able to rely on an objective outside party regarding the creative instincts ensures that there's someone focused on driving the project forward, rather than just making it fun. Balancing concerns of the team, as well as management, and quality assurance, is invaluable during the production process, and it is only made harder if the role of the producer and the creative visionary are merged..

The Technically Proficient Producer

There are number of advantages to having a technical background and applying those skills to a producer's role. Take a look at industry leaders like John Carmack of ID or Jason Rubin of Naughty Dog. Technical proficiency and expertise is always valued at successful companies, especially in the role of a producer. In this section, I will discuss some of the advantages of working with a technically proficient producer who can apply his programming background to managing the game's development process.

One of the principal advantages to working with a producer who has a technical background is that the producer is well versed in the technical aspects of the game's completion. This allows another level of problem solving aptitude to be applied when evaluating milestones (both from internal and external development teams). A producer's technical background often gives him or her the tools for solving a host of other challenges, including identifying dependencies within the schedule and understanding how the different design elements of the game relate to each other and to the capabilities of the game engine components and tools.

Another advantage offered by a producer with a technical background is his or her attention to detail and grasp of seemingly unrelated elements within a game's design or within engine architecture. A producer with technical skills can be relied upon to understand the issues related to basic engine architecture and design requirements of the game's toolset.

Generally, if you're technically inclined or creatively inclined, the role of being a producer for an internal team is well suited to your skills. Of course, this is a generality and many producers excel in any role. The next section discusses the differences in the details required of both internal and external producer.

Internal versus External Producers

This next section discusses the role of internal and external producers, diving deeper into the commonplace challenges than was discussed in previous chapters. Remember that any of the specialties mentioned in the last section can exist in either of the roles, internal or external. The producer role is so diverse that it'll require some element of each specialty at some point during the job.

Producer for an Internal Team

The producer for an internal team, either at a developer or a publisher, is charged with the daily management of the game or some aspect of the game, or even individual SKUs within a product line. The daily management of the internal team requires different set of skills than when working with external development teams.

The skills and specialized knowledge required for an internal producer depend largely on the size of the team and the duration of the product. If the product must be completed within a condensed timeline and production schedule (less than one year) there's a unique methodology to adopt to ensure that everyone is working toward that goal. This means that product enhancements and feature requests cannot vary from the specified game design and there must be a clear and concise process for bringing these decisions to a complete resolution. When working with an internal team, it is the small things that matter. Thousands of small things can add up and cause lengthy delays in the completion of a game.

Navigating through the Middle

A producer for an internal team, whether at a publisher or a developer, faces a tough challenge, regardless of what type of producer specialty that he emphasizes.

The challenge for an internal producer is getting the product through the middle of a project, called Production. That's where the euphoria of getting a new project started fades away like the sunset as you steer the project into the unknown. Getting through the middle of the project can be like entering a zone of despair, where your management or the publisher of the game are concerned because there's no visual progress on the project. It may feel as though everyone is breathing down your neck, the schedule becomes nearly impossible, and there's no end in sight to the frustrating challenges that await.

A balanced written schedule often shows everything on a project coming together at the last possible moment, but this is rarely possible or feasible. An effective set of proven tools is required to even begin production. Placing objects in a game world needs to happen as soon as possible so that the team can determine what's fun and why. Some systems (like rendering and gameplay) need to come together sooner than other systems, such as compatibility or mod features and special effects tools.

The internal team producer's key strength is to be able to convincingly demonstrate to upper management or the publisher progress in the game engine or against a well-defined schedule. Ensuring that the team has the right tools to begin work is the first step in the process.

During the production phase of the project (which usually corresponds to the Adapt phase in Agile Project Management) an internal producer inevitably comes up against the conflict between expectations and delivery of the product. This is usually the time between the Electronic Entertainment Expo (E3) demo levels that were showed to the press and the finalization of the product, where final game levels are coming together and being tested and the bugs are being fixed. Everyone gets used to seeing the gameplay that was shown at E3. When the rest of the game doesn't look that polished, they start to wonder why. This natural reaction can be frustrating for a producer.

As an internal producer, this is the time to adapt your approach to completing the game. Keep track of what features are being completed and how they are coming together. Be sure to document this progress against your schedule so that it is clearly defined when presenting to your management or the publisher. If you're an internal producer who is working with a third party producer, measure progress against clearly defined milestones. The trick to being able to stay on schedule is to cut features and content early and often. Work with the team leads to determine which features can be cut and how to do it. This tactic can help you make it through the middle and weather the toughest storm in game development.

Keeping the Team and the Game Focused

Relic Entertainment's Ron Moravek reminds producers that "nothing else matters other than finishing the game." What this means is that it is important for the producer to keep focused and ensure that the team is focused on finishing the game, and to keep external distractions to a minimum. Where can a producer add the most value to an internal team? The producer is not the art director, lead artist, lead designer, or the lead programmer and cannot add value in the same way that each of those positions can. But a producer can help define the essence of the experience of the game and focus the team on delivering that goal to users of the product.

This means that if you're a producer on a first person shooter-style title, make it the best FPS possible by adding value and clarity. Ask your team and yourself, "What are the three biggest promises the game experience offers?" Ensure that you have great answers to that question. If those promises are the best graphics, physics, and overall game balance, and then make deformable terrain andcinematic or special effects secondary.

THQ & Relic Entertainment's recent *Warhammer 40K: Dawn of War* product delivered arguably the best frontline combat action of any recent RTS. Was it an exceptional single player game? No. Did it use every unit and rule in the *Warhammer 40K* universe? No. But it delivered a well-balanced RTS with awesome frontline combat action. It delivered on its key promise to RTS fans: frontline combat action!

We're Not Here to Knit!

During a recent golf game, Ron Moravek from Relic Entertainment and his golfing partner came to a difficult area on a local course. Ron, sometimes the reluctant golfer, asked, "Should I get out my driver"? To which his golfing partner promptly replied, "We're not here to knit, Ron!" An unexpected answer, but one to which Ron promptly agreed.

While on the golf course, play golf. When working at a game developer, develop games. When faced with a team member who thinks that the key features and promises of the game are "too hard" or would be "very difficult" to achieve excellently, remind them that *we're not here to knit!*

Focusing the team on the goal of finishing the game and achieving the top promises of the game experience is just like golf. Play to win and get through the course with the fewest strokes as possible, getting closer the end with every swing.

Plan for a Broad Base when Building a Pyramid

The ancient Egyptians learned that in order to build a really tall pyramid, they needed to give it a broad base. This analogy applies to game development. To give your internal team the best chance of making a great game, start by building a broad foundation for the game. Here are a couple of ways to ensure a broad foundation.

Start with a clear essence statement and write it down. Clearly define the "promises of the gaming experience" to the gamer. Then, emphasize at your next team meeting, the three to five features of the game that are going to make the game great and sell tons of units. If you make just one bet on a single gameplay feature, your risk is too focused on a single area. The job of the producer is to manage risk, and by focusing the success or failure of the game on a single key element of a game, you're being an ineffective risk manager. By investing the efforts of the team on three to five key features and promises, you ensure that the foundation of this game is sufficiently large to begin production without the project ending up being a century-old game by the time it's finished.

The key thing to remember is that pyramids have three or four sides and they all focus on a single point at the very top. So should your game have three to five key features that are true selling points that focus into one exciting gaming experience that ties all points together.

Push for Quality

As an internal producer, the product's final quality is ultimately influenced directly by your input and focus. No other single role has as much impact on the product. A key aspect of the job is knowing when to say, "Is it good enough?"

In working on the original *Homeworld* game, Alex Garden and Ron Moravek kept pushing for higher quality from their team. During the final eight months of production, the game features were coming together but Alex kept asking that question, "Is this good enough?" One of the results of this emphasis on and push for quality was the inclusion of the Sensors Manager, a key feature of the *Homeworld* RTS that allowed the user to view the entire world map with the press of one button; this feature made the game infinitely more playable. The quality of the product was recognized in the industry and catapulted Relic to forefront of independent game developers.

Recommendations for Producers

While being a video game producer is always challenging, some internal producers make it unnecessarily hard on themselves by falling into some common traps. Here's a reference guide for what works and what doesn't in this role.

Remind Your Team of the Vision

On long projects, it is easy to focus on a specific part of the game and lose sight of the overall vision. Often there are 50-60 members on a team, and each member begins to develop his own personal vision of the game, causing different parts of the game's development to go in different directions. Remind the team of the focus of the game and why the project is going to be the best game in the genre with the key selling points.

Provide Stability and Confidence

When managing a team, or in any leadership position, remember to keep your emotions in check. If the producer is yelling or screaming at people or otherwise seems to be losing emotional control, then the perception among the team is that there's a huge problem with the product for which no solution exists. In such a case, the producer's reaction inflames an already difficult situation so that it is actually harder to find the right solution. In all of your actions, ensure stability and promote confidence by example. Save your frustration and emotional outbursts for the gym or your therapist's office.

Admit Your Mistakes

We all make mistakes. Being able to admit your mistake, make amends, and move on is extremely important for an efficient and harmonious working environment. Unfortunately, admissions of mistakes are rare in the game industry, as pride is so directly linked to creativity. Projects and their producers get entrenched in the direction they're heading and sometimes there's no turning back. Even when evidence of a bad idea or decision is clear, some producers just continue on the path toward the train wreck. If you've made a mistake, don't be afraid to admit it, stop work if necessary, and move in a different, better direction. Your team will respect you more, and your product can only benefit from your honesty.

Be Able to Assess the Game

Producers are often called upon to be objective critics of their own work and that of their team. Being able to assess a product unemotionally and objectively is one of the most valuable traits a producer can bring to the role and benefit the team. Many producers are very concerned about what they must do to prevent their project from being cancelled, and do not apply enough focus and objectivity to assessing where the product stands—whether it really is any good. Do you want to waste all of your time—and your team's—on a product that is lackluster and uninspired? It may earn some money for you and your company, but you'll never have the opportunity to get those years back; or you might miss out on another opportunity to work on a very successful game.

If the game is in a sorry state, evaluate and determine what would be required to fix. Then present the solution to your manager and determine whether it is worth the investment. If it's not worth the investment, then kill the project, as painful as it may be. A few days of pain in killing a project are a lot easier than many, many months of slogging through a project that's gone awry.

Don't Undervalue Process, but Don't Over-implement It

A process like that in the production of a video game is designed to reduce risk and uncertainty. And creativity is inherently risky and uncertain. Because these principles are diametrically opposed, the producer must find the right balance. Do this by creating the "wish list" of cool features or great ideas that would be valuable to implement if there is time and opportunity, but don't promise to implement these features if they deviate from the design or definitely add unacceptable risk completion of the product on time. Assess the feasibility of the ideas and formulate a plan which can be implemented.

Realize That You Don't Always Have the Right Answer

The role of the producer is concerned with solving problems. If there weren't any problems in software development, there wouldn't be a need for producers. However, there's one key rule to remember: When faced with problems, challenges, or interactions with another member of the team during which they turn to you for an answer—and a good solution—you don't always have to have the right answer right away. If you want to make sure your answer or solution is the best one possible, step back, think about it, maybe ask advice from others whom you respect, and only then provide an answer. You won't always have the luxury of doing so, but try to mull over your decision before acting on it, even in crunch times.

Don't Over-Manage the Team

One of the easiest traps to fall into as a producer is to start constantly telling people what to do and when to do it. While this may be necessary in some circumstances, most of the time it is simply over-managing the team. Work with your direct reports, the leads of the project, to determine what needs to be done and why. Don't try to do their job for them. Ask questions to help the leads understand your position. Instead of saying, "Make this unit color green instead of yellow," try questions like "What color do you think might work better to emphasize this unit's functionality other than yellow? What about green, as it emphasizes it functionality?" This gives the artist or designer time to think about what you're asking and possibly propose an even better solution than the one you're thinking of.

Don't Focus on Things Other than the Game

While it might be fun to work with the Marketing department on creating a great trailer or with the composer on creating a great score, unless you've been specifically charged with those responsibilities, don't take them on. Focus on making the game excellent. Find the ways in which the product can succeed and rise above the competition. Getting the game to the finish line is the ultimate goal. For the rest of the work, give your feedback when asked your opinion, but realize that you can't do everything so refrain from volunteering.

note

You'll find more on the daily practices of producer working with an internal development team in Chapter 8, "Tools for Your Success in Your Daily Routine."

External (Third-Party) Producers

External Product Development, or working with third party software developer, has its own unique set of challenges. Included in this section are some general guidelines to use when working in such situations, along with some suggestions for how to help ensure that the third-party software developer is making the most efficient use of its talent, management, and design ideas.

Working with a Complete Game Design

One of the primary reasons for failure to deliver the product on schedule is that game producers begin working on a product before the design is complete. While it is very rare to have a completed design at project start, listed in this subsection are some specific examples of how to structure a development agreement and ensure that there's a process in place for achieving a complete design before production begins in earnest across all components of the game.

However, an explicit milestone schedule cannot be written without a complete design document and technical design document. So how do you start a project without a complete milestone schedule?

It is nearly impossible to write an effective milestone schedule in situations where the developer doesn't believe in design documentation. As a producer, you need to predict and understand what the developer will be working on from one month to the next. If there is no formal review process, then there is no way to know if the developer is falling behind on adding features because you don't know what features are planned. This is a very dangerous position for you, as a producer at a publisher, to be in. Any problems that arise during development will come as nasty surprises, requiring extra money and schedule delays before the ship date arrives.

The design document for a game should describe a complete, releasable game. That is not to say that it should be finalized and then never changed during development. Details can be added to the document, features can be changed and improved, and sections not relevant to gameplay can be removed. However, nothing in the document should be blank or "TBD." Encourage your developers to design the game in general first and then add depth, instead of designing each level or design in complete detail on the first try. Otherwise, when it comes time to develop a feature, you may find your documentation lacking.

The developer and publisher should both agree on a nearly complete design before production begins. Milestones that are based on a complete design will be more accurate and require fewer changes over time. A complete design helps prevent miscommunication among programmers and designers at the developer, as well.

If the design cannot be completed before production begins, the first milestones of the project should concern completing the design. Have programmers and other members of the team work on tasks not directly related to the game, such as development tools, until it is done. Do not attempt to write milestones based on an incomplete design. Leave them TBD (it's okay to put that in the development agreement) and come back to them when the design is finished.

A design document should do the following:

- Describe a complete, releasable game.
- Describe every element of the game, including speech script, concept art of important structures, concept art to demonstrate the visual theme of each area, descriptions of major gameplay elements, complete stats for all important objects in the game, spell lists, NPC info, specific info about AI routines, and so on.
- Be formatted in a manner that is understandable to the developer and publisher.
- Be thorough enough that any art generation or programming is simply a question of translation.

- Describe all actions the player can take in the game in enough detail that programmers can determine how to organize the code to support that feature.

Working with a Complete Technical Design

A *technical design* is a design document for programmers. It should contain a complete feature list for the engine, describe the major data structures used by the program, and explain, in programming terms, how major tasks should be approached. This document will be controlled by the lead programmer on the team, and is useful to designers as well as programmers. Here's a real-life example of what happens with the technical design isn't shared freely with the design team.

Half-Life was a breakout first person shooter that heavily modified the Quake II engine to great effect. Teams of designers worked to design fun levels while teams of programmers developed special effects and other features. One feature they added allowed impressive arcs of electricity in a variety of forms. However, it was poorly communicated to the designers, so at first, very few of them used the effect in their levels. It was only after the designers were made aware of the effect that they started to weave it into the gameplay. That electricity was a defining element of *Half-Life*, and critical to the final game.

The technical design is useful to the producer because it lets him accurately measure the programming tasks required to create the game. Many developers are hesitant to create a technical design document, as programmers are not really the writing type—they'd rather be coding. However, without a clearly defined feature list, it is easy for programmers to just keep adding little features and lose sight of their greater goals.

The technical design document also helps prevent programmers doing work that will simply have to be redone later. It is a great tool for lead programmers, and can often save far more time and money than it takes to create.

Technical design documents should do the following:

- Describe what the engine is capable of and what features are available to the designers.
- Prevent feature creep (when game designers and programmers continue to add features to a game without discussing it with anyone else) and allow progress to be accurately measured.
- Be evaluated by someone at the publisher who has the appropriate technical skills.

Accepting Milestones

Accepting milestones is the process that publishers use to review the work submitted to them by external developers. The work of external developers is segmented into deliverable segments called milestones, which are submitted to the publisher for review. Acceptance is required before the developer gets paid.

If the milestones have been detailed, explicit, and followed accordingly by the developer, then the acceptance phase is easy. If the milestones were poorly written or were vague, then this will be a nightmarish process, as both developer and publisher will lose out in the ensuing conflict.

The following are crucial guidelines to remember when accepting milestones:

- You must respond with a written letter if a milestone is either rejected or accepted. E-mail is not acceptable for a rejection, as it is not legally binding. Use a format similar to the Sample Acceptance Letter found in the Appendix A. It is simple, and allows you to present detailed feedback on every tack to the developer.

- Give precise and detailed feedback. This is crucial in the case of a milestone rejection. It is possible to accept the milestone as described, even though there may be a request for new changes or modifications that may improve what was delivered. In this case, accept the milestone, but give detail as to what you would like adjusted or modified by the next milestone delivery.

- Understand the payment terms of the contract. Understand exactly what amount is due and when the developer is due to receive the money. Usually this is 30 days from the time that the milestone was delivered to the publisher, or in other cases, 30 days from when the invoice is received by the publisher. Currently most developers are paid within two weeks after submitting the milestone, but this varies from publisher to publisher.

- Understand the acceptance terms of the contract. A producer usually has ten days from the date of receipt to review and either approve or reject a milestone deliverable. This is not a lot of time to review the milestone and complete a detailed write-up. It is crucial that a review of the milestone is deliverable promptly. In most contracts, it is implied that if you do not give a developer written notification of a rejection, that the milestone is deemed accepted. So, by the terms of the agreement, the publisher may be forced to pay a developer for something that is not acceptable if a producer procrastinates in getting timely written feedback to the developer.

- Do not offer partial payments for milestones unless there is approval from the publisher's management. Do everything possible to avoid partially paying for milestones. They should not be paid for a scheduled deliverable until all the milestone items have been completed.

- Do not submit milestones for payment to Accounts Payable (AP) before the milestone has been reviewed and approved by your manager.

- Senior management must approve Alpha, Beta, and Final milestones. This includes the current QA requirements.

- The technical director should evaluate key technical milestones. This is crucial. Too often, producers simply look at what is written or visually presented to them. The technology is the skeleton, and the design/art is the skin and hair. It is crucial that the producer understands—or has others who are qualified evaluate—what is under the skin.

- The art director at your publisher should review key art-related milestones and provide critical feedback to help the developer's artist achieve excellence.

Reassess the Milestone Schedule Every Three Months

It is important to constantly review milestones and reassess the design and the criteria by which you are measuring progress. At the start of an 18-month-long project, it is difficult to determine exactly what the programmers at the developer will be working on in month 13. Many design questions will still be unanswered at the start of a project. By requiring constant milestone schedule reassessment, you guarantee you will have an accurate, complete milestone schedule throughout your project.

Use Microsoft Project to Track Task Dependencies

Many tasks require that other tasks be finished first. Modeling requires that visual design of a level be complete. A programmer implementing collision detection requires that the world be defined. Some tasks, of course, are unrelated—a musician, for example, can start work as soon as design is complete.

Microsoft Project allows a producer to track dependent tasks and other related efforts to making the game. Make certain that the developer you're working with has some sort of project scheduling system in place. Ask for a copy of MS Project whenever feasible.

A Step-by-Step Example

Here's a quick example of how to evaluate the feasibility of a proposed milestone schedule, as well as judge the milestone definitions for clarity.

1. Analyze the current design or pitch documents and determine what additional design materials are needed. If you have any questions about the design of your game, you need to get them answered here.

2. Write milestones defining what remains of the design process. Be sure to be explicit about the minimum amount of detail you expect in areas like interface, visual design, multiplayer capability, and so on.

3. Write milestones defining what remains of the technical design. The goal here is a feature list. You want your developer to carefully think through the technology they will be creating before they start working on it. Carefully consider how each feature relates to the game design. Use the Engine Elements (discussed later) as a checklist to review developer deliverables and process.

4. If practical, include a milestone at the end of the design process to reassess the milestone schedule. This will be your responsibility as well as the developer's, so be sure to schedule time for it.

5. Divide whatever design materials you have into as detailed a list of tasks as possible. For example, if you have a design for a world in a game, your task list would include items like "Design Visual Style," "Model World," "Texture World," and "Light World." This is a list of all the tasks that must be completed to get a finished game. Include as much detail as you can.

6. Repeat Step 5 with the technical design document to create a list of programming tasks.

7. Take the lists from Steps 5 and 6 and split the tasks into groups that will take about one month each to develop.

8. Using the task groups from Step 7, create a rough list of milestones. If appropriate, combine elements from the design and technical task lists. For example, if in one group, the developers are finishing the modeling of world 1 and implementing the terrain engine, that month's milestone could be to present world 1 in the terrain engine.

9. Overview your list of milestones and remove any vague language. Rewrite so that there is no question in your mind what each milestone entails. Ask a colleague to review it for you, as you could be too close to it to see ambiguities.

10. Schedule the project based on your milestone lists. You may want to return to your milestones after you have completed the project schedule, depending on the project.

11. Sit down and review the printed version of the schedule item by item (preferably prepared in MS Project) with your contact at the developer. This face-to-face meeting can stimulate a thought process that identifies any unforeseen circumstances before the milestone schedule is created. This helps the developer actually do the job that they were hired for.

The Final Word

Being a producer is a very challenging role. There are a lot of opportunities to make mistakes and stumble when faced with daunting challenges. Hopefully, the tools presented here can make the journey a bit easier. While there isn't one right way, and certainly what's outlined here is not the only way to work, it does provide a roadmap of techniques that have been successful in the past.

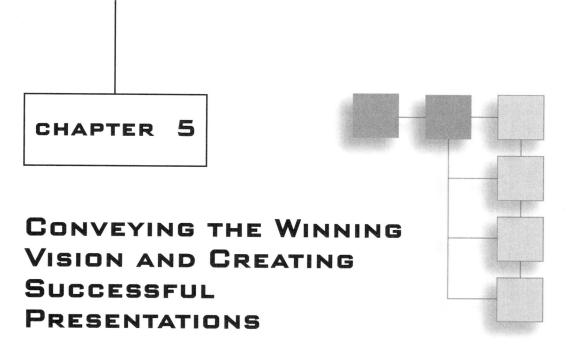

CHAPTER 5

CONVEYING THE WINNING VISION AND CREATING SUCCESSFUL PRESENTATIONS

All game development projects start with an idea. Someone writes down the game concept, why they think it might be fun, and why someone would want to buy this game. That's the way original projects are born. This chapter covers the key parts of a product presentation and provides some tips on how to be successful when presenting your ideas so that they can be produced into a great game. There are two parts to winning presentations. First is the proposal that is submitted to the publisher; second is the actual presentation to the publisher's staff. For our purposes in this chapter, the proposal means writing a game proposal document (the idea), submitting it to a publisher, and using it as a tool to get an appointment to make a presentation. The presentation refers to the documents used during the actual meeting with the publisher and those that you leave with the publisher after your meeting. The first part of this chapter is written from the perspective of the independent developer attempting to get a deal with a publisher. Later, I'll discuss the considerations that a producer at a publisher should consider.

note

This chapter addresses the steps required for a producer working at a developer to present an original concept to a publisher for consideration and acceptance. All other presentations are variations on this theme; this is the most common, but most challenging part of getting an original title into development.

A Winning Vision for the Brand

Most video game publishers are concerned with the development of a brand. If they're going to invest money and resources into a project, then they want to understand why the investment is going to work in the long term. This is most often done by associating the vision for a specific game with a larger vision for a brand. A couple of examples of successful brands within the video game industry are the following:

- *Command and Conquer Series*
- *Mario and Mario Brothers*
- *Myst, Riven, Myst III: Exile, and Myst IV: Revelation*
- *Balder's Gate*
- *Tony Hawk*
- *Grand Theft Auto*
- *The EA Sports Series*
- *Need for Speed*

Each of these brands began with a single idea or product and then blossomed into a much larger business. But the real upside to these initial products was the fact that the initial investment in the first game turned into a much larger business, with each of these brands generating tens of millions or hundreds of millions of dollars during the course of their business cycle. Good presentations and proposals play to the strength of a brand, explaining how the idea or concept could be turned into an entire business of multiple products.

Although an initial proposal does not need to address the specifics of how to build a brand out of this idea, it is good preparation and planning to ensure that you as a producer understand the big picture of brand management when presenting an idea to your internal management or when pitching a project to a publisher. Use the following checklist to identify the strength of the product and how it might fit into a business plan for a successful brand.

- Target demographic
- Price point
- Platform
- Learning curve
- Game genre (breadth of appeal)

Discuss why the target demographic is right for this type of game. If it is a racing game, ensure that the target demographic is aligned with that type of game, primarily males ages 18–35. Consider the price point and how your game proposal stands up to other games in the industry. If your game proposal includes a price point that is $59.99 when similar games are selling for $49.99, consider revising the proposal to reflect this market reality. The platform also has a big impact on whether a product makes a successful start and ends as a larger brand. A real time strategy game, such as *Command and Conquer* won't do well as a console title because the game type is noncomplementary to the platform or user control scheme. Be certain to address concerns like this before submitting your proposal. The learning curve is the time it takes for a user to learn how to play the game. Games that have steep learning curves will appeal to the hard-core gamers, whereas those with shallow learning curves have a much broader appeal. And lastly, consider the genre of the game that you're proposing. Is it a role-playing game with an appeal to only a specific type of gamer? Or is it an adventure game that almost anyone can enjoy? Consider the breadth of the game's appeal in your proposal and ensure that the other data supports the stated breadth.

Although most publishers don't expect a developer to have all of the answers, it is advantageous to consider the game development presentation and proposal from the perspective of a publisher. If you are a producer working at a publisher, these are typically the key points of a winning strategy that you'll need to address in detail before the project is approved.

However, this does not mean that unless your product can be clearly articulated as a brand, it won't be published. It just means that if you are thinking about these issues, you'll be that much further ahead when the time comes.

Writing a Winning Proposal

"You sell an original concept with description of unique gameplay, not through art style or cool technology. If the essence statement of a high-concept document can capture a truly unique gameplay concept, the product will find a home."

—Clyde Grossman, Senior Partner at Interactive Studio Management

There are no hard-and-fast rules for a winning proposal, so this book relies on what has worked well in the past as an example of what might work well in the future. There are also a lot of examples of approaches that don't work. This section addresses the types of proposals to write if you're looking to place an original title with a publisher and get a development contract.

Every written game proposal should clarify the game idea, player goals, and how the development of the game is to progress. Lastly, it should clarify the expectations for this title in the market, when properly supported by an effective marketing campaign. While creating a proposal to achieve those ends, the producer should come to understand and determine the resources, time, and talent (which equate to cost) used to make the game. In the end, it should communicate that your game has the potential to be great, sell millions of copies, be built into a larger business than just a single deal, and that the team will execute according to expectations.

Getting to Yes with a Publisher's Representative

The term *getting to yes* means achieving approval of a proposal so development of the game can begin! The first thing to remember about getting to yes is that you have to get the reader of the presentation to open it and read it, so there are a few basic steps to ensure that your proposal rises to the top of the stack at the publisher.

note

The steps in getting to yes are borrowed from Roger Fisher and William Ury, *Getting to Yes: Negotiating Agreement Without Giving In*

Keep in mind that the initial proposals are intended to pique the publisher's interest. Although you might be very excited about the idea, the publisher isn't yet to that point. You need to convey your enthusiasm and passion for this title, making it contagious and desired. Second, if you're talking to a publisher (such as Activision, for example), keep in mind that they (like most publishers) are only focused on building brands and understand which brands they are interested in. Activision might not be so interested in an interactive music party game (such as *Samba Di Amigo*), but might be completely interested in an FPS proposal. So, it must be clear from your proposal how your product develops into a brand. If this is the case, examine the current brands of the publisher and make a clear case as to why your product might fit into its own brand. Lastly and most importantly, the concept and the proposal need to convey a unique gameplay concept. It should not be a "me too" approach, in which the gameplay you're describing is simply, "better, more, faster, and deeper." That's not unique. That's evolution, not revolution.

Remember that the game design proposal and presentation is your idea. There's no template to use or form to fill out. Work with your development team to create the proposal that passionately conveys the idea you want to turn into a hit game. This isn't exactly a business plan, but it also isn't a work of fiction. Work to hit the mark in between by including just enough relevant business and market data points to add strength to your arguments and show them you're using valid criteria when judging the commercial ability of your game to perform. But, be certain to include enough emotion, conviction, and great ideas to demonstrate the talent and commitment to excellence of your team.

Form Follows Function

You might have heard this cliché before, especially when dealing with artists and creative types. The proposal and presentation must follow this rule as well. Understand where you want the proposal to take you and then develop a proposal that takes you there. The function or goal of the document shapes the form it takes. If you're creating a TV show style game like *You Don't Know Jack*, then the proposal might take the form of a TV show script.

When considering the future development of the *Myst* franchise, proposals were solicited from several developers, but the winning one came from a group called Presto Studios in San Diego, California. Their proposal included a technology demo, a business document outlining the business points, and a creative document bound into the form of a *Myst* "linking book," complete with parchment paper and calligraphy. It was impressive and it got my attention and the attention of the executive team. It conveyed that this team understood the franchise, knew adventure games, and were committed to excellence in bringing to life the details of the experience (which is a big part of why consumers buy products in the *Myst* brand). Needless to say, they were signed up to work on a title in the franchise and went on to develop the award-winning *Myst III: Exile* in large part due to the slickness of their presentation as well as their understanding of the market.

Focus your proposal and presentation on the strengths of your team. If your team is technology driven and has some great examples and tech demos to show, a futuristic and clean-cut proposal might be best suited to explain and convey these strengths. If your team has a great creative focus and artistic breadth, focus time in making the fonts, titles, headers, and overall page design layout follow in support of this concept. But stay away from fancy designs that don't provide readability or clarity of purpose.

Know Your Audience

When working on a proposal for an Asian publisher—at which many of the executives spoke only Korean fluently—one of the techniques I used was to focus the design and presentation style of the documents on the art style that we knew was pleasing to them, keeping the English content to a minimum. By including the numbers and financial elements of the proposal into a separate document book so that it could be reviewed independently of wading through tons of English documents. We consulted with an agent who knew and understood the local culture and asked for her advice when creating the proposal. When the documents were created, we rehearsed the presentation with everyone who was involved in presenting the game to the publisher. We rehearsed who would speak to which questions.

By taking these steps to know and understand our audience, we were assured of success and the project was approved. It was the first project using an external developer for this publisher and doing our homework really paid off.

Focus on the Key Elements

When you break it all down, a proposal for a new game is composed of the following key elements.

- A description of what the game is—the *essence statement* and *key promise* of an interactive experience.
- A development plan for how this experience is going to be created and why this team is capable of executing the plan.
- The reason why this game is going to sell millions of units and why it should be developed.

The essence statement and key promise are the most important parts of a game development proposal. They should not be more than one or two sentences, but they need to adequately convey the concept for the game as well as why anyone would want to buy it.

To address all of these points adequately and in a compelling way, a producer should understand who is most likely to buy the game and what the compelling motivation is for a user to buy this game. Showing how the team and the concept fulfills that gameplay promise is what the proposal should clearly articulate. The publisher may ask questions about who will buy the game, why it will sell, and how much it will sell for.

One commonly overlooked element within a game proposal is the focus on how and why the game makes money—lots of money. Just because it may be cool, new, and original doesn't always mean that it will sell.

note

Not all new games sell—even if it is from a hit-producing team whose games have been success-ful in the past. Take *Dikatana* (released in 2000), for example, from Ion Storm and John Romero. It was a great team with a cool idea, but it lacked in execution and, as a result, it didn't reach the mark of a critical or commercial success. But, their past success certainly brought the team to a place where they could get the development contract. The problem was in the execution.

One of the key elements the proposal should address is how to define the market for the game and supply some proof the market (consumers) will buy it. Resist including opin-ions and subjective statements, such as "Well, *Myst* sold well, so this adventure game should do just as well, especially because there aren't any other adventure games on the market right now." That statement includes some fairly broad assumptions. There's a rea-son why other adventure games aren't on the market right now, and it is that the market is highly competitive and certain genres (like adventure games) only have room for one or two leading products. The rest of the products in that genre aren't supported and usually fail commercially. Supply detailed, objective, and well-thought-out marketing data points to support your supposition that your proposal for a product delivers a promise to the market that they really want to absorb.

Describe the game experience and essence in detail. Create a sample sell sheet that might be used to help the reader understand and frame the game description and design with how the final product might be sold. A full creative design treatment for a game is often a long and boring document. So, propose and present a game treatment to the publisher that makes the game sound exciting.

Certainly the most important part of the proposal is that it must show that your team is able and qualified to develop this game.

Keep a Clear and Concise Voice

Because publishers get a lot of proposals and their representatives are always evaluating new opportunities for how to effectively invest their money, it is important to be able to concisely present the idea and passion behind the game proposals. In addition, publishers have limited time to actually read and analyze proposals; therefore, a principal goal of the proposal is to make that process easier by being concise, clear, and easily understood. Remember that *eloquence* is not synonymous with "interesting" or "exciting." Focus on making the product pitch attention getting, not necessarily eloquent.

Detail in the cover letter a way to orient the publisher to the team and the game. Then focus on the strengths of your team. If they have a history of hits under their collective belt, be certain to present that first. If the concept helps to define a genre or uses a license for an existing intellectual property that's well known and has other products in the market (such as a movie, TV show, book, DVD, or comic), add those details in as early as possible.

A good proposal doesn't lead with the game design document in its full depth; even if you truly believe that the product is very unique and truly poised for greatness, discuss the market first. Clearly articulate that message, and the opportunity to discuss the greatness of the concept will come later.

Focus on clear details such as Web sites and press materials in support of your proposal. Write with a voice focused on facts and outside proof, while avoiding exaggerations or big promises. The purpose of these documents is to grab the attention of the publisher's representative and lead them to the point at which they're asking for more details.

Keep in mind that the full creative design, budget, schedule, and proposed terms are often left for a follow-up later. Although these types of documents have more depth and facts, they are often left to later, after you have the interest of the publisher in the concept.

Getting to Yes with Your VP and Executive Team

All producers have supervisors and managers who are responsible for approving the funding of new projects whether at a developer or a publisher. However, this section discusses the role of a producer at a publisher. As a producer at a publisher, the biggest challenge to starting a new project is ensuring that you've properly addressed the concerns of your executive team and that sufficient confidence is built in the project, the concept, and the brand's potential. Although you might think that getting to YES is the hard part, actually, when you get to YES with your executive team, the challenge really begins and the work starts.

Presenting proposals internally is an important part of the role of a producer at a publisher, as well as a critical part of any independent game developer's continuing business. Examination of opportunity and an effective analysis is one of the ways to ensure that you start on the right projects with the right team.

When evaluating a new opportunity, ensure that it follows the topics and recommendations in the previous sections. When preparing to present it to the executive team at a publisher, you need to complete the following homework before such a presentation.

Understand the Goals of Executives

The goals of executives are to ensure that the company's money and resources are effective-ly invested in the right investments that generate excellent returns. While constantly realign-ing resource allocations with the right investments, executives work to avoid investments that aren't profitable or do not properly balance risk with reward. This is the principal moti-vating factor for executives, ensuring that risk is managed properly and that the investments made with company money are profitable and are the best use of those resources.

Separate the Issues

Separate the issues into specific and manageable ones. When presenting a proposal that might have several conflicts or challenges, you can separate the issues so that they appear more manageable than an opportunity that has many "issues." It is easier for executives to say "No" to a project when it is fraught with risk that has not been addressed on an indi-vidual risk basis. When grouped together, individual risks might seem more than they are when discussed and evaluated individually.

Separate the issues with a risk management plan and ensure that a plan is in place to address the risk. If the risk is a design risk, such as entering a highly competitive genre with a new and unique concept with a design team that has not worked in that genre before, offer a plan to compensate for that risk by including key milestone review points, a longer prototype and design schedule, or even hiring an addition to the design team who supplements the weakness and minimizes that particular risk.

Focus on Common Interests

By focusing on the common interests between the proposal (from a developer or a licen-sor) and the company, you're able to quickly and efficiently focus the proposal and pre-sentation on the potential benefits and positives of the proposal and the relationship.

Focus on the interests between the publisher and the developer. Then focus the proposal to appeal to the interests of the executive, such as a new product line, developing an exist-ing brand, or acquiring new technology and talent.

By appealing to these common interests and objectives of the company and the executives, you increase the likelihood of receiving a yes on the proposal. Avoid falling into the win-lose scenario by focusing the proposal on a scenario in which each party benefits.

Provide Options

One of the ways to ensure that a proposal is approved is to generate several successful options with varying degrees of risk and reward. Determine which options the publisher generally accepts and work to structure the proposal to fit within a range of options gen-erally accepted. Also have in mind (this means develop, but perhaps don't present) several other options that are generally creative. This could be things such as options on an engine or technology license for use in another game, or a license to the IP for other media, such as movies or television rights. By identifying a number of options, you have a greater chance of being successful in finding the right combination of factors to bring the publisher and the developer together with a great contract for a great game.

Provide options that specifically target the decision makers on either side of the proposal. If the developer is looking for a publisher with a solid track record of publishing well-tested titles and not rushing them to market, then highlight this portion when discussing the deal with the developer and include it in the presentation. When considering which VP or executive you're presenting the proposal to within your own publishing organization, target things that might be important to them, such as future brand development (easily creating other follow-on products that have a similar appeal within the same genre) and the applicability of the engine license to other products within a brand. Proposals are easy to accept when you're the decision maker who reviews a proposal with legitimate and accepted business points that cite precedent in support of the key points.

Outline Objective Criteria

If you're a producer at a publisher, one who is highly supportive of a new proposal from a top developer, one successful path in presenting and reviewing proposals internally is to outline the objective criteria for which the proposal and concept should be judged. This includes details such as feature lists, content depth, and schedule probability, as well as overall costs. By clearly defining an objective set of criteria with the initial presentation, you can more easily gauge and understand the expectations of management as well as show that the proposal meets or achieve internal criteria and goals for the company. Although executives might have their own set of criteria, establishing and presenting your own criteria helps the decision maker put it into perspective. It also shows that you've done your homework and it lends credibility to your arguments. However, each publisher has their own rules and procedures for presenting prototypes and game development opportunities, so follow those guidelines.

If you're a producer at a developer, use the technique of outlining some objective criteria on which to judge your proposal and any presentation given to a publisher's internal review team. Establish that criteria with the publisher's representative so that you can outline clear goals for the team creating the prototype and any presentation.

Preparing and Presenting a Winning Presentation

This section discusses the basics of how to prepare and present a winning presentation. Although there are no set rules on what documents go into a presentation, this section provides some examples of how to structure commonly used documents based upon other successful proposals. Do you have to include all of these documents in your proposal? No. But should you have them prepared and waiting? Probably, as it definitely helps your case if you look like a producer who is prepared for the hard questions. Being prepared and having done your homework if and when the time comes to start negotiations is yet another way to ensure that the proposal goes the way that you want it. By examining where a producer wants the proposal to go and identifying all the potential steps, pitfalls, challenges, objections, and upside benefits and potential rewards, you'll have the tools and have done the homework necessary to succeed.

Working with an Agent

Working with an agent to present your game concept idea to a publisher provides a number of advantages. Clyde Grossman, a former industry executive turned agent, outlines the following advice and benefits as to why clients use his agency:

- Agents know the publishers and which materials are appropriate for certain publishers.
- Agents understand what's commercially viable in the marketplace.
- Agents help their developers focus down to the essence of the concept and determine the right essence statement.
- Agents do presentations constantly, so they have the process down to a science.
- Agents help determine the right answers to difficult questions about technology, appeal, and anything else that might stand in the way of the deal.
- Agents handle negotiations. Not surprisingly, negotiations are often best handled by someone who has a lot of experience in negotiating.
- Agents provide help for the product during the entire development phase. They help developers identify problems in the product or the process before the publisher knows a problem even exists (or existed).
- Because agents are constantly watching several projects, they often recognize difficulties early, allowing for a way to solve problems with minimal impact to the product.
- Agents realize that making a deal is not going to be easy, and they help their clients through the difficult process of doing so.
- Commissions are paid out on a milestone basis, not on an up-front cost basis, so the agent shares the risk with the developer.

What's in a Prototype Presentation?

Each presentation is different. If someone tells you that a presentation must have X number of documents, that's not true for every case. The examples outlined in this section are some common documents that have been used in a number of successful new product proposals and presentations. For this example, assume that a prototype of the game exists and that it can be presented along with the documentation.

note

Having a prototype of the game that you're proposing is essential to new and original game ideas. If you're working with an existing, successful license, engine, and team, it would be less important, but probably easier to create. Prototypes are very helpful in showing that your team can develop and present a solid gameplay concept that's unique from an early stage.

Executive Summary

The most commonly used and offered document to lead a game proposal is the executive summary. This document explains the concept, the game, the market opportunity, and the technology used to develop the game in simple, clear, and easy-to-understand terms that an executive is used to seeing and reviewing. This document is generally an internal document used to frame the overall opportunity within context and without getting into specifics of the product.

You should include the following elements in your executive summary:

- **Product title.** Clearly detail which product this is for by including a sample logo and/or stylized text with the working title of the game as well as any subtitle. Include your company name and date as well.

- **Main heading.** Include the title of your game along with the proposed platform or SKUs that you're considering. Include the term *executive summary* at some point on the document so that the reader knows this is just a brief overview.

note

SKU stands for *stock keeping unit,* which means each individual product that is found on the shelf at a retailer. For example, if the game ships on PC, Xbox, and GameCube, then each version for each platform is its own SKU.

- **Quotations.** Use convincing quotations, if appropriate. Compelling quotations from literary works or historical works can put the proposal into perspective and attach some emotional connection to the proposal in a way that a good quote does. However, this is not recommended for all cases.

- **Story.** Consider if the story is the most important part of the presentation and proposal document. If not, leave it out or include only a minimal mention of the story. A common mistake is to include a ton of detail on the story and leave out the key details on the gameplay and the market opportunity. For example, this might be as short as a "As a spy in the future," which is very concise but perhaps good enough.

■ **Gameplay description**. Include some reference to the essence statement (explained later), including how the gameplay is going to deliver on the key promise of an experience to the user.

■ **Appeal**. Clearly articulate the key appeal of the game. For example, if it is an RTS that uses a 3D camera to immerse the user in intense battles in real time, provide a promise of unparalleled immersion in realistic battle views. Reuse or reword the essence statement for this section, and include a supporting phrase or additional detail of how the game accomplishes this promise to the user.

■ **Opportunity**. Discuss the *opportunity* for this game. If the game takes advantage of a new rendering technology or other advancement, discuss why the opportunity to deploy and use that technology in the game helps poise the game for success in the marketplace. If the opportunity is a cool and unique license, specify those details as well.

High-Concept Document

The high-concept document outlines the concept for the game. Included in this document is the essence statement or key promise to the user. The essence statement is generally a complete and vivid description of the main gameplay experience. The essence statement is not just a one-liner about the gameplay. It describes the essence of the experience. For example, the essence statement for *Super Mario 64* might be, "Explore visually stunning and colorful new worlds, defeat angry villains, and fight horrible monsters, while romping through exciting puzzles and collecting gold, all in an epic quest to save the princess from her imprisonment at the hands of the evil Bowser." The essence statement would *not* be, "Using a second-person removed camera, follow Mario through the colorful worlds of the kingdom of Toadstool in his quest to rescue the princess from Bowser in this action/adventure game fit for all ages." See the difference in how the essence statement vividly describes the promise of the experience for the user, rather than describing the game concept?

Consider the following tips when crafting your essence statement.

■ Use visual terms, such as haunting, gothic, and dreary to describe a dark world. Conversely, use vivid descriptors for describing bright and colorful worlds, such as dazzling, alluring, glittering, and shimmering to help the reader visualize the world that you're proposing to create.

- When describing gameplay or style, use familiar terms and relevant pop culture references to help the reader understand the specific appeal. For a dark adventure game, an example is "undertaking a haunting quest in a *Silent Hill*-meets-*Hellboy* stylized world." This gives the reader some excellent context about how to gauge your proposal and the appeal of your game. Other words, such as "chilling" or "global conspiracy" provide contextually accurate and vivid descriptions of how the gameplay unfolds within the world.

- After your essence statement is complete, go on to describe the key features of the game, such as special effects, special animations, fantastic level design, supernatural and magical abilities, gameplay integration with the world and story, music, sound effects, fighting, multiplayer, battles, and combat. Focus on five or fewer key features and then explain why and how those features are critical to the game and why users would buy and play the game.

Creative Design

The creative design documentation is about 20 or so pages long and it clearly describes the gameplay and gameplay conventions and systems. When making a proposal, it is generally recommended to have a draft of the proposed creative design for the game ready and accessible, but don't submit it to the publisher until they ask for it and are interested in the concept based upon their review of the high-concept documentation.

However, this draft is not expected to be the final form of the game. In fact, it is very likely that the creative design will change in response to the feedback from the initial proposal and presentation, so don't invest a ton of time explaining the details of the game; focus instead on the key gameplay systems and features, such as user interfaces, inventory control, and player interactions with the world. Core gameplay concepts and features can be left for later. Creative designs commonly change once a project is signed, so be sure to convey that there's some flexibility and adaptability in the design. Use this document to demonstrate control of the process, understanding of the nature of the genre, and the subtleties of the type of game, as well as efficient work processes and a commitment to quality.

Art Production Style Guidelines

The art production style guidelines can be the flavor of the presentation, but remember art style doesn't sell games. Gameplay is why consumers buy games. Use this document to clearly articulate how the form of the game follows the function of the game design and to give flavor to the proposal.

Discuss the guiding principal and inspirational references. Discuss the fundamentals behind the artistic style and visual presentation of the game. For example, if you're working in the science-fiction genre—creating a game that appeals to that market—discuss influences, such as Peter Elson, Chris Foss, and John Harris. *The Star Wars* films and *Blade Runner* are also good popular and appealing titles to reference.

Discuss the audio and visual treatment of the game and how the two components work together to form a compelling interactive experience. Discuss how the screen looks. (For example, is it clean or does it use overlaid interfaces?) Imagine how the story is going to be conveyed to the user. Is it going to be told in the form of a narrative voice, in dialogue between characters, or in scrolling text?

This is also the document in which to discuss how cutscenes using the in-game engine (commonly known as *non-interactive sequence*, or NIS) or even pre-rendered movies tie missions or levels together and how all the pieces fit together.

Address improvements that are considered for the graphical treatment of the game, such as where higher resolution textures are going to be used and how they'll add to the depth of the experience. Discuss advancements in the technology and how those advancements are going to be applied to the art style.

Certainly, the art style is the point at which you should discuss how different characters, units, or teams will look and how the protagonists are differentiated from the antagonists. In multiplayer games, discuss how teams (or races) are differentiated.

Discuss how any modable features are going to be included in the tools to which the end user has access. Are they going to be able to modify badges on their characters or units? Can they create custom artwork and apply it to their team?

Consider the orientation for the user and how the art style applies to that orientation. Is there going to be bright lights in the distance? Is there an up and down, and how is it depicted to the user?

It wouldn't be a video game without special effects, so be certain to mention how the special effects (particle) systems will look as well as show some examples of the direction of the special-effect treatment. For most video games, this is where the money shots come from for the box covers, poster artwork, and advertising and PR.

Technical Design Draft, Including Tool Discussion

Generally, there is no advantage to submitting a technical design document at the proposal or even at the presentation stage. First, it often confuses the matter about whether the concept is viable. Second, unless it really adds strength to the proposal, it can detract from an otherwise compelling and convincing creative concept. Finally, you will have plenty of time to flesh out the technical design after development of a game enters the pre-production phase and work begins in earnest on the concept.

However, for those rare occasions in which a technical design documentation, tool discussion, or high-level technical document is required at the proposal or presentation stage, consider the recommendations in this section.

By including a brief discussion of the specific capabilities of each game feature, this can help the audience understand why this game will sell. Such a technical feature document might be separated from the feature list and arranged in sections by function, including Data Layout, Debugging Features, Rendering, Special FX, Networking, Sound, Movie Playback, Animation, Character Integration, and so on. Then briefly discuss each section of the entire technology toolset, explaining why this technology is most appropriately used for your game. This should be no more than 8–10 pages long.

Finally, including a complete feature list of each feature that you anticipate using in the game, is generally overkill at the presentation stage. But if you choose to complete that task, it can be the first step toward creating the "Programmer Task Definitions" outline structure, which is required to plan the project's schedule.

Although including the programming task for each feature is a long and involved process, at the presentation phase, the producer should work with the lead programmer or technical director to at least identify the key features that are needed for the game as well as outline them into a structure that is easily fulfilled and completed if and when the project is green-lighted. Then as the game's development progresses, update this documentation with the details of how the features are actually implemented. This means that the technical design document should be divided into chapters based upon features. Keep this in mind as you structure your design documentation for the pitch so you can use it as a foundation for the full technical design when that milestone becomes due.

Schedule and Budget

Often, a schedule and budget are immediately included in the proposal for any new game project. Although including them occasionally has some advantages, I don't recommend doing so. I recommend preparing this document but not presenting it until you're asked how much the project is going to cost by the publisher or your management.

Present the creative concept and the ideas behind why this game proposal will be successful; after that interest has been secured, use the budget and the schedule to start discussing the details and demonstrate control of the situation as well as a complete understanding of the work required and its long-term potential. Get them excited before stating the proposed cost.

The budget and schedule section should include the following documents:

- Total budget and proposed milestone schedule (by month).
- Publisher's financial model (discussed later) showing projected sales, using relevant data from a reputable marketing source, as well as key break-even points for break-even units, break-even price, and royalty earn out.
- High-level schedule showing the following phases of development (prototype and proof of concept review, pre-production, production, testing, Gold Master release, and post-release support).

Build of Prototype and Build Notes

Unless you're a well-established, hit-driven developer who churns out golden products every two years, most publishers want to see a working prototype before they seriously consider funding the proposal.

How do you complete a prototype if you're short on cash? There's a few ways to do that. First is to short-list a few publishers and propose to them the funding of the prototype. Some publishers will do this if you have a good reputation for solid game development. The second way is to use one of the existing free toolsets or modable engines that allow users to create their own content to complete a prototype that shows your concept. Although not as good as a production prototype, prototypes created using the mod technology from another game can be created relatively easily and inexpensively. Some games (such as *Half-Life: Counter-Strike*) were presented and created purely using the mod tools available to the public.

Most game developers create prototypes to generate interest. Some prototypes demonstrate a particular technology asset, whereas others are a demonstration of a particular type of gameplay. Sometimes a prototype does both. But decide what you want your prototype to do before starting work on it and focus your efforts on one or the other.

The most important part of a prototype is that it should be fun to play and demonstrate the concept that it is interesting to play. It should be a small, but well-polished demonstration of great gameplay, with a focus on clearly articulating what makes it unique.

So what are *build notes*? Build notes are the notes that you create and provide to whoever is going to be evaluating the game. Include specific examples and text as you might find in a readme.txt file on a retail version of a game.

Figure 5.1 shows an example of the first page of a build notes text file from a recent prototype. Sometimes, when the gameplay style requires it, a walk-through of what the player must do to complete the prototype is very helpful for the reviewer, who normally doesn't have time to guess and use trial and error to get through many prototypes a week. An example of what a walk-through might look like on this action-adventure game from Gnosis Games is also shown in Figure 5.1.

```
*****************************************
* Broken Saints by Gnosis Games        *
*****************************************

Install details:

---------------

The game requires UT2003 and the BonusPack to run properly. There will be
shortcuts created to assist in starting the game.

Please select the folder in which Unreal Tournament 2003 is installed!

This is commonly "C:\UT2003".

Minimum Requirements:

---------------------

OS: Windows XP or 2000

CPU: 933MHz or faster

RAM: 256MB or more

Disc Drive: 16x or faster CD/DVD drive

Hard Drive: 200MB of free space

Video: DirectX 9 compatible video card

Input: Keyboard, Mouse

Preferred video cards:

GeForce 4 Fx/ ATI Radeon 9800 - Or greater

Controls:

---------

<Movement> -------- A and D are used for turning left (A) and right (D).

<Movement> -------- W and S control moving the player forward and backward.

<Fire weapon> ----- V attacks.  Only during vision sequence.

<Action/Use Item> ---------- Space bar.

Known Issues:

-------------

•      When players open crates in the first bunker room, the camera does not
look at the items players can pick up.

•      After players open the crate across from the main entrance, the camera
shifts to an off-kilter angle.
```

Figure 5.1
The Broken Saints team put together comprehensive build notes with their recent prototype.

After discussing the prototype, you'll need to consider how to make the actual presentation if and when you get a meeting with the publisher. At this meeting, the challenge of the day is to present the creative concept and demonstrate the essence of the gameplay with outstanding acumen.

The Actual Presentation

If you've succeeded to the actual presentation stage—at which you're presenting the prototype and game proposal to the right people—you should consider the guidelines discussed in the following subsections when making the presentation.

Know People's Names and Roles

Another person's name is the most important thing that you can remember when making a game proposal. Work with your contact and do the homework to know who is going to be at the meeting, what their roles are, and perhaps what their general concerns and focuses are.

Don't Get Stuck on the Story

In talking with some industry executives, I inquired about how the search for new content and IP development was going. They told me a story about a recent developer who seemed fairly together and talented, who they'd invited to make a presentation to their product review committee. When I asked how the presentation went, it was fully explained to me, "They made the classic mistake. They focused on how cool the story was and how deep the player could get into the story."

The moral of this story is to not focus on some unimportant part of the game, but to clearly articulate why this game has the potential to sell millions of units (because of its gameplay, not its story, as stories drive books and movies sales, not game sales).

Expect the Unexpected—You Don't Know Jack

Early in my career, while working at Spectrum HoloByte, I was responsible for arranging the product submission and review meetings. One of the products that we received for consideration was the now well-known *You Don't Know Jack* product, in its prototype phase, which didn't look that much different from the final retail version (which just had more content and more polished user interface screens). After the product was demonstrated, the review team discussed it. They were intrigued. Some people were excited. But no one knew how to market it because it was out of the ordinary and unexpected. It didn't fit into the "mold" of the types of products that the company was interested in publishing. Unfortunately for the company, Spectrum HoloByte passed on publishing it. It was only many months later when it was published by Berkeley Systems and the game went on to be a hit mass-market game did the decision-makers who'd passed on the proposal consider that they'd missed a great opportunity.

If you're presenting a game proposal, keep this story in mind if your product is slightly out of the ordinary and perhaps perceived as a mismatch for that particular publisher. Tailor your presentation to address these types of concerns and do your homework so that no question from the publisher is unexpected.

Get the Game Concept Across Quickly

I always laughed when I read a proposal accompanying a prototype that said something like, "Although I don't expect you (the reviewer) to get it at first, it just takes time to understand the gameplay." Successful prototypes and successful games are ones that the end user understands within 90 seconds—one minute is better. If the prototype is already too complicated to get this point across in five minutes, then how fun will the game be after two years of development? Go back and refocus the prototype so that anyone who plays it finds the fun in the first minute and gets the concept right away.

Don't Try to Improve the Company

Although it is rare for someone to come to an office and think they know your own business better than you do, it does happen. Don't be one of these people; guard what you say so that it focuses on the positive and beneficial aspects of your proposal versus what the company might or might not have done wrong in the past. No one is perfect, but there is no need to call out past mistakes when it serves no advantage.

Show, Don't Tell

This is the mantra for all who want a game project to be green-lighted. If you can show something, a picture truly is worth a thousand words. You might tell your manager, your VP, or your producer at the publisher, "This is the right team for the job. We have the best talent and most diversified team." Instead, try showing why this is the right team and explain that "Our last two games have sold X number of units and are well supported by the fan community. Our tools allowed fans to create several mods, the most successful of which is played online thousands of times per day. Our games and accomplishments have won a number of industry awards and recognition. If you check our proposal under the awards and industry accomplishments, you can see for yourself what a team committed to excellence can accomplish."

Focus on Technology

If the prototype is a technology-focused demonstration of a game, include a spec sheet of what is actually happening on the screen and why it is remarkable. Discuss the specifics of the technology (polygons per frame, texture depth, size, lighting, and special effects). Focus on the aspects of the technology and try to throw in more than just a little fun for good measure.

License Focus

If your prototype is focused on a license that has already been secured, perhaps to a movie or comic, focus your proposal and prototype on how this license is fully realized, exploited, and how it might work with sequels and add strength to an existing brand or provide a foundation for a new brand. Prototypes based on a license give special attention to the characters and world. The prototype should adeptly demonstrate the gameplay innovation that your team is considering for employing with this license.

Know the Numbers

Knowing the numbers means that you (or someone on your team with you at the presentation) should have the numbers associated with what it took to create the prototype, as well as what investment would be required to take the prototype phase to the next level. You should also know what the entire project is estimated to cost. This also refers to the need to understand the publisher's business, including risk assessment and estimated return on investment. Publishers have financial goals that they are required to meet. The easier you can make it for them to see how they can get to those goals, the more likely you are to get your project approved.

Do Your Marketing Homework

Only a few games sell more than a million units each year. Saying that your prototype is just like the next *Grand Theft Auto* is not a good example. Do your homework to understand what average titles are selling in a specific genre and market (both North American and European). Be able to discuss the competitive features of each title with which your prototype might compete. Understand the high- and low-case sales scenarios. Although these points might not be discussed in the actual proposal and presentation, you want to be prepared if and when they are brought up.

Have a Quick Checklist for the Presentation

Going into a presentation unprepared can kill the proposal before anything has even been said. Here's a quick checklist that's proven helpful.

- **Test the gameplay demo and provide working hardware.** Don't expect the publisher to supply hardware that conforms to your specs and has all of the right drivers. Bring your own hardware.

- **Bring gameplay on videotape.** Prepare for the unexpected by supplying videotape with your presentation. It should demonstrate the essence of the gameplay in this videotape. This prevents the situation in which someone might want to play and present the game to others, but is cautious of looking like an inexperienced player. It also assures that you have a working demonstration of the gameplay, regardless of anything else that might work against a presentation's polish.

- **Know who is going to sell which parts**. When going with a team, be certain to clearly delineate roles between those who are presenting with you. Establish clear guidelines as to who is going to answer the business-, technical-, creative-, and production-related questions. Separate the questions into topics and assign an expert to each area, and stick to that.

- **Bring a backup.** Be certain you have backup copies of all documentation, on CD, as well as CDs of the prototype if that's possible. They'll come in handy. You can even image a computer's system disk, with the prototype build installed on it, and burn it to CD; then, it is ready for a quick installation at a moment's notice.

- **Know your message.** Live, sleep, and breathe the essence statement and focus your energy on explaining the essence of the gameplay.

- **Rehearse.** Practice the presentation at least three times before presenting it. It is surprising how many small mistakes can be eliminated with this easy step, ensuring the final presentation is slick and polished, just as the prototype should be.

Preparing for the Hard Questions

A valuable piece of advice came from Alex Garden, the CEO of Relic Entertainment. Although I like to pride myself on being prepared, organized, and fully functional, having all the right answers and knowing where to find the few answers that I don't have, Alex often challenged me with questions that made me think about the problem in a way that I'd not considered. He gave me a valuable piece of advice two days before an important presentation to one of the publishers we were working with: "Sit down and write down the top 5 most difficult or challenging questions you can think of related to this presentation. Then send them to me, and I want to see your answers before you go." He was certainly right to insist on this because during the presentation, I was asked four of the 5 hard questions I'd written down and fortunately prepared for.

The following is a list of some challenging questions to prepare for before any meeting or presentation.

With what degree of certainty can you predict when this product is going to be complete if we give you the green light?

There hardly ever is a right answer to this question, but focus the question on a demonstration of your control and grasp of the tasks at hand and how your team is organized to provide the best chance of hitting the predicted completion date.

What would you say are the biggest risks with this product and how are they being addressed?

(continued on next page)

Preparing for the Hard Questions (continued)

You should be able to reference a risk management plan (in the Appendix D) that addresses these.

Do you have all of the right talent on the team if we wanted to start tomorrow?

The answer if very rarely "yes" because most talented people are booked up from project to project and a team is almost always growing until the testing phase.

Why are your project costs so high?

Defer this question to whomever prepared the budget. But a general rule of thumb is $10,000 USD per month per employee. So, if you have a 20-person team, a cost of $200,000 per month is fairly reasonable. The longer the development timeline, the more a project costs.

What are the biggest competitive challenges this game faces?

Refer to your notes on the competitive analysis and demonstrate an element of control and knowledge in this area by referring to your marketing homework.

The Final Word

Getting an original title, like any new idea, signed up and a project started is a challenging, but rewarding task. Keep in mind that the most successful titles in entertainment software came from an original idea at some point in their past. Hopefully, what's included in this chapter helps turn your proposal into a reality.

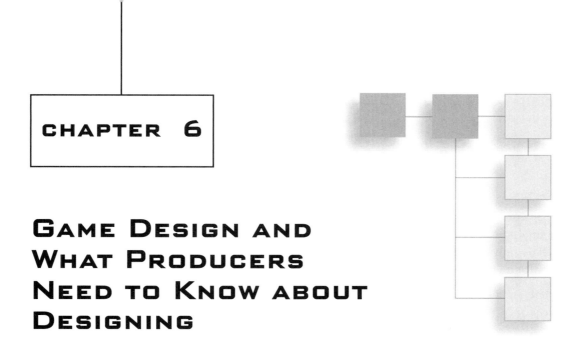

CHAPTER 6

GAME DESIGN AND WHAT PRODUCERS NEED TO KNOW ABOUT DESIGNING

The role of a producer actually has little to do with designing and more do with finding the best idea and best-defined game concept and ensuring that the final game meets the essential gameplay promises to the consumer. Naturally, the producer needs to ensure there's the right team to complete those gameplay experience promises.

This chapter discusses the role of the producer as it relates to a game's overall creative design, level design, and all of the design work in between concept and final product. In this chapter are the essential pieces of knowledge each producer should understand when working with game designers. By understanding and respecting these fundamentals, a producer can make the design process more efficient and help produce a higher-quality game design.

Can Producers Design Games?

Having a dual-function role—being both a producer and the lead designer of a video game—is extremely challenging. Each role has its own essential demands and constraints. Each is its own full-time job. Really, the responsibilities should be separate, and there should be both a producer and a lead designer on a game, with the producer focusing on the production of the game and the lead designer focusing on the creative vision.

However, that doesn't mean that the producer is prohibited from making design suggestions or otherwise helping to refine the design into its core elements and key promises of experience to the user. This is the fun part of creating a video game's design.

Producers and Game Design

There are generally too many other things going on for a producer to be working on designing a video game, but it really depends on how your game and team and company is structured. In some cases, like at EA, producers *are* charged with designing parts of the game, as there are very few if any game designers.

Whether a producer should handle design depends mostly on the type of project and the scope of the design responsibilities. For an original IP title like an RPG or adventure game, it might be risky to place the design responsibilities on a producer. If it's a racing game that needs only minor updates, revisions, and improvements, a producer, assistant producer, and/or an associate producer may be able to handle the design responsibilities easily.

Here are a few truths to consider about producers and designing video games:

- A producer cannot dictate the design of a video game. He can only guide it.
- A producer charged with designing a game is a bottleneck to the creative process in most cases.
- A producer must be ready for interruptions and constant distractions. Such an arrangement is generally contrary to creative endeavors that require focus and complete attention.

Myths about Producers and Game Design

There are a few common misconceptions concerning a producer's role and the process of designing a video game. This section will attempt to disperse some of those myths. But as you read each myth, remember that every project and producer is different. These are broad generalizations that apply to a common set of circumstances in the game industry, but not to every case.

- **The producer *always* leads the game's design and creative vision.** The producer doesn't always have to lead the game's creative vision, telling others when and where to include design concepts, features, units, or characters. But a good understanding of how this vision is coming together is important. A producer should have an excellent grasp of the concept and how the game is going to deliver on the promises of the user experience embedded in the game design. Working with the lead designer, the producer can help guide this vision to fruition.
- **The producer is *always* the one with the best ideas.** Remember that the producer does not always have the best game design ideas, but their input *is* required to make sure that the design ideas that are being contemplated in a game design are actually feasible and producible within the scope of the game.

- **The producer can usually find time to focus on designing.** The role of a producer is one of constant interruption, prioritization, and re-prioritization, with changing objectives, goals, and circumstances. This type of demand and the constant interruption is generally not conducive to focusing and clearly identifying the key goals of the user experience, as well as how they are going to be implemented and complement every other system. Designing games takes focus, clarity, and assurance that the design team is working in harmony and communicating well. If you're a producer who wants to design games, make sure that the communication is taking place within the design team and then communicate those ideas and goals to the rest of the team. Find time to focus on the procedural and production challenges first, and then consider how the design challenges fit into that role.

Female Producers and the Video Game Industry

From an interview with Tracy Rosenthal-Newsom, Project Leader for the *Karaoke Revolution* series of video games, Sr. Producer at Harmonix Music, game developer in Cambridge, MA.

Q: *What are the biggest challenges you see for women who want to help shape a game's creation in a producing role?*

A: I don't believe that gender alone limits a producer's power to shape the creation of a game. Effective producers produce effectively. All producers find challenges when shaping their game. However, as a female producer who is interested in creating games for the mass market, I do face some specific challenges.

Our industry has historically created most of its games for boys and men by men. In order to design games that reach both genders, we need development teams where both genders are well-represented. Unfortunately, the pool of female producers, designers, artists, programmers, audio designers, and testers remains small.

At Harmonix Music, women have made up about 25 percent of our *Karaoke Revolution* development teams, which is actually high compared to industry norms. We work within a collaborative iterative design approach that allows for a wide-range of design ideas to emerge from all contributing members. Most notably, every discipline of our *Karaoke Revolution* development team (production, design, code, art, audio and QA) has included female representation.

Another challenge persists at the publisher level. Publishers seek to replicate their previous successes and are naturally reluctant to take risks with new types of games. As a female producer who is interested in designing new gaming experiences for a more mass market, my challenge is to convince the publishers that following the same old formulas won't always be good for the bottom

(continued on next page)

Female Producers and the Video Game Industry (continued)

line. We need to diversify our products by creating gender-neutral games for the mass market. We need to persuade the publishers to finance games made for both the casual gamer and the "newbie gamer" who currently doesn't play video games but wants to try. We need to help the publishers break out of their established marketing practices in order to access an untapped population of new gamers unlike the old demographic. This is more likely to happen with new blood in our work force. New ideas will come from both women and men; the best designs will emerge from well-balanced teams of both genders. It is up to female and male producers to assemble well-balanced teams in an effort to effect change in our industry.

Q: *What direct impact have you had on a game's design that has helped its overall appeal to the mass market?*

A: As the project leader of the *Karaoke Revolution* series, I was involved at each step of the design and production of the products. From the time the concept was brought to us by Konami, every design choice our collaborative team made was with the intent to create the ultimate party game for the mass market. Even with the primary audience targeted at bi-gender late teens and young adults, we learned early on in play-testing that children and middle-age adults of both genders loved the game as much as our primary audience. We executed our design with this mass market in mind.

Designing a Producible Video Game within Constraints

In order for producers to add value and ensure effective communications within the process of developing video games, there are a few areas of game design and game design constraints with which they should familiarize themselves.

A producer constantly checks to ensure that a game in development runs on the target platform at all stages of development and conforms to the design outlined by the designers. A producer must understand the platform on which the publisher is going to ship the game. These details include understanding that there is a limited amount of RAM and data space on the media, as well as the limitations of the technology. While it is challenging, it can be fun as long as you know the rules and work within them. Here are some common constraints that are faced by game designers and producers. All of these issues must be considered when undertaking game development on multiple platforms.

Multi-Platform Simultaneous Releases

Developers and publishers plan games to ship on multiple platforms. The decision that this game is going to ship simultaneously on multiple platforms is usually made right at the beginning of a project. Driven by marketing forces—such as the need to release a

Lord of the Rings title on all platforms simultaneously in order to coincide with the release of the film—the multiplatform simultaneous release is a requirement for most hit titles. Interface and memory concerns concerning all platforms tend to be addressed during the initial stage of development rather than during a typical port (the process of converting a game to work from one platform to the other) process.

Significant differences exist between the various types of hardware platforms—such as the Sony Playstation 2, Xbox, GameCube, and the PC, along with a whole host of handhelds—and there are some advantages and disadvantages. But all platforms have certain criteria and constraints that affect a game's design. Those constraints apply differently depending on the type of game being made. And in the end, games need to support the key features of their platform, whether it is the graphics, the user interface, or the game features.

Some platforms have unique niches in the market. For example, Nintendo Game Boy grew from a niche market to the Game Boy Advanced, and is now one of the most popular hardware platforms in history for playing games. Platforms are targeted to appeal to different demographics. Nintendo appeals to a younger category then other consoles. Xbox and Sony Playstation 2 appeal to a more mature audience.

As a game producer, you may have tremendous freedom to do your job, but one of the keys to success is to help guide the design process through the constraints of the hardware, the market, and the schedule. These types of constraints are very specific and immovable. Hardware technology for consoles is fixed, and for PCs it is very complicated. Your game must work on a console and the PC and it must be completed in about 24 months, during which time the technology may change. To create a detailed design for your game before beginning production, a producer should work with the design and programming teams to research all of the potential technology hurdles for your game. When working with the designers, keep in mind that it should be a flexible design, work on all platforms, and exploit the strengths of each.

Working with Design Constraints of Console Games

As a designer, you should review the key challenges that you may face when designing a game, and work out solutions to overcome those challenges. But the most important step is to understand the potential challenges before starting on a game's design.

Advantages of Producing and Designing Console Games

The advantage of designing games for console gaming systems is that the specifications are published, known, and unchanging for the life of the console. When you learn how to create a game on a particular platform, you can eliminate any number of inefficiencies and focus on the strengths of the platform and the game. For example, Xbox is known for its higher quality graphics and powerful graphics processing unit (GPU), expanded memory, and hard drive. As a result of the powerful GPU, it can draw more polygons per frame and per scene than other consoles. It can also store saved games as well as other relevant data on its hard drive.

Games that are developed for the Xbox may contain more polygons and look better than other games on other consoles. More importantly, key routines for drawing polygons or using the key features of the console's applications programmer interface (API) are clearly outlined in the platform's documentation.

Another advantage is that you need not concern yourself with compatibility across multiple types of hardware, as is a concern when developing games on the PC. This is beneficial because it allows you to focus your knowledge and expertise on how to achieve the best results on a very specific hardware specification. When developing games for consoles, remember that the critical advantage is to focus your ability to exploit the strengths of that console.

A third advantage is that customer support costs for products developed for consoles are extremely low when compared to the games released for the PC. This is because there is little chance that a player will experience trouble when playing the game for the first time.

Lastly, the games developed for consoles generally sell more units than games developed strictly for the PC. Console products generally sell more games because consumers buy gaming consoles specifically for gaming purposes, whereas PCs have multiple purposes beyond entertainment value. Console games are generally easier to learn to play than most PC games. Thus, the financial rewards for game developers and publishers are generally higher for products developed for the console than those for the PC market.

Disadvantages of Producing and Designing Console Games

While consoles offer many advantages to the game development process, there are also some disadvantages that every producer of a console game must face. One of the key disadvantages of developing games for release on a console is the fact that a game developer is limited to the input methods that are compatible with the console.

There are very specific hardware constraints that must be adhered to. For example, if a game uses more than 64 MB of RAM, it cannot be played on any of the current consoles. It can be played only on the PC. As a result, the game design must account for key hardware constraints before and during a game's development cycle.

Specifically, consoles generally do not support keyboards or mice. This limits the types of games that can be developed for the console. For example, real-time strategy (RTS) games do not sell well when developed for or ported to consoles because they require multiple inputs from both keyboards and mice to support their key gameplay features. A good example of a failed RTS port to the console was *Starcraft* for the Nintendo 64 console. The interface and controls were not sufficient to control the vast numbers of units on screen at a single time. As a result, a very successful RTS was unsuccessful as a port to this console.

The second disadvantage is that before beginning to develop a game, you must seek and receive the hardware manufacturer's approval. Furthermore, after the game has been completed, it must be tested by the hardware manufacturer—Nintendo, Sony, or Microsoft. You must receive approval from the manufacturer to actually manufacture and ship the game to retail stores. This means that not every proposed game can be developed. These are rigorous processes that ensure only specific titles are approved and developed for each console.

Proprietary hardware investment is another disadvantage when developing on consoles. Consoles not only require a PC for each game developer working on the team, but also require "development kits," which are emulators of the final version that include proprietary tools, libraries, and coding templates for use in the game.

You also need to use development kits to test the game throughout the development cycle. These hardware items are often very expensive because of their proprietary nature—costing $15,000 or more in some cases, depending on your relationship with the hardware manufacturer. This is more than four times the cost of an average PC used for game development.

Some development kits, such as those for Nintendo and GameCube are also, by legal and contractual obligation, prohibited from leaving the country. This can be a problem for developers who use offshore resources. It can be very difficult to get development kits set up in certain countries outside North America and Western Europe.

When developing on multiple consoles, there are many factors that affect art style and how a game looks. Polygon count and memory constraints form restriction for how a scene is rendered on-screen. To get the best look on all consoles, you may need to build more than one entire set of models and textures and use techniques like switching models in real-time in order to maximize the frame rate speed at which the game runs.

note

In 2003, it was suggested by Jason Rubin of Naughty Dog Software that "Games have now reached a point at which graphics are no longer our primary selling point, and very soon we will have to concentrate on new things to attract the consumer's attention." What this means is that photorealism can now be achieved with extra investment in art production quality and graphics style. Future games will need to branch out in their art styles. For example, *Jet Grind Radio* and *Viewtiful Joe* are games that have embraced a new art production style, one of a surreal cartoon world. The investment in brilliant graphics should not overshadow the investment in new types of gameplay. New types of gameplay and new art styles are the solution to the diminishing return on investments in graphics quality alone.

When developing for a console, you must examine the advantages of that console. For example, Playstation 2 and Xbox are well-known and respected for their applicability for racing games because they can render a succession of millions of polygons at very fast frame rates. Successful titles, such as *Gran Turismo, Project Gotham*, and the *Need for Speed* series are well suited for console platforms because their interface is easy to use and the vehicles are easily controlled and exploit the rendering strengths of the console. These strengths appeal to console users as they try to master the skills needed for racing. Carefully consider the type of game that you are designing. If it requires a lot of user input and controls, then the console is probably not the ideal platform for this game.

Simulations such as *Microsoft's Flight Simulator* or RTS games such as *Warcraft III* or *Command & Conquer* are not suited to the console's strengths because these use large amount of memory and require more user input than can be easily supported through a console controller. These types of games require a mouse and keyboard and are best suited for distribution on the PC.

On consoles, there is a limited ability to save games. The Xbox has more flexibility because it has a hard drive included in it. Both Playstation 2 and GameCube require the user to purchase separate memory cards with read/write memory. There are specified parameters for the file size of saved games. The solution to this challenge is to carefully consider the size of the deterministic data set while designing a game rather than waiting until the game is many months into production. This can be an expensive proposition to fix later.

Finally, the game cannot be patched after it is released. What this means is that any bug, defect, design flaw, imbalance, or other material imperfection in the interface is encapsulated in the game forever once it is manufactured. Because of this, all hardware manufacturers have rigorous testing standards for all games published on their console. This means that you should plan for a lengthy quality assurance process to refine the key selling points of the game to ensure that it meets the quality standards enforced by the console publisher and the manufacturer.

Working with the Design Constraints of the PC

There are many considerations that a producer working on a title for the PC must take into account, but the major one is the target specification of the PC. This is generally defined as what kind of system specification a gamer can buy for $1,000. A typical requirement of most game producers is to forecast the price of PCs and estimate a target specification at least two years ahead. This estimation process generally begins when the development of a PC game starts. At several points during the development process the producer needs to revise it to ensure accuracy.

For example, a PC that costs $1,000 today is probably not going to be manufactured and available for sale in two years. Look at the latest and most advanced high-end specifications currently available when a game's development is started. A high-end PC with a

Pentium GHz processor and Gigabytes of RAM that costs $3,000 today will probably cost only $1,000 in approximately two years. This specification will be a common computer with a wide installed base in every market worldwide within two years.

This is how game developers determine the target platform, commonly known as the *target system spec.* Game developers who are working on a title for the PC generally expect to release their game two years from the start of development.

A typical $1,000 PC in 2005 includes the features listed in Table 6.1.

Table 6.1 The $1,000 PC of Today

Component	Spec Today
CPU	GHz Pentium
3D Accelerator Card	128Mb nVIDIA 5700 or greater
Hard Drive	60Gb
RAM	512Mb - 1Gb

The *target spec,* also referred to as the *recommended specification,* means that the game should run optimally on that specification. The minimum system specification will be less stringent than the target, but the game will not run optimally and not all features will be included, perhaps by elimination of hardware transform and lighting (T&L) or reduction in the graphical feature set.

A team cannot always push for the biggest and best minimum specs for their upcoming product. Often the publisher actually insists on lower minimum specs especially for games for the casual gamer. This is to ensure that the game can appeal to the largest possible installed base. So-called "family" games are at the extreme end of these criteria, with the minimum specs being quite low to meet the needs of this demographic.

Advantages of Producing and Designing PC Games

There are several advantages in developing games for release on the PC platform. First, anyone can develop a game in any genre for the PC. Game developers have total freedom in this regard. With the exception of some minor legal ramifications or restriction on online gambling, almost any game can be published for the PC platform.

The PC platform has a relatively robust hardware specification because it includes 3D hardware acceleration, RAM, hard drive space, and a sound card, and can render in multiple resolutions. It is a more complex hardware specification than a console and, as such, it offers a lot more possibilities in terms of how it may be used to its maximum potential.

The PC has been around for more than 20 years as a gaming platform. Therefore, there are a number of relatively easy-to-use, off-the-shelf game development software solutions (called *middleware*) available to license, such as sound engines, physics engines, video codecs, graphics APIs (such as DirectX or OpenGL), and object-oriented coding architecture standards. These are standard middleware solutions that are tested and proven to work when incorporated into a game's architecture according to documented guidelines.

Developing games for the PC has the added benefit of a lower cost of goods, compared to the costs of goods for a console. This means that extra CDs can be included to support the game's depth, additional content, or new features, without any major impact in the overall costs of goods. Generally, games developed for the PC have a cost of goods (COGs) of about four to five dollars per unit, which is about 50 percent less than the COGs for console.

The game code or art content can be updated after the product's release. By supporting automatic patches and updating, games can continue to evolve after they've been purchased by a consumer. This also allows for online gaming, additional content, and patches to fix game bugs, errors, defects, or imbalances in the game's design.

There are several ways to exploit the strengths of the PC. Principally, the advantages of the PC are focused around use and control of the game through a keyboard or a mouse. Flight simulator games and real-time strategy games use a large majority of the PC's strengths. The depth of a game's features on a PC game commonly exceed the depth of features on other platforms. You need to use the keyboard to provide a greater depth of input choices, features, and gameplay.

Secondly, first-person shooter games are especially popular on the PC because it provides for a first-person perspective on a fast-paced, 3D world filled with action, shooting, and danger. The game mobility you get from combining the mouse with the WASD keys on a keyboard just cannot be duplicated on a gamepad. This type of interactive experience requires a stronger interface and ability for the user to control the experience.

The PC offers tremendous ease when saving games, as there is vast storage space in its hard drive. PCs also have more processing power, which can make up for some types of unoptimized code.

Moreover, when you consider the huge number of players on the Internet and on computer networks, multiplayer accessibility is an important strength of the PC.

Finally, the PC is capable of providing higher resolution graphics than any console that is restricted to the PC. This is important issue when you're creating a game that requires a higher level of detail, texture depth, and immersive experience. Offering the experience of a world in as close to photo resolution as possible is a great strength of high-end PCs. Use this strength to include a strong art style with tremendous depth and level of detail.

Disadvantages of Producing Games and Designing for the PC

Although the PC is flexible and powerful today, there are some disadvantages in developing for such a complex platform. When designing for the PC, you need to account for and identify problems in it.

Since the PC has a variety of games published on it, there is no standard set of game tools similar to the ones consoles manufacturers supply with their hardware. There are many tools and many engines, but they do not work with all applications and for all games. As a game designer, you must sometimes create your own proprietary tools for building worlds, creating levels and units, placing sound effects and special effects, and so on. Building proprietary tools and plug-ins for 3D software such as 3D Studio Max takes time. It takes even more time to get the tools working as according to your needs. If you license existing tools and technologies, you incur substantial expense.

Compatibility Testing

The main disadvantage of designing a game for the PC is the sheer complexity of the PC. There are multiple hardware configurations, as well as required software configurations, including the multiple versions of Windows that must be tested—95, 98, 2000, NT, and XP. This testing process is called *compatibility testing*.

As a producer for a PC title, you face the challenges of ensuring that your game works on all versions of the hardware within their specification. This can be potentially thousands of possible combinations, and is always very time-consuming. You may need to use outside testing companies for at least some of this testing, and you may incur a substantial extra expense.

The Game Code

The game code and game design must be versatile rather than specific. There are generally one or two ways to code for a console optimally, depending upon the desired results and the specifics called for in the game design. With PCs, because there is more flexibility, there is more room for error. There may be two or as many as ten different ways to code a feature into a game to achieve the desired result. This requires a broad degree of flexibility, discipline, and experience to code for the PC effectively and efficiently. To counter this disadvantage, a very complete technical design and feature set is required prior to beginning development, allowing the developer to clearly identify the entire task list, features, and potential challenges and prepare accordingly. Compared to developing on a console, where most of the challenges are defined, this is a big disadvantage.

Competition

Because the PC platform offers so much freedom and few barriers to entry, there is a lot of competition in the market. The top two or three titles in a genre make 80 percent of the revenue. In any year, there may be thousands of PC games released through retail channels.

From those thousands of titles, only the top five percent are profitable projects. This means that only those titles that innovate in entirely new and compelling ways can distinguish themselves in such a crowded market. The alternative is to do sequels to existing PC titles that are part of a successful brand, and have been successful in the past. As a result, the market can stagnate, with some titles showing little innovation at all.

In the midst of all of this competition, the fiscal reality is that PC titles rarely sell the typical volumes that console titles do. It is rare for a PC title to sell more than 1 million units worldwide—unlike console titles.

Working with Design Constraints of Handheld Games

There are several handheld platforms on the market today. The majority of the market share is controlled by Nintendo's Game Boy and the Game Boy Advance. Other platforms include Nokia's N-Gage, Sony's Playstation Portable, and the Zodiac from Tapwave. Together, these handheld platforms comprise the handheld gaming market worldwide.

Consider the advantages, disadvantages, and potential problems encountered when developing games on a handheld platform.

Advantages of Producing Games and Designing Handheld Games

One of the key advantages when developing for the handheld platform market is that the platform hardware is clearly defined and it eliminates compatibility testing challenges.

An abundance of existing content is ready to be converted, or "ported," to the handheld platform. Games ready for porting, some developed more than 10 years ago, include classics such as *Centipede, PacMac, Jeopardy,* and *Wheel of Fortune.* These old classics have been around for a long time and have a broad marketability. These games also include the types of gameplay that appeal to the broad demographic (everyone from your kid sister to top executives to some grandmothers) that owns handheld platforms and cell phones.

The porting process is relatively straightforward in a handheld platform. They don't require any new game design, as they are known quantities—fun games that appeal to a large audience. Because this porting process is a known factor, many of the challenges that a designer faces over a long and involved project on either a console or a PC have been removed.

Handheld consoles are widely distributed and have a large installed base (meaning the number of people who have purchased handheld or portable gaming hardware). For example, the Nintendo GameBoy has outsold the GameCube by more than 10 to one. This increases the potential for sales of units on the handheld platforms.

Creatively, the handheld platform allows developers who miss "the old days" of computer gaming to create games that excel in gameplay and design without having to push the technological boundaries of sound and graphics.

Disadvantages of Producing Games and Designing Handheld Games

There are many disadvantages when working on such a constrained and defined platform. The primary disadvantage is the system limits on file size, RAM, and total game size. For example, the entire N-Gage game must fit into less than 3MB of RAM, with the application being limited to 64Kb. Most processors on handheld platforms have less computing power than do home computers from the early 1990s.

Most handheld games do not have sufficient networking capabilities or bandwidth to make it feasible to play against another person. Although certain phone games are naturals for multiplayer applications, the lack of bandwidth required for fast action is a significant constraint. Networking is not typically considered a key feature of a handheld. This is because of the high latency that is associated with such devices and their peripherals.

Players are constrained to a small screen size, such as 200x300—or 176x208 in the case of N-Gage. There is a very limited amount of screen size that can be clearly drawn to such a small screen. To compound this, the limited color and sound support do not add to the depth of the game.

Finally, the user has limited power supply. Short play times are paramount. The user must be able to have a ton of fun in a very short period of time; this is often difficult to design for with an original title or concept that requires hours just to learn how to play.

Based upon the strengths and weaknesses of the handheld platform, what are the problems that might be encountered and how can they be solved, or designed for?

Technical Constraints of Game Design

Progress in the video game industry is largely driven by advances in technology. As technology progress, so does the complexity of the considerations required by game developers. How should the new and expanded capabilities of hardware be used in games? How should you plan for the advancement of hardware technology?

When developing for any platform, you need to use specific APIs provided by Microsoft, such as Direct X 9.0 and its subsequent versions and supported SDKs, as well as the development tools provided by hardware manufacturers such as Sony or Nintendo. Intel and 3D-accelerator card manufacturers also offer tools and development solutions for game developers. These tools become more robust with every revision. Direct X 9.0 provides more and more choices about how to implement game graphics, sound, and music. This progression ensures that game development becomes more complex, while providing an improvement to the overall visual appeal of games.

Games such as *Homeworld2* are extremely complex in their gameplay design and use of technology. Use of a 3D camera, multiple levels of data, and limitations on the effective use of polygonal rendering and frame rate posed challenges to the developers at every step of the game's development. This is not an uncommon story in the game development industry. The consequences of these challenges were that the game required additional testing to ensure that the proposed solutions were effectively employed, that the frame rate was sufficient and camera controls improved enough to be useful to a wide variety of users.

It is important to consider the technical limitations and constraints when designing a game because it is easy to design beyond the means of the technology that the market has embraced. A game designed beyond the common specifications of the marketplace might be a great game, but would face tremendous challenges in being commercially successful.

Graphics

As game development progresses, more games get closer to photorealistic graphics displayed in real-time. More importantly, pre-rendered graphic standards of yesterday, such as those used in the movie *Toy Story*, are fast becoming the standard for real-time graphics in present day games.

PCs show the most active and visible progression of technology, as players constantly upgrade their machines with the latest 3D accelerator hardware. Console games take leaps and bounds over longer periods of time—three to four years—because the console hardware cannot be upgraded once the platform is on the market. A new version of the console must emerge on the market and game developers must learn how to use all of its features (see Figure 6.1).

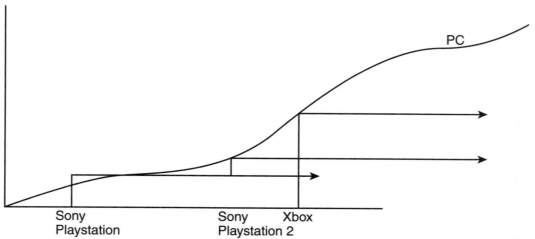

Figure 6.1
This figure shows how graphics quality and complexity improves over time, depending on the console. Notice that the PC platform constantly improves, while the consoles remain relatively flat.

With the PC, the graphics rendering capabilities differ widely depending on the type of the machine and the 3D accelerator card. The advantage of developing for the PC is that there are constantly new features to use as new 3D hardware accelerator cards are released on the market. The disadvantage is that the platform is constantly changing and the standards can be confusing and time-consuming to develop for.

Specifically, PC cards are moving away from the GeForce 1 and 2 standards set by their manufacturer, NVidia. Most games in 2005 will require GeForce 3 or higher. What does that mean for gaming? It means that most games will use even more normal mapping. *Normal mapping* is a procedurally different way of doing bump mapping. It appears to give bumps to the surface of textures. The games will use the same complexity as in "in-game" polygonal models but with higher quality effects, as they use normal mapping. How is this done? Normal maps are generated offline and then used during real-time gameplay to give the illusion of higher complexity poly models.

The advantage of using a console is that its graphics rendering architecture and API are a known, documented set of features that don't change. Game developers develop an expertise at using this architecture and these features after developing several games for a single platform. However, the software cannot exceed the limitations of the hardware no matter how good a game developer is.

A final rule is that PCs will always exceed the technical limitations of a console over the long-term, but the complexity of the PC holds it back from mass-market acceptance.

Memory

Memory is one of the constraining factors that apply to all video games, regardless of platform, genre, or market. A console memory is fixed with the specification published by the console manufacturer. With PCs, it is one of the variables that make developing for the PC challenging. Upgrading or downgrading the computer's memory is very easy to do. So, how do you develop a game with memory constraints in mind?

The first rule to remember is to keep the game within a specific minimum memory specification, such as 32 Mb on the PC and only 6 Mb on a console. This impacts the size of the world that the game can have and also the complexity of how the world is rendered.

As a game developer, you must remember to use the different types of RAM that are available within a platform. All platforms have certain restrictions (and some provisions) for program memory (the game code), sound RAM (for music and sound FX), and texture RAM (for rendering graphics). While some platforms have specific provisions for each type of RAM, other platforms include RAM in a common resource pool. It depends on the platform you're developing on.

Using more memory may make the game run slower because using more memory means more missed *cache calls*, or calls to the CPU cache which preps the data before it is loaded into memory, and processing more data. Keep memory usage minimal whenever possible.

Program Code Memory Usage

Different languages produce program code of various sizes. Also, compilers for the same language produce program code of different sizes. You need to keep track of the amount of RAM used for stack space and static data. Test your optimization options early and often. Once per build would be ideal because you can identify when and why a change in the program code memory usage occurred.

Texture RAM

This is the most common and widespread consideration of games today. For each texture, there are different MIP levels, which take 33 percent of the largest size of the texture. To cut down on texture usage, use the top MIP level for the highest detail texture and discard the highest detail texture.

note

Note that bit depth (8, 16, 24, 32, and so on) and texture compression have a large impact on texture RAM usage. The more bit depth, the more memory that's used.

Some hardware renderers will allow you to exceed the amount of RAM they have, and will copy textures from system RAM to video RAM as needed. This will cause a significant speed penalty to your graphics engine. Keep in mind that different texture effects, such as bump mapping and environment mapping, are all texture-based considerations that must be accounted for in your texture RAM budget.

Video Buffer RAM

Video buffers include render buffers (usually two for double-buffering), Z-buffer for proper depth-order rendering, stencil buffer for shadows and other effects, accumulation buffers for motion blur and other effects, and render-to-texture for shadow and lighting effects. At higher resolutions, these buffers take larger portions of available video RAM. Oversampling also increases the resolution of these buffers relative to the final screen resolution.

Models and Animation

More polygons generally mean more RAM. The same applies to more complex rendering effects on models. Additional texture layers, complex animation skeletons, and model format can also affect the amount of RAM used by models.

Animations may take a lot of RAM depending on how complex they are, and how many there are. To reduce memory usage by animations, you can use the same animation for different models. A larger model would play the animation slower than a smaller one, and it may have different animation parameters to make it seem smaller. You can also use animation blending (blending between a running animation and a leaning animation makes a running around a corner animation redundant) and representation (quaternions are not only simpler to blend and interpolate, they are smaller than matrices).

Sound

Sound data can use up a lot of memory, depending on how it is used. Some types of sound, such as speech and music, can be streamed from the disk, thereby reducing memory usage. Sound that is used frequently or must be low-latency, such as footstep sounds, must be kept in memory. Techniques for reducing memory usage of resident sounds include storing them with lower-quality settings. For example, explosion sounds need lower quality settings than music. Other techniques include instancing and playing back at different speeds, blending, or stitching together with different sounds for more variation. Compression, especially loss frequency-domain compression algorithms such as MP3, can tie down the perceived audio quality in a game.

Level Data and Game Data

In some types of games, level data can be quite large. This is usually because levels contain a large number of textures and models. Levels may also contain a large number of enemies, which affects the size of the game data in that level. If level data is a concern, your level production pipeline should report the amount of level data required and warn the user if he is exceeding the budgeted allowance.

The amount of data used to store the game state can be quite large. Also, this data can grow as the game proceeds. The program should be regularly profiled using a controlled worst-case scenario to test this. The worst-case scenario would involve the maximum number of players, all enemies on-screen, and the biggest level, all being drawn simultaneously.

Remember that all the data that fits into memory must be installed on a computer or used on a console from a storage device. Often, the data used in memory is just a small fraction of the compressed data included in the storage device. The next section reviews the considerations of the storage device.

Storage Device

Read-only devices cannot be used to store data such as saved games. On consoles that use CD-ROMs or DVDs, an additional storage device, usually a memory card, must also be available. Different devices have different read speeds. You can usually read faster from a CD-ROM than from a DVD and faster still from a hard drive. To further complicate matters, different devices have different seek speeds. CD-ROMs and DVDs have much slower seek speeds than hard drives. Memory cards are generally the fastest. Because of the slow seek time of CD-ROMs and DVDs, try not to read two files at once. When streaming music, it should be stopped or streamed from RAM during loading. This can impact a game's design when you need to stream music, sound effects, and a movie from the storage device at the same time.

Big File Systems

If many small files are packed together into a single larger file, this reduces the number of file open and close calls and speeds loading. This process is called a *big file system*. Within the big file, individual files may be compressed or otherwise optimized to further improve load time and/or reduce storage size. You may see a significant speed boost on loading if your files are arranged in the order they will most likely be loaded. This is due to the elimination of many small seeks of the hard drive or other storage media. Games installed on and read from a hard drive generally list the required minimum amount of free hard drive space that is required before installing a game to that drive. This is to ensure that there will be enough space to install the game and enough space for storage of temporary files and user data. During the install procedure is where the big files are copied to a user's hard drive.

Games on CD-ROM and DVD must fit within the maximum size of the medium chosen. Some of the space on the CD-ROM or DVD may be needed for OS code, copy protection, publisher promotions, or additional content. A big file system will help optimize the space on the duplication media if it uses compression algorithms.

Storing Files on a Memory Card

Did you ever own a Nintendo 64 or an original Playstation? Remember the memory cards that you could buy separately? Of course, GameCubes and PS2s still use memory cards, so they are not quite a thing of the past. Memory cards are used for storing user data on systems that are based on CD-ROMs, DVDs, or ROM Cartridges. Memory cards have very limited storage compared to a CD-ROM or DVD. Also, there may be limitations on how much of this limited space your program can use. Memory cards are usually based on flash RAM, which is very slow to write. Limiting the size of stored data is very important to avoid long save times.

Other Design Constraints for Any Game

As a producer, you're often principally responsible for being the guardian of the game design and for ensuring that it stays within the constraints of the project. This next section discusses some of the common business or marketing constraints on a game's design.

Genre and Target Demographic

The brand definition directly affects genres and target demographics. Brand definition is a clear delineation of which brand a game fits into. Is it a strategy game that fits into the *Command & Conquer* brand? Or is it a science fiction, outer space 3D strategy game such as the games in the *Homeworld* brand? Is it a platform game such as *Mario 64*? Obviously, when creating a RTS game for Nintendo, you would face significant challenges, considering that the RTS genre does not do well on consoles and the Nintendo demographic is children between ages 10 and 17 who may not understand the concepts behind an RTS very readily.

Knowing the audience requires research from market research companies such as National Purchase Diary Group, Inc. (http://www.NPD.com). Purchasers of video games are typically males between the ages of 15 and 45 who have a fairly large disposable income. Review this information with the Marketing department before starting design work just to see what type of games certain age groups are buying.

Key Feature Requirements

Marketing departments of large publishing organizations often have key feature requirements for certain brands. Pivotal brands, such as the *Myst* series, *Command & Conquer*, *Call of Duty*, and *Need for Speed* have key features that are required in products in the brand. For example, all *Myst* products must work on a typically lower-end PC that is at least two years or older. That means the rendering system must include features that use the lower-end graphics cards' features as well as the higher-end features, such as dynamic lighting. This also means that the product must scale between the various hardware specifications seamlessly.

The features of a game are often linked to their unique selling points. Game features are principal elements of a game that make it more interesting, exciting, and fresh compared to other games in the market.

Marketing teams usually have some input that determines the key features of a game, but the final decision on whether the features are included in a game is made by the development team. The key issue is whether or not the game features are competitive enough.

For example, the multiplayer first-person shooter game, *Return to Castle Wolfenstein*, published by Activision, includes the following game features:

- Epic environments
- Intense, story-driven combat
- Fearsome firepower
- New character classes
- Enhanced communications
- Additional game modes

These features were derived from the game's innovative gameplay and technology deployment into quantifiable aspects that are communicated to the consumer on the packaging. A risk in not identifying the features clearly and concisely is that the game may look like every other game on the market, with no unique feature or appeal. This is why effective product placement and advertising requires almost a year of lead-time to develop and prepare properly before publishing.

With the *Need for Speed* series, a marketing requirement for designers is that the software offer support for external hardware, such as a steering wheel and foot pedals, as well as be able to play the same game on all platforms. These are requirements that are set by the Marketing team for the strengths of the brand, and designers must include these features in their design.

A strong RTS brand, such as *Command & Conquer*, must include real-time 3D graphics, special effects, and a rotatable camera. These are the marketing requirements because that is what players of that brand have come to expect, as they are a standard feature of all RTS games on the market.

Competitive Product Analysis

The competitive product analysis involves reviewing all competing games in a genre and analyzing them for competitive purposes. During this process, the designer generally creates a matrix of product features and selling points and analyzes which are important and why.

When developing a game, the designer reviews how product features are implemented in a game and considers ways to improve an existing feature design. This means that games in a competitive genre need to get better and improve over time, otherwise they will fail. For example, *Homeworld2*, the sequel to the game *Homeworld*, a real-time 3D RTS game, improves on many different features of the original product, as well as on competing products like *ORB, Hegemonia*, and *Earth and Beyond*. This was achieved through the use of a competitive analysis to evaluate what made those products better and how could the development team improve upon the ideas demonstrated in the competitive product.

After this analysis, the *Homeworld2* team reviewed their designs for the game's menu system, user interface, and background creation methods, as well as a few minor gameplay elements. As a result, *Homeworld2* was able to significantly improve the interface accessibility to the user by evaluating their previous work as well as that of competitive products.

License Constraints and Licensing Your Game's IP

Licenses are important to video games because they provide a unique connectivity to another intellectual property, such as a movie, TV series, or a comic strip.

Licensing of video game characters or the use of other intellectual property licenses in video games is very common and often lucrative for both the licensee and the licensor. This section covers how licenses to video game characters and other intellectual property restrict and empower game designers and what you, as a producer, should know about working with licenses. It is common for the video game industry to use licenses to other intellectual property in developing video games in order to ensure the continuity of a brand and to capitalize on another hot product in a different market. The most common license is that of characters and story.

Game Characters, Genres, and Target Demographics

A common license applied in video game development today is the license of a character. Unique characters play a pivotal role in the success of a video game, so a logical business approach is to apply that success to other media.

A popular and familiar video game license is that of Lara Croft, from *Tomb Raider*. Edios, the publisher of the *Tomb Raider* products, licensed the *Tomb Raider* intellectual property to Paramount Pictures for the development of a series of movies.

Unique character development is critical to developing a successful video game and creating a value in that intellectual property. Once a successful brand featuring a principal character has been established, interested parties enter negotiations on the terms of a license agreement. A license agreement covers the terms under which the two parties, the licensor and the licensee, may agree to work together. The license agreement covers points such as duration of the license, how and for which products it may be used, and how much is paid in consideration for using the rights to the character.

When you create a design for a product that uses a license, there may be some guidelines for using that license. In the case of *Tomb Raider*, a license to use the main character, Lara Croft, would require that the game use the character in a way that is consistent with the movies and the other video games.

Other guidelines provided by a license may be related to the genre and target the demographic of the license. A puzzle or adventure game using the *Star Trek* license might be a mismatch with the genre and demographic, considering that *Star Trek* appeals mostly to males and the puzzle or adventure genre interest is 50 percent male and 50 percent female. Secondly, a license provides guidelines in terms of story, art direction, and overall game experience to the game designer; this means that the game designer does not have total freedom to design a new game, but must encompass the key elements of the license, such as character, story, and weapons. Generally, the game designer can develop an entirely new part of the story, or create new weapons or characters, but these must "fit" within the creative aspects allowed by the license.

In general, a producer for a video game project that uses a license is responsible for helping focus a game designer's ideas and contributions that add to an already successful intellectual property. This keeps the project moving toward a concept that is producible and manageable.

Key Game Features

A license must be matched with the right technology and game features. For example, a game using a license to the *Matrix* movie series would need to exploit unique particle FX, high-resolution graphics, video playback, and dynamic sound. The other key features would need to be action, adventure, shooting, and story progression. These are all elements that have some content provided by the license, but in the end it is up to you as the game designer to make an effective and compelling use of the elements provided by the license.

When using a license, consider features that support the game's previous expectations of interactivity and take them to the next level. In *Myst III: Exile*, the game builds upon the previous features of *Myst* and *Riven,* but includes a new form of camera—one that rotates 360 degrees in any direction—while still providing the point-and-click interactivity that users came to expect from the previous products in the license.

You need to consider in your game design key competitive game features that use the strengths of the license's guidelines. Do not try to force a new feature into a licensed product just because it is cool, new, or unique.

Requirements of the Licensee

The last consideration that is of paramount importance to the game designer is the requirements of the licensee. For a game that uses the *Star Trek* license, there are other guidelines provided to the game designers—the game cannot show the USS Enterprise being destroyed, for instance. Paramount Pictures has an entire licensing department set up to handle requests from licensees on clarification on how the elements of the *Star Trek* license can be used in video games and other products.

Referencing the appeal of the genre and demographic in the *Harry Potter* license is actually one of the requirements of the licensee. The licensor did not want movies or video games created that did not have direct appeal to the same demographic (children) as do the books. Therefore, this was made a requirement of the license agreement.

Lastly, the requirements of the licensee can be specific, as in such titles as the *Pool of Radiance* series, which uses a Dungeons and Dragons license. Because Dungeons and Dragons exists as a separate game outside the game industry, one of the requirements of using this license is that the rules of the Dungeons and Dragons games must be generally followed when creating a new product. This applies specifically to combat and how combat rounds are completed, with each player taking a turn and a roll of the dice being completed substituted with an element of chance.

The main point to remember is that different licensees have different requirements. Some are purely guidelines, while others are strict constraints. The important thing to do is to confirm whether you are working within a guideline or within a specific constraint before you begin working on your design. That ensures that there is no wasted work and the design meets the expectations of the licensor. There is usually an approvals process, during which the licensor approves or vetoes the various aspects of the design or the game; this is another potential area for conflict and challenges.

Game Theory

Is there really such a thing as game theory? Yes, there is, and it has actually been around for a long time. Game theory has been applied in the field of economics, as it is a part of mathematical analysis that enables decision-making in conflicting situations. Such a situation arises when two or more players, with differing goals, act on the same system or share the same resources.

Game Theory, as it relates to video games, is the concept that all players make rational decisions for their own benefit. Given two alternatives, a player selects the one that will work to his best advantage. Two or more well-defined choices or sequences of choices exist in every case. In every potential combination of these events the players creates, there's a win, lose, or draw that may terminate the game. Each intermediate step is clearly defined as well. There is a potential reward for each participant associated with each action.

Even though perfect knowledge of the game and of the opposition is assumed, it must be understood that the players do not have this knowledge at the beginning of the game. Although impractical, except for the computer opponent, a game designer must assume that the player fully understands the rules of the game as well as the rewards for other players. As a producer, you should also understand and apply this concept to reviewing design documentation.

The concept of game theory is used principally when programming computer opponent strategies and difficulty levels. The game's artificial intelligence routines reference a range of responses by a human player. By understanding that a game is a sequence of meaningful decisions, each with an opportunity for a winning outcome for the player, game designers can predict a range of rational decisions by players.

note

The game theory is especially important in massively multiplayer online games (MMOGs) because it defines the ways in which players interact within an online world that is populated by users 24 hours of day. All interactions between players must conform to game theory rules. MMOGs need to be designed to allow for a greater element of randomness in all interactions between players.

Game theory is an important concept for a producer to understand. It is one of the fundamental rules of game design and every game must include some element or degree of game theory—otherwise, it is not a game, but a movie or some other linear experience lacking a degree of interactivity expected by users of a video game.

Game Design Documentation

Now that we've covered a few of the rules related to what a producer should know about designing video games, the question arises: "How do all of these ideas and concepts get conveyed to anyone else?" That's where game design documentation comes in. The purposed of game design documentation is to communicate ideas; as the old quote goes, "Without communication comes chaos." Good (meaning *clear*) game design improves the chances that a good game emerges after many months or years of effort.

Producers and Game Design Documentation

I have a reputation in certain circles as being anti-documentation. I consider this a badge of honor. In my opinion, the single worse thing that you can do to kick off your Pre-production (phase) is to sit down and write a 100-page design document.

—Mark Cerny, DICE speech February 2002.

Clear and concise game design document is imperative to implementing a good game. But here's where a producer can play a pivotal role in the game's development. Game design documentation is meant to be a guide for the team during the design and production phases of a game, with the later designs building on the earlier designs filling in the details and clarifying the individual systems of the game as defined in pre-production.

Joshua Gordon from *Gamasutra* states, "Without question the biggest problem I find during the design and implementation of games is the lack of interactivity amongst the various team members of a project." The primary role of a producer is to ensure that this interactivity and communication occurs. But in order to ensure that those interactions are fruitful, the design document can't be the size of *War and Peace*. More importantly, it must hone in quickly on why the game is fun and reverberate that theme throughout the rest of development cycle.

Here's a quick summary of key questions and points to remember when considering game design documentation and how to judge whether or not your document is an effective guide for the game's creation.

■ Is it artistic? Does it convey a sense of what the designers really are envisioning? Sometimes a picture is worth a thousand words. Have the designers asked the art director to sketch what a specific concept or feature might look like?

- When reading the entire document, what does it convey in terms of the "big picture?" Can the "big picture" be conveyed without hundreds of pages of diatribe and waxing eloquent from the philosophers on the design team?

- Be prepared to discuss feasibility with the designers in design review meetings. Come prepared, have your notes and questions ready. Think ahead in how the design impacts both the art and programming. What is the overall look and feel of the design? Why are the characters appealing and how does the player relate to the characters? How to do the levels relate to the story and the gameplay? Is there a special level that has promise to show off what the game is really like at an early stage? How does the current design measure up?

- What do the menu and interface items look like and how well are they implemented? Does the interface look too complex? Is there a mock-up of what an actual screenshot might look like? If not, get a designer to sit with the art director and work on a few possibilities of what the final screen and interface looks like. Then review it with the art and programming teams and then revise as appropriate.

- Allow for revisions right up to the last possible moment. A design document should be updated to reflect the actual state of the game at the present time. Encourage the team to update documentation as features and items are implemented so that an accurate record of how a feature works or why a unit or character behaves a certain way. This saves a lot of time later when trying to track down causes for particular bugs.

- Remember that concept drawings are worth their weight in gold. They can save time and money by clearly defining an element before any amount of time during production is invested in creating it. To minimize the risk of starting production on a game element, unit, character or other piece of the puzzle, create one first, then try it out and show it around. Take screenshots if this is a model and send it out to the whole team. Get feedback on the first one before having a team member continue on creating any more.

- Ensure that the designers have tons of reference material. Especially reference material from movies, books, and other games. Make sure that the entire team has the same reference material so that the designers are not working with reference material from the *Matrix* while the artists are thinking that this next game is like *Star Trek*. Homogenize the reference material to reflect a consistent voice and style in the game's design documentation.

Most importantly, remember that the job of the producer is to ensure communication amongst the team on a constant basis. Only through constant revisions and re-reading of the documentation can a producer ensure that he understands what the team is making and why.

Elements of a Producible Video Game Design Document

There are many parts to every producible video game and when even one is lacking, the chances of a great game coming together is severely diminished. Instead of describing what is supposed to be included in each section of a game's design documentation (as every game and company has a different situation and every game is not going to need the same elements of documentation or level of detail), I recommend that every producer read one of the excellent books on game design listed in Appendix C. Gamasutra (http://www.gamasutra.com) is also an excellent reference source to become familiar with and use on a daily basis.

There are many books, articles and studies that go way beyond the scope of this book in describing how to create an excellent game design and document it so that it can become a reality. Suffice it to say that the game's design documentation should include the following parts:

Major Game Design Components

- Essence Statement
- Core Concept or Gameplay Promise
- General Gameplay Description
- Game Flow Chart, including use cases
- Technology Requirements
- Interface Design and Use
- Character Design
- Minimal Discussion of Story or License Use

Secondary Game Design Components

- Artificial Intelligence Design
- Behaviors Data Table
- Damage
- Death Sequences
- Demo/Attract Mode
- Difficult Levels
- Document revisions
- Enemy Description

- Export Pipeline Documentation & Procedures
- Gameplay Specifications (Hardware Target Spec)
- Level Briefings
- Lexicon
- Memory Map and Footprint Estimate
- Mission/Level Design Checklist
- Modability
- Model Lists
- Multiplayer Design (Maps and Gameplay Descriptions)
- Multiple Views
- Music and Sound Effects Lists
- Object Description
- Pause Game
- Player and Camera Behavior
- Rewards Table
- Save Game Methods
- Score

- Scripting
- Simulation Time
- Sound Design
- Special Effects
- Specialized Art Requirements (loading screens or on-screen text areas)
- Start Up

- Story
- Terrain Features
- Transitions
- Voiceover Lists
- Weapon Systems
- Weapons Data Table
- Winning Sequences

While this list is fairly comprehensive, your particular project may have more or less documentation depending on the type of game. Use this list as a quick reference guide to make sure your design team has thought through the basics.

Technical Design

The technical design portion of the game design documentation explains how certain features will be implemented. While during the early stages of the project, the technical design may only include a general discussion of basic features of the game and its toolset—and include topics such as polygon count, rendering capabilities, and frame rate—as the game progresses in development, the technical design needs to be updated to reflect how features were implemented. As features are implemented, the technical design documentation becomes the "Programmer Task Annotations."

note

Each programming task needs to include an allowance for updating documentation as a task. Don't mark a task as complete on the schedule until the technical design documentation has been updated to reflect how the game feature was implemented.

Here's a quick list of some common elements that comprise a technical design document.

- **Automated build creation**. A key point to ensure that the game stays on schedule. Be sure the design includes an allowance for creating builds automatically so that the game can be tested and played on a daily basis with a constant stream of new features being included.
- **Camera**. Discusses how the camera works and interacts with the world. Camera collision should be discussed here.
- **Commands**. How commands are handled from the user.
- **Computer opponents and enemy AI**. Discusses how these AI functions work.
- **Front end**. Establishes parameters for minimum resolution, optimal resolution, and scaling of the UI.

- **Game data**. Clear delineation of how data is stored, created and modified, as well as how the designers can manipulate it.
- **Game Logic, multiplayer**. Any special discussion about how the MP game works.
- **Game Logic, single player**. Any special discussion about how the SP game works.
- **Graphics and Rendering**. Minimum system specifications, as well as poly and texture budget should be established in this section.
- **Infrastructure and architecture**. Is the game mod-able and how data-driven is the game's architecture and engine capabilities?
- **Initialization and shutdown**. A list of the modules used to start up and shut down the game and how they work.
- **Localization**. All games today require easily modifiable localizable data, allowing for simultaneous worldwide releases. This should be discussed in this section.
- **Movie Sequences or in-game cutscenes**. Discussion of playback using the in-game animation engine or a movie encoder/decoder like DivX or BINK.
- **Networking**. Clarifies how the networking code works.
- **NPC, Unit AI**. Discusses how these AI functions work.
- **Optimization opportunities**. Includes opportunities for making the game run faster.
- **Scripting system**. Answers the questions: Is the scripting system familiar to the designers? Does it use LUA or a similar language?
- **Simulation**. Discusses how the simulation works, whether an RTS or a racing game, there's some element of a simulation in there. Cyclical redundancy checks (CRCs) between clients are commonly discussed in this section.
- **Sounds**. Often left until the last moment, how the sound engine works should be discussed and planned early on.
- **Tools**. Items such as the Mission Editor, sound effect placement, special effects placement, background creation and implementation, and any mod tools made available to the fans.

Tools Requirements

Thomas Carlyle once said, "Man is a tool-using animal. . . . Without tools he is nothing. With tools he is all." This has never been a truer statement than when considering the steps required building a game. Complete and effective tools are generally required before beginning production of any game. See Chapter 7 for a list and description of some common tools.

The Creative Design Review

The creative design generally includes several reviews, both internal and external. When entering the creative design review (which might happen several times during a project), expect skeptical attitudes, in-depth questions, and challenges to assumptions. In order to be prepared for these circumstances, I recommend preparing for such meetings by working with the design team to complete some preparatory steps, such as creating use case scenarios and completing a competitive analysis.

Use Case Scenarios

A *use case scenario* is a description illustrating, step by step, how a player is intended to use a system. By capturing the system behavior from the user's point of view, a use case scenario clearly defines how the system should work. Often included in use case scenarios are examples, drawings, and descriptions of all of the steps of the interaction in a linear form. This is an extremely practical way of describing the challenge in clear terms and specifying the functionality.

Establishing use case scenarios early helps define a goal-oriented set of interactions between game players and the game system being considered and designed. Creating a strong use case scenario is an excellent way to ensure capture of all functional requirements in a game's design. This is especially true when the game is going to be coded in an object-oriented coding language like C++, where complete understanding and definition of system is required to ensure that it is coded without adversely affecting other systems.

note

> One useful reference for creating use cases is *Applying Use Cases: A Practical Guide*, by Geri Schneider.

Often, design documentation is written in a style appropriate for other game developers and the perspective of the player is diminished. By including use cases as a requirement, the perspective of the player won't be inadvertently neglected.

Ownership of the Creative Vision

This is often a sensitive topic and one that creates conflict within game development teams. Who pioneers the concept, and who can follow through on the creative vision? Often, the person who pioneers the creative vision is someone other than the person who can execute on all the details required to realize the creative vision in a finished product. This section discusses how to manage the ownership of the creative vision.

Assigning Ownership

As the producer, it is generally your responsibility to ensure that the ownership of the creative vision is entrusted to the right individual. This assignment should go to a person who is confident, enthusiastic, organized, and passionate about the product, and who can articulate a clear creative direction. This is a very unique set of skills and traits, and a game's quality and the quality of the creative design can be fully realized by a person who uses and employs these skills.

Managing Ownership

Managing ownership of the creative vision is a bit like being a policeman confronted with a group of otherwise law-abiding citizens out on a night of drinking. You want to be nice and to give them the benefit of the doubt, while at the same time making sure that they don't hurt anyone or do something stupid.

One of the ways to effectively manage ownership of the creative vision is to evaluate the progress of the creative design against other measurable benchmarks practiced by other teams. The second way is to seek feedback often. A common theme of game project postmortems is to seek feedback "often and even more often." Get other designers within the company to review and provide constructive comments to the person charged with the creative vision.

Lastly, seek out feedback from Marketing on the overall goals of the product. Does the creative vision still meet those goals? If so, how are the promises of the game's design going to be met? The owner of the creative vision should be constantly asking himself these questions and revising the answers.

Protecting the Creative Vision

One of the producer's role and obligations to the team is to help protect the creative vision from outside (external) factors, influences, or distractions. When a producer truly believes in the originality and potential of a creative vision, it is his responsibility to run interference between those who are external to the team—such as executives, Marketing, game critics and licensors—who want to influence the game's creative direction. When there are too many cooks in the kitchen, it can cause a project to be delayed or fail no matter how talented the team.

Realizing the Creative Vision and When to Say No

Feature creep is when a game development team keeps adding features that expand the scope of the game to a point where the process gets out of control. A producer's job is to manage this situation—often referred to as "killing feature creep." It is the producer's job to protect the creative vision and do everything possible to help the team realize its full value and ensure that it reaches the marketplace as a screaming success; this also means that it is the producer's responsibility to be the first point of challenge, conflict, or constraint when a creative vision exceeds what's producible within the time or budget.

Often the most successful games are not the ones most creative at implementing *all* of their features. *Grand Theft Auto San Andreas* included an update to the *Grand Theft Auto* game experience. Polishing the implementation of one or two new features from previous versions led to a solid implementation and a top selling game. This means being able to tactfully say "no" to the design team when it's getting too ambitious, while offering a constructive counter-proposal or solution.

If you're working with an outside publisher who holds the creative vision, this can be much more difficult. Try to have the difficult discussions on where an ambitious design may lead before starting work on the game. Trying to address changes in the game's design once work as started is generally not recommended. Let everyone (your team, your manager, the publisher) know that your goal is to make a great product, but that adding features during production can add risk and costs.

A Final Word

This chapter covers a tremendous amount of material, giving you a good start on what you need to understand to be able to help guide the design of a video game project. While this chapter may have seemed fairly in-depth, there really is a wide breadth of resources and references that are simply beyond the scope of what I can discuss here. I encourage you to refer to the resources and reference sections of Appendix C, as well as online at http://www.gamasutra.com to ensure that, as a producer, you have a firm grasp of the concepts required to help turn a winning game design into a successful game. It could be the most valuable skill and knowledge base that you develop in your career.

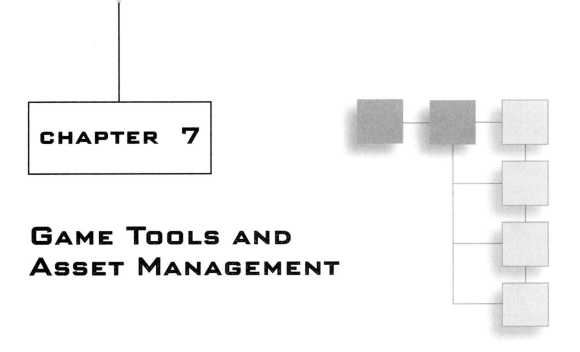

CHAPTER 7

GAME TOOLS AND ASSET MANAGEMENT

efore starting any new project, in addition to finding the best group of people to sur-
round himself with, a producer must make sure that his team has the right set of
tools—ones that will allow them to create the best game possible.

—Stephane Morichere-Matte, Lead Programmer, Relic Entertainment/THQ, Inc.

Being a producer is not just about starting game projects or making sure that marketing has the details necessary for them to start selling the game; it's also about ensuring that the team has the tools needed to accomplish the essence statement outlined in the game's design. Today's industry professionals have a large library of development tools at their disposal. Tools are available for almost every purpose. In this flood of tools, it can sometimes be difficult to choose the correct tools for each task. This chapter covers examples of excellent tools available and the best way to use them. This chapter is specifically focused on the role of a producer at a developer. However, a producer at a publisher should have a cursory understanding and knowledge of the tools and requirements of any development team with which they're working. That's just part of being a good producer, risk manager, and effective leader.

Having the Right Tools

Having the right tools can save your project money, strengthen presentations, reduce overall project risk, and help the team focus on what makes the game fun. One of the common themes that kept coming up as I was researching this chapter was the role of the producer as a good risk manager. One of the ways to manage risk is to use effective and efficient tools. But to do that, a producer needs to understand and rely upon the input of the team leads on the development team as to which tools they're going to need and when and how to get them. This also means that the producer must rely upon and focus the efforts of each team lead so that they understand and develop the knowledge about the type of tools that their team is going to need. This comes back to risk management. The producer needs to know, understand, and work with each team lead to develop solutions to risks before they impact a product's features, schedule, or budget. One of the ways to do this is to ensure that they understand the requirements of the game design, the overall production effort, and the tools needed so that the team can realize the potential of the game's design.

Before even examining the available tools, you first need to outline and understand the tools that your team might need. This means that you must understand the design of the game. For example, an RTS is not going to need a physics engine that features true vehicle simulation, but a racing game would certainly require that sort of extensibility. With these types of considerations in mind, the following sections provide an overview of the types of tools available and necessary to complete a video game development project.

Pre-Production Steps

Throughout the development of the game, your team must rely on the technology you provide to develop an excellent game. Therefore, it is crucial that the team has the best tools available for the task. It's important to identify which tools are needed and how to acquire them in the pre-production stage.

This means that the design must clearly specify the requirements of the game, the requirements of the tools, and the anticipated end-user support of the product post-commercial-release. To do this, a producer must ensure that there are flexible procedures and encourage communication between the game's designers, the tools programmers, and the artists.

During the pre-production phase, sit down with the designer and create a high-level design for each feature set in the game (gameplay, weapons, units, character interactions, movement, combat, and so on). Then identify the tools most commonly needed for those feature sets. Then pair up a tools programmer with a representative from the programming team responsible for tool programming to ensure that the needs of the design team are clearly articulated. The tool should have exactly the right features, no more and no less than what would make it optimal for providing the right depth to the gameplay, with the ease of use to the designer balanced against the development time. Then use the same procedure, pairing up a technical artist and a tools programmer, to develop the required plugins and add-ons for the art tools that are required to move the art assets into the game.

After that process is complete, run a few tests. Have an artist perform some tests on the tools, exporting the art asset (a character or a unit) into the game engine. Ensure that it works properly and efficiently. Check the exported asset for bugs and document the process that was used to create the asset and then every step that was required to get the art asset into the game. That is called the *art pipeline identification*. After the art pipeline has been identified and documented, a producer has a greater understanding of what steps are required to get an asset into the game and how long it takes. From there, it generally involves some difficult math to do the estimations on how many objects and art assets can be made over the course of a development schedule. When this process is complete, you are able to determine (roughly) how content heavy or light the design is. Then, you can move onto the next steps and build a prototype.

Try to Get It Right the First Time

When building the prototype, it's extremely important to define the art pipeline as soon as possible. For example, a team started working on a prototype for a game, but started off with a badly defined pipeline. Hurrying through the development of the prototype because of a short deadline caused other problems that cascaded through their entire development cycle. Their level designer often had to do the import/export process before getting the assets into the engine, artists were waiting for assets to be approved before moving on, and they had problems with getting their animations and rigs to work in the engine they were using. It was reminiscent of rusty and worn-out clockwork gears being forced to work by physical force. All it needed was some sharpening and a bit of oil. It didn't take long for the team to realize how much time was being lost from not having a defined pipeline. They customized the tools they were working with and spent two days polishing and defining a working pipeline. From there, the development of the prototype was smooth and they barely met the deadline.

The lesson learned was that it's better to spend the two days defining an effective workflow and a pipeline so that everybody can do their work unhindered. The amount of time each team member spends on trying to fix things one by one adds up to days of work.

note

A common scenario on game development projects with large teams comes from a lack of communication. The designers often outline the best-case, most-complicated feature they could possibly want—such as 200 futuristic weapons with 1000 different weapons special effects, each for a special part of the game. Players can even trade weapons, upgrade them, and their effectiveness changes depending on the player's stats. Plus, this tool for weapon customization needs to ship with the game so that the players can use it as well. Then, the programmers go off to create this type of feature set in the game's development. Only a few weeks later does it come out that this type of design requirement might take a lot longer to develop as well as increase the number of art assets required for the feature.

Finally, the producer realizes that this design element is going to take a lot longer than expected and cost a lot of money. Does the game really need 200 different weapons and 1000 various special effects? Does the tool really need to ship with the game? Does the design team actually need a special tool to modify and create the best and baddest weapons the world has ever seen? Well, probably not. The game will probably be just as fun with only 30 weapons instead of 200. Does the modability really add value to the game? Will it actually sell more units? Maybe, but maybe not. Consider if it is worth the risk of an added month or two of development time because the programmers working on the tools are delaying working on the sound tool and other asset integration tools, which can speed along the process of bringing the game together.

Testing for the Tools You Need

As the project leads work on defining the game/art/tech design of the game, they should also focus on how those designs will be implemented.

Many of the tools you will use can be bought commercially, whereas many of them will need to be created by your programmers. Or, in a combination of the two, your programmer could modify existing tools through the use of plug-ins. Both 3D Studio Max and Maya support various plug-ins and have a highly modable architecture. Most of the good commercial tools can be tested for an evaluation period. It's essential you know your tool before deciding to use it on your game.

Use your team to test those tools well before making a decision. Building a prototype might be the best way to do this. Use the development of the prototype to define the pros and cons of tools. Document your needs and your successes well so your tech team can start building the rest of the tools you need as soon as possible.

After the development is in full motion, it can be very costly to have subpar tools. Designers need good world-building tools, audio designers need good tools to implement their audio, and the pipeline for art needs to be smooth. A setback on any of those can be extremely costly and might lead to an unmet milestone. Remember that when developing a video game, it takes time to get the art assets into the game world and running on the engine. The goal is to get that entire process—from creation, to exporting, to integration into the game—to happen as quickly and efficiently as possible. Game development projects often have thousands of art assets that must all go through the same process; so, for example, if you can cut the integration time for each asset from 15 minutes to 10 minutes with more than 3000 art assets that still need to go into the game, the added efficiency just saved more than 15,000 minutes (or about 250 hours) of production time.

Much information is available from fellow development teams regarding how to acquire the tools you need and which of those will serve your purpose best.

Create Use Cases

To define your software specifications, the design team should create frequent use cases. Document every feature and every aspect needed to portray that feature. Be very detailed in the use cases creation—the more detail, the better. Create diagrams and documents for each feature. The designers and programmers then define the specifications needed to make the game happen. It's very important to get this done as soon as possible and be as detailed as possible. You want to create the tools you need right at the start. You can then test and tweak those tools while producing the prototype.

What Producers Need to Know about Tools

When it comes to selecting or creating tools for the development process, the producer does not have to know every detail of each tool. The producer should accept the guidance of his fellow professionals from each department. When selecting game components and middleware, the programmers will know the nitty-gritty details of each solution. The producer only needs to know the basic function of each program. Way too many programs and tools are available for the producer to know the details of them all.

If you're working with a good team, rely upon the professionals. The audio professionals know which audio tools to use, the programmers know the middleware engines, and the artists know which art tools to look for. Instead of knowing all the details about the tools, the producer should be working closely with the leads of each department to establish a smooth pipeline for the tools that get selected.

Programming Tools

There are a lot of resources available to programmers. Here's a list of some of the commonly available tools for programmers. Each section is divided into a "what the producer needs to know" section, as well as a more detailed description of its use.

OpenGL ES—Khronos Group

OpenGL ES is one of the de facto graphic standards used today. Khronos Group includes some tools that are useful in getting the most out of the technology.

What the producer needs to know

OpenGL ES is the standard 2-D/3D graphics API (Application Programming Interface) for embedded systems.

More background

OpenGL has long been the industry-wide standard for high performance 2D/3D graphics on devices ranging from mobile phones to PCs to supercomputers. OpenGL ES is the version used for Embedded Systems (ES). Embedded systems are products with micro-processor-based control systems. These systems are ranging from mobile to automotive, communications, mil/aero, consumer, and even medical.

OpenGL ES provides a low-level API between software applications and hardware or software graphics engines. This standard 3D graphics API for embedded systems offers a variety of advanced 3D graphics and games across all major mobile and embedded platforms.

OpenGL ES was awarded the *Game Developers Magazine* Front Line Award in 2003.

IncrediBuild—Xoreax Software

IncrediBuild is a powerful tool from the entrepreneurs at Xoreax Software in Israel.

What the producer needs to know

IncrediBuild is a development tool that dramatically speeds up Microsoft Visual C++ (6.0, 7.0, and 7.1) compilation and builds. This can decrease the time it takes to do incremental builds. In crunch time, that's very important!

More background

Slow compilation time has always been one of the C++/C programming language's weakest spots. Whether it's a few hours wait for a full product build, or 10 minutes spent several times a day, waiting for an incremental build to finish on a developer workstation leads to frustration, loss of productivity, and wasted time.

Now, for the first time, IncrediBuild offers a unique and effective solution. Through the use of Xoreax's Distributed Compilation technology, the compilation speed of any Visual Studio 6.0 or .NET project is boosted, without requiring any changes in the code or project files. Through its seamless integration with the Visual Studio development environment and a strong command-line interface, IncrediBuild makes a natural enhancement to the Microsoft Visual C++ development environment.

In my experience, Incredibuild increased production efficiency significantly on several projects. It allows the development team to create incremental builds for testing in record time and with fewer errors in the autobuild process. Incredibuild's technical support is also known for their responsiveness.

Microsoft Visual C++ IDE

Microsoft Visual C++ has been the backbone of commercial video game development for many years.

What the producer needs to know

Microsoft Visual C++ IDE (Integrated Development Environment) is a standard IDE for C/C++.

More background

The programming languages C and C++ are used for almost every commercially successful game. The main reason for this is because they lend themselves well to object-oriented programming (OOP). OOP works best for big programs and/or any software built from a large amount of code. The reason for this is because OOP code is extremely easy to organize and manage. It is not as fast as other programming methods, so it's not as useful for smaller programs. But it is good for reusing code, and any big software developer should always reuse code whenever possibe.

Out of the two languages, C++ lends itself better to OOP and is, therefore, used more often in game development. One definition of an object in OOP is: "An object is a software bundle of variables and related methods." This basically means that it's like a real-world object except it has its state and all of its behaviors. Then, the blueprint of the variables and related methods in the object are referred to as a class.

A few IDEs for C++ are available. Microsoft Visual C++ IDE is one of the most popular. This IDE has reached its seventh generation and has come a long way from its first. Aside from it having all the compiling features you need, it now has many methods to speed up the coding process and workflow greatly. If you want to code in C++, a tool of this sort is a must-have.

Visual Assist X—Whole Tomato Software

Anything that helps speed up the coding process is a friend of the producer.

What the producer needs to know

Visual Assist .NET offers powerful editing features for Microsoft Visual Studio IDE that speed up the coding process.

More background

Visual Assist is a Visual C++ plug-in that was developed to boost the productivity of your C++ programmers using Microsoft Visual C++ IDE. Visual Assist introduces powerful editing features that are completely integrated into the Microsoft development environment. This plug-in was considered by many a "must-have" for Visual C++ IDE versions 6.0 and lower. It is not as useful now because the features of the plug-in have now been fully integrated into the IDE itself.

The most popular features of this plug-in are Enhanced List Boxes, which allow easy access to member and completion list boxes while writing code, and a Suggestion List, which offers good suggestions to the words you are typing. The Suggestion List only needs one written letter to work—it then suggests a way to complete the word. Enhanced Syntax Coloring makes the code easier to read and debug because of more meaningful coloring. Goto allows you to move your caret to any symbol in your code and press the Goto button to jump to the declaration or implementation of the symbol. Underline Spelling Errors basically underlines incorrectly spelled words with a squiggly line as you type. Auto Recovery frequently saves backup copies of the files you modify. If the IDE crashes, this Visual Assist offers to use either the last backup copy or the last manually saved file.

All the features of this plug-in are useful and increase productivity. However, its features have now been implemented into the IDE itself, so it's useless for those who are using the most current version of the Microsoft Visual C++ IDE.

VectorC—Codeplay

Specialized platform development tools are powerful tools for console games. While most are proprietary, here's one that works for the PS2.

What the producer needs to know

VectorC is a powerful Vector optimizing compiler mainly geared toward PS2 game development.

More background

VectorC is a vectorizing compiler. It allows for highly optimized compilation of both PC and PS2 programs without having touse an assembly language. VectorC compiles, optimizes, and vectorizes both C and C++ code.

VectorC {PC} Professional Edition is the full-featured compiler used for PC programs. This version can optimize and compile for both C and C++, but the C++ function is missing one feature—exception handling. VectorC does standard, nonvector, high-performance optimizations, as well as vectorizing optimization. VectorC {PC} PE has been designed to integrate seamlessly into Microsoft Visual C++ IDE.

VectorC {PC} Special Edition is a version of the professional C compiler at a much lower price.

VectorC {VU} is a C/C++ compiler that generates micromode code for the Playstation 2 (PS2) vector units, VU0 and VU1. This is the only compiler available for these components of the Playstation 2, which previously required assembly language programming. VectorC {VU} is a Win32 compiler that works within CodeWarrior and Visual Studio 6.

VectorC {EE} was mostly created to take full advantage of PS2's Emotion Engine (EE). VectorC {EE} optimizes existing Playstation 2 software using software pipelining, memory access reduction, and vectorization. You can recompile your existing game engine using VectorC {EE} and, thereby, improve its performance. It can also be used to write portable code that still gives maximum speed.

This program falls short in that although Codeplay promises the best vector compiler on the market, there are not many who use it. This mean it's hard to know if they deliver on all their promises. Detailed information about the compiler is hard to obtain unless you're a registered PS2 developer.

XNA and DirectX

Every time a new version of DirectX comes out, there's a host of considerations and updates that game developers must be aware of. Here's the scoop on XNA, which was introduced to game developers at the Game Developer's Conference in 2004.

What the producer needs to know

XNA is the future development platform standard for PC and Xbox game development. XNA includes a new and divided DirectX with the addition of the Xbox Audio Creation Tool (XACT) and Performance Investigator for DirectX (PIX).

More background

For a long time, Microsoft has made industry-standard APIs for development on their PC platform. They've made the low-level API standard for graphics and sound that game developers have worked with for a decade. Now that Microsoft has joined the console gaming race with their Xbox console, they have plans to create industry standards for cross-platform graphics development.

Their newest product is called XNA. XNA was first introduced at the 2004 GDC. The current XNA framework supports Windows, Xbox, and mobile technologies. In the future, Microsoft hopes third-party developers will develop XNA for other console systems, such as Playstation 2 and Nintendo GameCube. Whether Sony and Nintendo agree remains to be seen.

XNA includes the latest version of DirectX with the addition of Xbox tools, such as the Xbox Audio Creation Tool (XACT), which allows composers and sound designers to create dynamic effects and apply real-time processing, and Performance Investigator for DirectX (PIX), which has been available for Xbox development for some time but has now been released for PC.

DirectX (an advanced suite of multimedia APIs built in to the Windows operating systems) is one of those industry standards Microsoft has created in the past. DirectX is a Windows technology that enables higher performance in graphics (full-color graphics, video, 3D animation) and sound (surround sound) when you're playing games or watching video on a PC. With the introduction of XNA, DirectX will undergo some changes. In the past, DirectX has been equipped with the following components:

- **Direct3D.** Graphics
- **DirectSound.** Sound
- **DirectMusic.** Music
- **DirectPlay.** Networking
- **DirectInput.** Input

Following are the changes DirectX will undergo with the next version of Windows, Longhorn, and the introduction of XNA:

- Direct3D will become the WGF (Windows Graphic Foundation) and will provide the base for the Longhorn desktop.
- DirectSound and DirectMusic will be replaced by XACT and Longhorn's API.
- DirectPlay will have added Xbox live technology.
- DirectShow will be replaced by a new media SDK.
- DirectInput will stay the same.

Microsoft does not expect this new standard to be cross-platform for all the next generation consoles, but the plan is to begin with all Microsoft platforms and slowly move on to others. The expectation for this new standard is high, and if it delivers on its promises, it might mean reduced costs for game development studios.

Interview with Luke Moloney

Luke Moloney is one of the founders of Relic Entertainment and is Lead Programmer on *Homeworld* and *Homeworld2*. I caught up with Luke between his business travels to provide this feedback for producers.

Q: What is the one lesson or topic that you value most highly?

A: I think one of the biggest lessons a new producer or engineer could learn is that almost everything takes longer than you think it should in video games. Too many times I've heard veteran programmers criticized as "lazy" when making time estimates for tasks that sound overly generous. When readjusted to be more "realistic," these tasks inevitably end up incomplete, or completed to a poor standard of quality.

Q: What is the most important trait a producer can display: leadership, understanding, flexibility, or even just how to ask clarifying questions?

A: All of those traits are important and must be displayed in varying degrees. It's very important that on any development team the programmers are working together with artists, designers, and producers toward common goals. To this end, a producer must work hard to ensure that programmers are working on tasks that are directly in line with what artists and designers need. Very often, programmers like to work on features that are "cool" from a technical point of view, but are unusable or overly complex for artists or designers. Having artists and designers do mock-ups and clear demonstrations of what they want can help programmers better understand what they need programmers to do. At the same time, a producer must make sure that the requirements specified by the artists and designers are actually going to be used. Very often, artists and designers will specify a technical requirement (such as "environment mapping on all surfaces!") that is difficult to implement and will only be used on one or two cases. This is an inefficient usage of programmer resources.

Q: What recommendations do you have for producers in how to be successful?

A: I hinted earlier that some producers may find time estimates from some programmers to be overly generous. At the same time, a producer should be wary of time estimates that are too optimistic. This is a common problem with less experienced programmers. A good producer should compare time estimates against actual time taken for all tasks and develop a general rule to apply to time estimates from each team member to help ensure a more accurate schedule going forward.

A producer and a lead programmer have plenty of opportunity to interact, so use [this] to build a positive relationship. When the time comes and the lead programmer wants to throw away and rewrite a large portion of a game engine's code, use the relationship to help explore if that is really necessary. Such refactoring can be a good thing, but usually takes a long time and introduces many bugs if done to established, tested code. The costs and benefits of such a process need to be care

(continued on next page)

Interview with Luke Moloney (continued)

fully weighed. If a producer deems such a task to be too costly or dangerous, it may be a difficult task to convince a programmer without making him or her very upset. Just blindly trusting the opinion of a programmer in such a case can be very costly.

Q: What tools do you think producers underutilize or should do more research about that would make the programmers' jobs easier?

A: I've yet to work on a project that had a decent task planning solution. I've used Microsoft Project, Excel, Perforce's task list, Outlook scheduling, File Maker, Test Track, and others. In most cases, these tools are only partially used, or are used in conjunction with one or more other programs. I think a producer could serve a team well by using just one of these programs, and making a central task list that incorporates bug reports, development tasks, and progress updates. Using multiple programs means tasks will inevitably slip through the cracks, unless a great deal of effort is expended keeping the data in two tools in sync. Also try to ensure that multiple tools don't assign tasks to developers multiple times. "'I've already fixed that darn bug; why is it saying it's still open?" is a common frustration heard toward the end of a development cycle.

Q: What experience have you had in working with producers and determining reasonable schedules for a project, as well as tracking the team's progress through that schedule?

A: As I mentioned previously, it's a challenge to determine realistic time estimates from the estimates given by programmers especially. Programming tasks are usually off by about 50 percent either too long or too short. The challenge for a producer is to find out if they tend to be too long or too short. Time estimates must always be compared to actual time taken to determine how a developer tends to estimate. Also bear in mind that this can be useful for identifying exceptionally good or poor performers within the team. Note, however, that poor time estimation skills alone do not identify a poor performer or vice versa.

Also, schedules usually need to be revised on a per-milestone basis. An understanding that the schedule will change is important as otherwise one might be inclined to use a scheduling tool that makes rescheduling difficult. Don't be afraid to revise your schedule. Keep the old versions around; they might be handy when it comes to doing a postmortem.

Art Tools

The art tools also double as world building tools in many cases. There's a lot to know and consider when deciding what art tools to use on your project, so read on.

Maya 6.0—Alias

Maya is one of the two dominant 3D applications used in the industry today and the most used program in high-end computer graphics (CG) films.

What the producer needs to know

Maya is one of the many 3D software packages used in the game industry. It's highly customizable and can handle all aspects of 3D art: modeling, rigging, animation, rendering, material editing, and cinematic visual effects.

More background

Maya does a great job at generalizing in 3D development. It's great at all sections: modeling, animating, effects, and rendering. Maya is very customizable, and each artist can customize its graphical interface to best fit their individual workflow to save time in development. In regard to game development, Maya's strongest points are its material and UV editor, rigging and animation, and the very powerful MEL scripting language. The new version 6.0 adds a big function to its material editor by now understanding Photoshop .psd file formats and its layers.

What detracts mostly from Maya is its Polygon modeling tools. Maya started out as a NURBS (Non-Uniform Rational B-Spline) only program and still has inferior polygon modeling tools compared to Discreet's 3D Studio Max. Users have also complained that Maya's once revolutionary GUI hasn't been updated as the program has matured with new and useful features. The most popular package of Maya for game developers, Maya Complete, is considerably cheaper than 3D Studio Max and XSI.

3D Studio Max 7—Discreet

Discreet's 3D Studio Max is one of the most widely used art tools in the game industry today. While it offers some key advantages, there is no single solution that's always better than the others.

What the producer needs to know

3D Studio Max is often on the forefront of the 3D software packages. It's also highly customizable and can handle all aspects of 3D art: modeling, rigging, animation, rendering, material editing, and cinematic visual effects.

More background

3D Studio Max is the dominant leader in game development 3D applications. A big reason for this is their early dominance in the 3D software industry. 3D Studio Max's success in game development comes mostly from their polygon modeling tools. This application focuses its modeling tools on polygons instead of NURBS and, therefore, has the best tools for the job of all the 3D applications. 3D Studio Max is also known to have the most time-efficient workflow embedded to their "out-of-the-box" product.

This new version, 7, finally integrates the revolutionary tool Character Studio into the program. Character Studio greatly improves character rigging and animation. Although it is still inferior to Maya's and XSI's animators, it is getting closer. The 3D Studio Max 7 package is currently more expensive than Maya but is still cheaper than XSI. 3D Studio Max falls short in its rigging, animation, and material editing. Maya has the best material editor, whereas Maya and XSI both share the best rigging and animation tools of the three top competitors.

note

Both 3D Studio Max and Maya have a large following of supporting communities and plug-in creators. Tutorials can be found on the Web for just about any feature in either program. But what really adds to the flexibility of both programs are all the available plug-ins. Literally thousands of plug-ins are available that introduce new features and/or workflow improvements.

XSI 4—Softimage

Softimage is the workhorse of the animation industry. However, that doesn't mean it is only good for animation.

What the producer needs to know

XSI is a full 3D package capable of all aspects of 3D development. XSI is mostly known for its cinematic ability and its great animation editor.

More background

Of the three biggest 3D competitors, XSI is trailing far behind 3D Studio Max and Maya in game studio usage. The main reason for this has been their license fee structure. Only developers with prestigious cinematic departments use this tool in North America. (However, XSI 4 is currently the most popular and most used application in game development in Japan.) With the new version, XSI 4, Softimage makes a noteworthy attempt at overcoming this disadvantage. Every available package of the application has been dramatically dropped in price.

The new version, XSI 4, is considered by many the biggest update since version 1 of the program and many expect it to bring XSI a lot closer to the two dominant programs in the 3D field. The new version greatly improves the program's modeling tools, bringing it close to Maya's standards.

XSI has an advantage over the competition in animation and rendering. The other applications are still behind on animation, but both Maya and 3D Studio Max now have similar rendering technology. XSI's GUI is also very advanced; those who take the time to learn it find it a very productive environment in which to work.

note

Programmers don't like to learn other people's code. When faced with a choice of modifying someone else's code and creating a plug-in or creating a tool from scratch, it is common that programmers opt for the latter. This is generally the wrong course of action and a good producer works to challenge this tendency.

Photoshop CS—Adobe

Adobe Photoshop is one of the most used tools in game development today, so be sure that you have access to a copy.

What the producer needs to know

Photoshop is the worldwide, cross-industry standard for digital art creation, so make sure that it is a cornerstone of your production efforts. It's equally useful to novices or seasoned art professionals, helping to convey key creative concepts and scenes.

More background

Photoshop is used in every phase of the development, from pre-production to finalizing and marketing. It is far superior to any competitors and is an industry standard in every serious company.

Concept artists use it to produce paintings of your game environments and characters. All in-game textures are created with the use of Photoshop and their great tools. Designers use it to draw level plans and front-end mock-ups. Screenshots that are released are touched up in Photoshop to make them look better.

Photoshop has been dominant in the industry for many years, so it fits into any pipeline and any artist can get into a time-efficient workflow. Often-used complicated maneuvers in the program can be made into a simple action and any artist can apply it with a click of a button, making many tedious and time-consuming tasks efficient.

It is a lot easier to have an artist sketch a scene to give the rest of the team an idea of what the game feature might look like in action compared with months and months of development before what's on the screen is realized as being insufficient or contradictory to the needs of the design.

Encourage your artists to use this tool liberally to sketch ideas, characters, and otherwise convey the sense of gameplay at early stages of the game's development. Gameplay ideas or level design setups can only provide so much in text form. Having artists draw out those levels and features in action helps inspire the rest of the team working on them.

FaceGen Modeller 3.0—Singular Inversions

Face modeling tools are becoming increasingly important as audiences demand more realism in their characters.

What the producer needs to know

FaceGen Modeller is great for making high-quality face and head models very quickly.

More background

The FaceGen Modeller series has received numerous awards, including *Game Developer Magazine*'s Front Line Award in 2003. FaceGen Modeller is a powerful and amazingly straightforward 3D head and face creation tool. It is a fast and effective way to create realistic or caricature face models in a very short amount of time.

As an artist's tool, it allows the efficient creation of a 3D head in not much more than a click of a button. The model and tool are very flexible, allowing the artist to tweak it to look the way they like with a series of sliders. The sliders determine sex, gender, race, weight, emotions, and feature definition. Most details can be tweaked with simple sliders. The mesh made in FaceGen can easily be imported to any of the main full 3D applications. Their SDK is flexible and can be easily integrated into almost any engine.

Artists also have an option to make a detailed 3D model from a photo using the Photofit feature. To make the model, artists must provide photos made following their specification. Those photos are then sent to a Singular Inversions online service, and after a few minutes, the detailed 3D head/face is delivered to the artists, ready for implementation.

The only setback of the program is that there is no way to create the photosimulated head manually, only through their online service.

Zbrush 2—Pixologic

Use of art modeling tools that reflect traditional art creation methods can make the creation process more familiar to traditionally trained artists.

What the producer needs to know

Zbrush allows artists to create very high polygon (poly) models similar to real-world sculpting. It is great for multimillion polymodels to make normal maps from.

More background

This new 3D application from Pixologic is causing awe throughout the industry. Zbrush is a revolutionary new approach to 3D modeling. With this program, modeling is done much more like traditional sculpting.

This tool will be very useful in next generation game development because games can handle a much higher polycount. Meshes made in Zbrush can easily be used for normal maps, which most next generation hardware will be able to handle well. The current version Zbrush 2 is a big step up from the 1.5 version. The GUI has been redone to be more intuitive and less time-consuming. New material types, modeling techniques, and sculpture brushes are just a part of the upgrades from the previous version. The software is being developed with good guidance from games industry professionals in order for the software to fit its needs.

Granny 2—RAD Game Tools

RAD Game Tools has provided stable tools for game developers for many years.

What the producer needs to know

Granny 2 is the latest version of the industry's best commercial import/export tool. Granny can get any art asset, including models, textures, and animations, into the game almost instantly.

More background

Granny 2 is the current version of the Granny 3D tool. This tool is an extremely powerful middleware tool for 3D assets in game development. Artists create models in Maya or Max and then bring it into Granny.

Granny can be used as a mass exporter for your game. Bring all the 3D assets into Granny and it will smoothly export them in the file format you need for your game engine. Artists can also use Granny to manipulate those meshes. Granny features a powerful animation function. It can be used to manipulate existing animations, create new animations, perform animation blending, and inverse kinematics. Then, Granny exports those seamlessly into your game engine.

Granny can handle vertex animations and vertex editing. It generates normal and texture maps. Your artists can freely work with high-resolution textures, which Granny turns into the proper size for the game engine when exporting.

Granny can serve as an engine construction toolkit and be used as a full run-time system or as pieces of a custom run-time system. Granny does preprocessing as well, including compressions, conversions, centering, and extraction.

The Granny 3D toolkit is available for Win 32, Mac OS X, Xbox, Playstation 2, and Nintendo GameCube development.

Game Components

Game components are the basic building blocks of a fun game, like physics, rendering and world creation, called middleware. Each of these tools has substantial documentation and background materials so that any team can make the most of the solution.

Havok 2—Havok

Havok sports one of the most-developed real-time physics engines ever. If you want your game to look like real life, consider Havok!

What the producer needs to know

The Havok 2 engine is one of the best middleware solutions for realistic in-game physics.

More background

The Havok physics engines are considered by some the best things in game development since 3D graphics. The Havok engines allow for realistic and rag-doll physics simulation in games, and its dynamics have been the reason for many new gameplay additions to recent FPSs. Havok and Havok 2 have both won the *Game Developers Magazine* Front Line Award in 2002 and 2003.

Havok Game Dynamics SDK is the fastest, most flexible, cross-platform game dynamics solution available on the market today. Havok can now deliver up to 10 real-time physically controlled rag-dolls on the PS2. The Havok team has been focused on building game specific solutions that are respected for their usefulness. Such a focus has made Havok the number one provider of middleware physics to the games industry.

RenderWare—Criterion

Electronic Arts recently made an entry into the tool-creation market with the purchase of RenderWare. This speaks volumes about this tools use and value at industry leader Electronic Arts.

What the producer needs to know

RenderWare offers solid engines for graphics, physics, AI, and audio for a good price.

More background

Criterion's RenderWare is the industry's current leading middleware provider, with over 500 in development or released titles under its belt. RenderWare has a large portfolio of development tools. Its middleware includes graphics, physics, AI, and audio solutions.

Criterion has always provided extremely reliable customer service, which has led developers to seek their middleware again and again. RenderWare is currently available for Playstation 2, Xbox, Nintendo GameCube, and PC. Everything indicates it will also be available for next generation platforms. RenderWare's complete middleware solution serves best for small developers. Bigger developers and publishers usually build on top of specialized middleware such as the Havok physics engine.

The weak point of this solution is the learning curve for developers to understand its integration. The RenderWare package is a large and complicated solution. The RenderWare package is very general and provides a very broad solution. Because it doesn't focus on one thing, it falls short of some other specialized middleware.

Gamebryo—NDL

Gamebryo is a stable, real-time engine that allows game developers to quickly get a prototype up and running.

What the producer needs to know

Gamebryo is a very reliable 3D graphics run-time engine built on the NetImmerse middleware.

More background

Gamebryo builds on the award-winning NetImmerse middleware and enjoys all the experience NDL had with that middleware. Gamebryo is currently being used for over 70 titles—at least a title for each game genre.

Gamebryo is a 3D graphics run-time engine. It has a powerful rendering engine that has a brand-new pixel and vertex shader system. The shader system supports custom-made shaders as well as shaders from RenderMonkey, cgFX, or HLSL. Gamebryo also provides some "off-the-shelf" shaders.

Gamebryo has an advanced motion system that can handle almost any animation type possible to produce in 3D Studio Max and Maya. The system can also share animation data among characters and blend animation layers.

Most of the commercially successful games using the Gamebryo middleware are of the RPG and simulation genre.

Quazal—Quazal

Quazal is a network architecture middleware that's making in-roads into the MMOG market. It is pioneering new and uncharted territory.

What the producer needs to know

Quazal offers a family of game networking middleware. Quazal's products offer networking for games with 2–32 player support. It even includes scalability up to a grand-scale MMOG, with 32,000 player clusters support. But that requires a lot of computers!

More background

Quazal provides great solutions to online gaming and community infrastructure. Quazal has three distinct products: Net-Z, Rendez-Vous, and Eterna. All of those are flexible and reliable infrastructures for online experiences. The Net-Z was the first of the line. This is a networking solution for online games with 2–32 player servers.

Net-Z is an easy-to-use and flexible in-game networking engine. There are two variants to Net-Z, each of which meets different needs. On one side is the classic Net-Z object-based networking, which uses the concept of duplicated objects to push information from a Duplication Master to a Duplica. This system allows the use of latency masking and band-width reduction techniques, such as dead reckoning. Also, full fault tolerance and load balancing is supported with this variant of Net-Z. On the other side is the deterministic SyncSim approach. This is best used for games that cannot allow any divergence between stations, and runs as a synchronized simulation. Sports games, fighting games, and other similar genres benefit the most from SyncSim.

Second in the line is the Quazal's Rendez-Vous. This structure is not for game worlds but for online lobbies and communities. It provides all aspects of a full-scale lobby service, including authentication, matchmaking, friends lists, competition, teams, messaging, and more. It has great level of flexibility with a database back end that is open to developers and Python-based scripting for developers to add and pick and choose the best features for their game.

The third product is the Eterna. The Eterna is an MMO networking product that will undergo some radical changes in the near future. It is mentioned in more detail in the next section, "Other MMO Engines and Middleware."

Flexibility is one of the Quazal product line strong points. All products allow developers to tune and update features as needed and make integration easy. The Quazal products also come with detailed and very accessible documentation. The main weakness of the Quazal product line arises from its flexibility: With such an open-ended product, it can be hard to find the most effective work techniques. The Rendez-Vous is also a new product, so its stability has yet to be confirmed.

Other MMOG Engines and Middleware

MMOGs are being developed more frequently in the industry. The process of developing such a title is both long and very costly. Dealing with such a massive game world can be very tough and developers often spend most of the time getting it to work. This leaves lit-tle time for gameplay innovation and beautiful art creation. To change this around, mid-dleware developers are racing to produce the best package for the job so that developers can spend more time on the game and not have to worry about the framework.

Most of the biggest developers of MMOGs make their own proprietary tools and engines, but teams with fewer resources are going to third-party developers to look for the greatest middleware. Listed below are some of the leading MMOG middleware and basic information about each.

Big World—Big World Pty Ltd.

Big World includes the following features:

- Dynamically reconfigurable server infrastructure
- Advanced 3D game engine
- World editor, particle editor, and model viewer
- Live management tools

The Big World product is a complete MMO middleware solution. It's an end-to-end package of client, server, and tools technology. Big World is a fairly flexible product that is only available for serious MMOG developers with funding. It is not aimed at educational institutions or nonfunded start-ups.

Terazona—Zona Inc.

ZAF (Zona Application Framework) includes the following features:

- A flexible, user-definable means to group players and objects to intelligently determine who receives which updates, thereby making efficient use of available bandwidth.
- An API for abstracting away underlying communication complexities.
- A relevant nomenclature for game development projects.
- Common game functionalities such as chat and user profile persistence.
- Reliability through automatic server fail-over, when deployed in "cluster mode."
- An administrative console to control and monitor the system.
- A game master interface for solving user problems and configuring the game.

ZGF (Zona Gaming Framework) includes the following features:

- Game Master Interface
- NPC Observer Framework
- NPC Map Loading Interface
- Entity Manager Framework
- Cheat Response Framework
- Security Framework
- Contract Framework

Terazona has three levels of availability: Terazona Community Edition (up to 500 players), Terazona Standard Edition (up to 2500 players), and Terazona MMOG Edition (up to 32,000 players per server cluster).

Audio Tools

It is important that a producer understand some basic constraints and freedoms offered by audio tools today. Audio is such a large component of the interactive experience, and a producer should be able to have an intelligent discussion with their audio professional.

Multitrack Digital Sound File Editors

These are tools of the audio professional that help make the game sound better. ProTools, Nuendo, Vegas, Cubase SX, Logic, and Digital Performer all have their strengths, so read up and then talk to your audio professional to find out what applies to your game.

What the producer needs to know

Multitrack digital sound file editors are sequencing software packages that composers use to mix and arrange music. Discuss with your audio professional whether this product is required for your game and what the benefits would be in creating linear and nonlinear music.

More background

Multitrack digital sound file editors are mainly used to record, mix, and arrange music. These editors can also be used to record game dialogue and foley sound effects. These programs offer a multitrack/channel interface that makes sequencing and arranging very straightforward.

These programs are usually very big. Some are specialized and some are not. Some are great at recording any audio and dealing with music, whereas others have capability to edit sound effects heavily as well. Consult your audio director and composer about these packages before purchasing a license. They will no doubt have enough knowledge of the current packages and preferences for those they usually use.

Stereo Digital Sound File Editors

Sound file editors make up the backbone of sound effects. Consider SoundForge and Peak for your new project.

What the producer needs to know

Stereo digital sound file editors are editors that are used to master sound effects.

More background

These programs can be used to record quality audio, but their ace is in their audio editing features. These applications traditionally offer a simple, intuitive interface that lends itself well to editing single tracks of sound effects. They offer dozens of effects to apply to audio, and each of those effects can be tweaked to make the best effect for your needs.

These programs are great for producing excellent sound effects for games, but they are not good for dealing with music. Consult your sound effects person about the best choice of software.

Sound Effects Libraries

There's more than a virtual ton of sound effect libraries out there. Hollywood Edge, Sound Ideas, and a ton more are available for a reasonable license fee.

What the producer needs to know

There are about 100 different sound effects kits on the market. Depending on your game, you might need to have custom sound effects created, or perhaps you can alter existing sound effects from these libraries. Hollywood Edge and Sound Ideas are only two of the most popular kits available, and the person charged with your sound effects should have a good idea of what samples they have, what they'll need to license, and if anything needs to be created specifically for your game. Review this resource with your sound person and ensure that they have a good understanding of the many choices they have in this area after you've outlined the sound effect requirements for your game.

Surround Sound Encoders

Sound and Surround sound encoders have emerged since the dawn of video games. A few good examples have distinquished themselves in the marketplace, including SurCode and Nuendo.

What the producer needs to know

These are tools for implementing audio and music in the game. Everyone uses different tools but there are some recommendations. Discuss this with your composer or audio director to determine the best solution for your particular game, whether 3D sound is a requirement, and how big of a role sound and music will play in the interactive experience. One of these solutions might be a good solution for you if your game engine does not support 3D positional audio or if your design has very specific requirements for positional sound.

Sound Implementation: GameCODA—Sensaura

GameCODA was recently acquired by Creative Labs. Here's what you need to know about GameCODA.

What the producer needs to know

GameCODA is like 3D Studio Max but only for sound. It provides a nearly complete solution for implementing sound on multiple platforms. This or a custom tool that has similar functionality is required to complete the game. Discuss this with those who are charged with implementing sound and music in your game to determine if it is the right solution for you.

More background

GameCODA is a cross-platform audio integration middleware. It is compatible with PC, Playstation 2, Xbox, and Nintendo GameCube game development. Since it was first announced at the GDC in 2002, it has been used on single-platform and cross-platform titles from Lionhead Studios, Activision, Codemasters, and SCi.

This tool is useful for any developer for sound integration, and is extremely useful for any team working on a cross-platform title. Having one middleware for all versions saves both time and money. GameCODA is not only a usable cross-platform, but has also been developed so that the same high-quality sound can be used on all platforms. There's virtually no difference between the major consoles, although Xbox currently has the richest audio engine.

When GameCODA was developed, it was meant to be used by programmers, level designers, sound designers, and musicians. Level designers can place audio with a 3D component interface, which can be used with their level editors.

World-Building Tools

World building tools and efficiencies in the game building pipeline are a producer's friend.

Unreal Engine 2—Epic Games

Unreal Engine 2 is a complete game development engine providing a very polished level editor, animation system, physics, 3D graphics engine, rendering, and AI.

What the producer needs to know

The Unreal Engine has been one of the strongest 3D engines available for a long time; it has an impressive library of titles and one of the biggest mod communities in the industry.

More background

You can acquire the Unreal Engine 2 in two ways. Companies can license the full engine from Epic Games. Unreal Engine 2 is a complete game development framework targeted at today's mainstream PCs, the Microsoft Xbox game console, and Sony's Playstation 2. However, anyone who buys Unreal Tournament 2003, Unreal 2, or Unreal Tournament 2004 gets a free version of the Unreal world-builder level editing tool. The level editing tool comes with a powerful scripting language.

The level editor and scripting language allow players of the games to edit and add characters, art assets, gameplay modes, and heavily modified (mod) version of the game. Many full conversion mods have been made with the Unreal world-building tools, which don't have any resemblance to any of the Unreal games.

The full engine, Unreal Engine 2, is a complete game framework. Its production-proven tools and feature-rich code base enable a game development team to begin authoring all aspects of a product from day one: art, models, levels, gameplay code, user interface, and new features. Many high-profile commercial games have been developed using the Unreal Engine 2.

Neverwinter Nights Engine—Bioware

There's a ton for game engines. Here's what's available.

What the producer needs to know

The Neverwinter Nights Engine is a complete game engine that Bioware and Bioware affiliated development companies use to create large-scale RPGs.

More background

The NWN Engine was first used for the award-winning RPG Neverwinter Nights by Bioware in 2002. The toolset has since been the groundwork for numerous titles from Bioware. The engine has not been licensed commercially but has been used for Bioware's in-house titles as well as other Bioware affiliated developers.

Each game published using the NWN Engine comes with a free toolset called Aurora. The toolset includes a 3D level editor and a scripting language. Bioware hosts a community of game fans and developers. Their community is one of the biggest in the industry and they have received awards for their support to their community. Members of this community are very active in making game modules (mods) using the Aurora toolset. Many of these mods have been very successful in this community, and some are being sold online in Bioware's store.

Quake 3 Arena Engine—ID Software

Here's another game engine for the game developer's everyday use.

What the producer needs to know

The Quake 3 Arena Engine is an older, yet powerful game engine; it will be available as open source by the end of 2005. This can be a viable choice for developers with a limited budget.

More background

ID is one of the leading game engine developers and has been developing and licensing 3D engines for longer than any other 3D engine developers. They have licensed their engines from their whole popular Quake series.

ID Software has taken the stance of letting their product speak for itself. They do not commercially advertise their engines, but developers can contact them to acquire a license. Their most recent incarnation, the Quake 3 Arena engine, has been very successful and has been used for hit games, such as *Call of Duty* (Activision), *Return to Castle Wolfenstein* (ID Software), and *American Magee's Alice* (Rogue Entertainment).

The game, Quake 3 Arena, comes with a free world-building tool, Q3Radiant. Quake 3 Arena also has a very active module (mod) community.

Source—Valve Software

Care to say *Half-Life 2*, anyone?

What the producer needs to know

The Source engine is a new product from Valve Software that offers a complete game development engine, providing a very polished level editor, animation system, physics, 3D graphics engine, rendering, and AI.

More background

Valve Software just recently released its Source engine technology to be licensed by any third party. Valve used the engine to produce the highly anticipated *Half-Life 2*. The Source engine technology has been just as anticipated in the development world as the game was in the gamer world.

Source offers new technology for character animation, advanced AI, real-world physics, and shader-based rendering. Source builds its physics system on the currently most advanced physics engine in the industry, Havok 2. Source is expected to be one of the main world-building engines in the next few years to come.

Half-Life 2 comes with a free Source world-building level editor and scripting language. Fans can use this to build game modules, or mods. Because the technology is new, there haven't been any big mods done with Source yet. However, one game other than Half-Life 2 has been published using the engine.

Scheduling Tools

Although there is no holy grail yet for the scheduling of software development projects, the best solution usually involves several tools and applications, coupled with clear and workable procedures and methods. Top this off with a good producer and you have a complete scheduling solution! However, one or more of the following applications are recommended as critical to any project manager, producer, or anyone responsible for bringing together even a small part of a video game and taking it to market on schedule.

Microsoft Excel

Microsoft Excel is the foundation of all software projects with their ease of use and versatility.

What the producer needs to know

Producers should know this product very well. It is one of the best choices for scheduling and management of a project. By setting up the right spreadsheets, the producer can track the hundreds or even thousands of assets and components of a video game as they flow through the production cycle.

More background

This powerful spreadsheet-based program is widely used for scheduling and resource management throughout the industry. Although MS Excel doesn't have many of the advanced scheduling features of Microsoft Project, its simplicity lends well to management of small-scale projects and individual departments of large development teams. In Excel, links can be made between workbooks and other Excel files. It is extremely flexible and is most effective with managing tasks and resources.

Microsoft Project

Microsoft Project, despite its complexity, remains one of the most used project management software packages

What the producer needs to know

It's also suggested that the producer get to know this tool well. It's an extremely powerful scheduling and management tool.

More background

Although this massive scheduling and management tool has its flaws, it has everything to successfully manage a large-scale project/team/company. This program is designed for managers to easily schedule and manage task lists, resources, milestones, team meetings, and finances, and it does those things very well.

Project has extremely strong and flexible scheduling features. Tracking tasks, milestones, resources, and overall progress are done automatically. Microsoft Project also has strong resource allocation features and will report overallocations, which can then be easily leveled within the program. All this can then be reported to each team member with the server features. Each team member only receives information from the schedule that concerns him.

Alienbrain Studio 7—NXN Software

Alienbrain Studio 7 has come a long way since the old days.

What the producer needs to know

Alienbrain was originally a digital asset management tool but its most recent version is a good solution to management for the whole team, including version control.

More background

Alienbrain is a very user-friendly digital asset management tool. In this tool's first five versions, it focused on being an excellent digital art asset management tool. Since then, it has become a great management tool for the whole team.

Alienbrain supports all major art asset file formats used in game development. It can be integrated into Maya, 3D Studio Max, and Photoshop seamlessly. The GUI is extremely friendly for artists. In addition to asset management, Alienbrain keeps track of tasks and their level of completion.

Before version 6, Alienbrain was lacking in code management and version control, but in 2003 NXN Software introduced Alienbrain Engineer—a product add-on that obliterated Alienbrain's former shortcomings. New code version control and code merging systems were introduced that made Alienbrain on par with Perforce. These features have been polished even further for version 7 and come closer to being the "one-stop" management tool for the whole development process.

Alienbrain's worst enemy has always been its price tag and that has, unfortunately, not changed.

Creating Proprietary Tools

When you have to create proprietary tools on your team, you need to remember a few rules. Although it is recommended that you keep the proprietary tool development limited to specific helper tools—such as profiling and art exporter modifications—sometimes creating another might be unavoidable. The following sections discuss some recommendations for when that is the case.

Design Specifications Clearly

Communication is essential in every phase of development and there's no exception when creating your proprietary tools. The programmers charged with creating reliable tools should constantly communicate in detail with the users of each tool. Level designers should give detailed specifications to what they need in their world-building tools and gameplay integration tools. Use their knowledge when planning the production of your tools. There are always essential features that go into each tool, but they will need loads of additional features to have a fast and solid workflow.

In addition, the engineers should always design the tool software before coding it. Designing the tools, classes, and components in detail before coding can save time in the long run.

When features have been implemented, be certain to have each department test their tools. Some features can be made more comfortable for the users and further polish is unavoidable. Be certain to have each department make a detailed specification list before your programmers start building the tools. The more detail in those lists, the less time programmers have to spend building it.

Communicate and Demonstrate the Tools

When the tool has been developed, its users have to learn how to use it. Have "how-to" documentation about each feature included in each tool. If functionality travels only by word-of-mouth, most of the users will never know about it. Although creating documentation might sound like a daunting task, it will save a lot of time in the long run. If there is no documentation, the engineer (or anyone who knows about the feature) must explain new features to everybody, including newly hired people. That is a daunting task!

Test the Entire Pipeline

When the users know about the features, they can give feedback and broken tools can be fixed fast. Test every tool individually for pipeline efficiency (see Figure 7.1). After all the major tools are ready, test them all to check for pipeline errors in the way they work together. Be certain there are no problems with the pipeline and that it's as smooth as possible. A smooth pipeline will save you a lot of time in development. Fix any errors right away and then retest it. Don't assume it works; fixing one problem can often cause others.

To do these types of testing efficiently, get the internal QA (Quality Assurance) team involved. They will systematically find problems and errors, and programmers can fix the tools quickly.

It's important to have one person who can make sure every user question about the tools gets answered. The users will feel better and the pipeline will stay smooth.

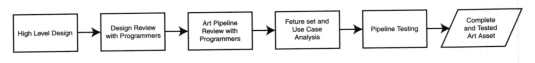

Figure 7.1
Pipeline definition and testing.

Update Proprietary Tools

It's inevitable that the data format for the proprietary tools will get stale over time. Upgrades and enhancements to the game's development and progress along the production cycle change over time. As new formats and features are added to the game engine, updates to the tools are also required. It's best to create a schedule with milestones for your tools development. Make that schedule match the one for the game development. As new features are introduced, new tools are as well.

There is a large information base freely available about what to do and what not to do when it comes to proprietary tools development. Almost every postmortem written has a mention of their tool's development in either their "what went right" or "what went wrong" sections.

There is a whole section for postmortems on the Gamasutra Web site. Use the experience of fellow developers to your advantage and apply the best ways to your tool's development. There is an especially good article on Gamasutra, written by Paul Frost about his experience developing tools for *Asheron's Call 2*; check it out.

Asset Management and Procedures

With the thousands of assets that go into a game today, there's no way around having asset management software.

Version Control Systems

Perforce, Visual SourceSafe, CVS, and Test Track make up the bulk of the tools available for this purpose.

What the producer needs to know

Any project with multiple programmers working on the same source code needs a good version control and code management program. You can choose from many that are available, so consult with your technical director before purchasing a license.

More background

During software development projects with multiple programmers, the source code is edited and updated constantly. To prevent programmers who are working on the same code at the same time from breaking the code, a good maintenance program is needed. These types of programs offer a GUI to do this as quickly as possible. These programs track versions well by allowing programmers to merge their code with whatever others have been working on. They also highlight code others have worked on so when a programmer accesses the code, he knows what has changed since he last saw it. A tool of this type is a clear must for any game development project.

Of the top competitors, CVS (Concurrent Versioning System) is the only free program. CVS handles everything it sets out to do well but the GUI is not up to par with the more advanced commercial products, such as Perforce.

Negotiating Tips and Suggestions

In helping a good producer get the right tools for the job, a few tips are worth mentioning. I've had great success with third-party hardware manufacturers, such as NVIDIA and ATI, when I've requested that they provide the latest versions of their hardware to the team for free or at a reduced cost. Ensuring compatibility with the latest software is the role of the developer relations team. I've even had them provide a laptop for demonstration purposes when it came time for a press tour. This was a tremendous help and all I had to do was to mention how great it looked on the NVIDIA laptop.

Alienware has also provided specialized hardware at reduced rates or in trade for cross-promotions that are targeted at hard-core gamers. In working with these two companies, I've found that it is relatively easy to find a win-win solution when approaching their Marketing department. They've been extremely flexible and helpful in providing custom hardware solutions on an emergency basis when the need arose.

The Final Word

Are there some final words of wisdom? Certainly, there's a lot to know about game development tools. Unfortunately, there's more to know than can be covered here, but this should provide a quick reference for you to ensure that you're familiar with some of the latest and greatest and how they fit into the process. The most important message is to understand that without the right tools and a clearly defined production pipeline, games take a very, very long time to develop. The better the tools are, the more time can be invested in making the game fun, rather than just putting it together and fixing it so it doesn't crash.

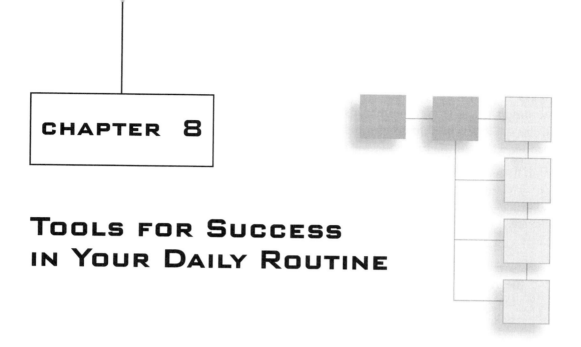

CHAPTER 8

Tools for Success in Your Daily Routine

This chapter discusses some common tools and techniques used by successful producers in managing past projects. Although this chapter is not all encompassing, more than a few techniques and tools are discussed that might make your daily routine slightly more formalized, focused, and streamlined. The trick is to review what is outlined here and select what works for your team and specific situation. The best producers embrace some formality and process structure, ensuring that a good process is not undervalued. But be cautious not to over-implement it. It is very difficult to mold creativity into a structured process.

Processes for Producing a Video Game

This section details a few specifics on procedures and processes that a producer should use to keep track of what's going on during the project and to ensure proper and effective communication between the team, management, and publisher.

Daily Delta Reports

The first and most valuable process I've found in practice at successful developers is the use of the Daily Delta reports and reporting structure. This section provides a quick look at how it works. In this system, on a daily basis, each team member completes a short list of what he or she accomplished or finished that day. If he didn't finish anything, the team member should state what he worked on, but it is important for each team member to try to accomplish one thing—or finish one task—each day.

Team members should subdivide their tasks into manageable portions and focus on accomplishing them. Although this isn't always possible, it is the goal to try for. The Daily Delta process is used to communicate back to the team the following morning. The procedure works in the following way:

1. E-mail daily reminder for Daily Delta with the subject line "Daily Delta: [Date]" at 5 p.m. each workday. This takes about 30 seconds.

2. Each team member simply replies to the Daily Delta reminder e-mail, describing, in bullet-point format, what was accomplished that day. This takes about 90 seconds to two minutes.

3. The next day, one of the first things the producer or the assistant producer does is read through all of the replies to the Daily Delta reminders. This takes about five–nine minutes, depending on how many there are. If someone is missing or sick, the producer or AP notes that in the report.

4. Then, whomever is responsible for publishing the Daily Delta report separates all of the responses into three categories: Design, Art, and Programming. Then, he cuts and pastes each Daily Delta report from each team member into the department section that they're a part of. Artists go into the Art Section, for example.

6. A published report would look something like what is shown in Figure 8.1.

Daily Delta Report Method Benefits

The Daily Delta process is a concise, easy, and efficient way to track the progress of a large team. Despite the initial resistance some teams might offer when you're trying to introduce a new procedure into the production process, rarely does the resistance last beyond the point when the team starts to realize and reap the benefits. Here's a list of the benefits offered by the Daily Delta process.

- Includes low overhead and time requirement.
- Provides a daily record of what's occurred that spans an entire project.
- Can be easily referenced by department.
- Can correlate easily to the schedule (if you require that the tasks follow the same naming structure—meaning that each team member must report work completed on the task as it is spelled on the schedule).
- Ensures communication among large teams in an efficient manner.
- Provides an efficient way to review decisions and resource allocations, measuring the effectiveness of those decisions against goals.

<u>**Project X Daily Delta - Thursday, April 28th, 2004**</u>

"The greatest use of life is to spend it for something that will outlast it."
William James (1842 - 1910)

<u>**Programming**</u>

Programmer 1 (NAME HERE)
- Occlusion task
- Fixing JArchive

Programmer 2 (NAME HERE)
- Meeting with 3rd party licensee people

Programmer 3 (NAME HERE)
- Reviewed 3rd party license technology & wrote up lessons

Programmer 4 (NAME HERE)
- meeting with BW guys

Programmer 5 (NAME HERE)
- Fixed some combat crash bugs
- Working on the Automated Build System

<u>**Design**</u>

Designer 1 (NAME HERE)
- Got the spawn tool working
- Combat meeting

Designer 2 (NAME HERE)
- Knee specialist (urgent surgery coming up – doh!)
- Meeting with publisher's agent
- Considering some professional stats help

Designer 3 (NAME HERE)
- Player Housing

Designer 4 (NAME HERE)
- Finished Skill Tree Creation
- Read a few design documents, particular art style related

Designer 5 (NAME HERE)
- research in gameplay balancing
- backstory

Designer 6 (NAME HERE)
- Finished first draft of AI Planning requirements from design.
- Animation meeting

<u>**Art**</u>

Artist 1 (NAME HERE)
- Review Nicks Concept Art
- Added to Style Guide
- Added to Creature Doc

Figure 8.1
A Daily Delta Report example.

(continued on next page)

- Looked at the required scale variations for our buildings
- started rough scale mock up

Artist 2 (NAME HERE)
- shoulder and elbow deformation testing

Artist 3 (NAME HERE)
- Finished :
  007_Battle_Circle_003_Gate.psd

- Started and altered :
  010_Herbalist_Revised_003.psd

Artist 4 (NAME HERE)
- finished up on ported combat anims

Artist 5 (NAME HERE)
- Extra requests for new combat system

Contractors Go in this Section - Like Sound Guys or External Reviewers

Contractor 1
- Web development strategy
- Billing system feedback documentation
- Review Style guide

Figure 8.1 (continued)
A Daily Delta Report example.

Source/Version Control Reports

You have many version control tools to consider, but the one that seems to have the most benefits for game developers is the software package called Perforce. Most version-control software can generate list reporting on the status of every file used to compile the game. Most version control software offers this type of functionality.

note

When using version control software, take the time to learn and understand its features and how to use it properly. It is a product's lifeblood. Once, when I was checking out a file while talking on the phone, I accidentally checked out the entire database, checking out every single file that was not otherwise checked out to someone else. This caused a work disruption and was quite embarrassing when one of the programmers came to me to ask why I'd checked out his code.

Using Wiki

If you've never heard of Wiki, then I'm glad you're reading this. I'd never heard of it either until someone referred me to Jamie Fristrom's article on a "Manager in a Strange Land: Collaborating with Wiki" (December 19, 2003) on Gamasutra.com.

Wiki is a collaborative documentation and brainstorming tool. But depending on how it is used, it can be a great way to manage design documents. If you've tried and failed when attempting to set up an internal Web site to manage and record the design process—and it was just too much work—here's the solution.

note

Wiki is free for download at http://openwiki.com. After you get it installed on a server, you'll need to update it (it automatically tells you what it needs to download from Microsoft for it to work properly). It is about as easy to install as QuickTime Pro.

Wiki works this way: To simply add or change content within Wiki, you just double-click. Documents that lend themselves to constant updating, such as creative and technical design document subsections, are excellent candidates for management through Wiki. Wiki supports complexity from the very highest level of documentation to the very lowest level, down to and including one- or two-sentence descriptions of every single task on the programming task list. It makes it really easy for programmers to annotate their tasks with the details when a feature is implemented and tested.

It is an easily accessible place to put FAQs for version control, as well as check-in and testing procedures for all art assets, or even pipeline description and troubleshooting tips for testing the current build of the game.

There's always a small concern that someone on the team might change content that's important. But, fortunately, Wiki has a version-control feature that backs up all previous revisions, edits, and changes, so a producer can see who changed what and when.

One of the drawbacks to using Wiki is that it doesn't play nicely with printers. The documentation, although readable, is rarely presentable in its raw form off the printer. It is a bit of work to translate and reformat it into Microsoft Word for a design review presentation or a milestone submission, but not impossible.

You can also send out updates to design documents via e-mail and then attach the link to Wiki in the e-mail. Although it is rare that anyone reads the entire document, this is a good measure to follow when you've scheduled a meeting to discuss a specific feature and everyone attending the meeting needs to come up to speed on the latest iteration of the design document.

Finally, Wiki makes it easy to update documents, collaborate with the team, and track changes and updates, but that doesn't mean that the team will do it. You must infect them with Wiki, and, like a virus, the process will spread. An example of Wiki is shown in Figure 8.2, below.

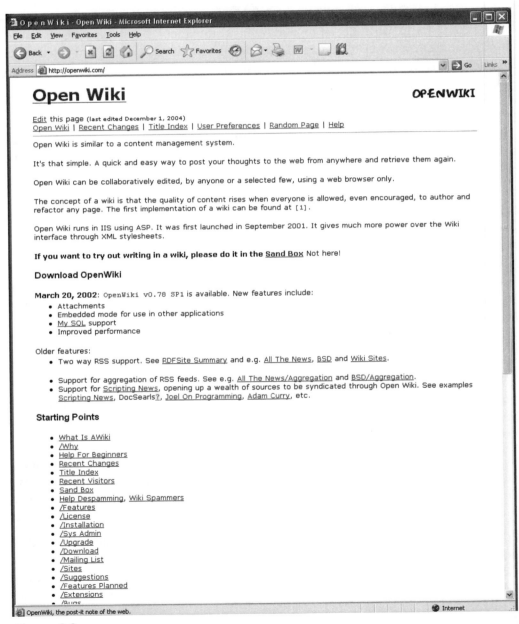

Figure 8.2
The Wiki tool

Team Meetings

The first thing to remember about a team meeting is that they are very expensive, so be certain that they're valuable. Each team member sitting idle for 15 minutes costs approximately $15. So, if you have 30 people in a team meeting for 30 minutes, that costs about $900. Would it have been better to invest that money elsewhere? Keep this in mind whenever you have an urge to schedule the entire team for a meeting.

Although team meetings are expensive, it can be equally expensive to not have them on a regular basis. The key to efficiency is to set up an agenda and format for the meeting. In my experience, a team meeting at least once per month works out just fine. During team meetings, you should focus on the positive aspects of the game's progress, show that you have a plan of how to accomplish the challenges ahead, and, above all, ensure that the team takes a positive message away from every team meeting.

Leads Meetings

When working at a developer, one of the most valuable processes is the weekly Leads meeting. This is the time when the lead programmer, producer, assistant producer, lead artist, art director, and lead designer discuss the upcoming goals for the week, the upcoming milestones for the month, and the challenges that lay ahead. Although no producer can reasonably offer solutions to challenges in all of these areas, it is the role of the producer to foster creative problem solving, candid discussions, and clear resolutions from each Leads meeting. The following list is a format for the Leads meeting.

- Review accomplishments
- Outline the problems
- Generate options
- Propose solutions
- Build a consensus
- Make a decision
- Communicate the course of action to those persons affected by the decision
- Keep a record of the decision and the course of action

Ensure that someone is taking notes at the meeting and that the meeting minutes are published as soon as is practical after the conclusion of the meeting.

Executive/Steering Committee Meetings

One of the meetings that isn't necessarily enjoyable, but is still important to do, is the meeting with the executives and/or a steering group. At this meeting, you, as the producer, generally run the show. The executives are there to review and evaluate the team's progress and the goal is to get them to understand how their investment in the project is yielding results.

note

It is valuable to arrange a steering group for your product if you work within a large organization. Leads from other projects, marketing managers, and other senior people can often add value and objectivity to the direction of product development.

For executive meetings, it is best that the producer drive the agenda, have it published beforehand, and bring up critical issues that require executive decisions—such as policy issues and strategic directions—with advice and facts being provided to support your position. Include time to answer any questions and demonstrate new features and the overall progress of the game. Understand that critical feedback is valuable, but not all of it will be possible to implement. Understanding this and determining how to implement the most valuable feedback from an executive meeting is the talent of being a producer. Above all, be prepared for this meeting. Demonstrate control of the development process and earn the continued confidence of your executive team.

Risk Management Tools

Because the principal responsibility of the producer is to manage risk, a comprehensive stable of risk management tools is an essential part of the job. The following sections discuss some examples of tools that have been used to successfully manage risk in the past.

Risk Management Worksheet

When managing risk for a project, the first step is to identify the risk. Including every possible risk on a list is a great start for this process. Brainstorm with the leads of a project and identify the risks. Include everyone with a stake in the project: art, programming, sound, design, marketing, and production. Do not try to qualify or quantify any of the risks; just focus on making the list of risks and then categorize them. A sample appears in Figure 8.3.

The second step in this process is the quality and quantitative evaluation of each risk identified on the risk list. Correlate quality with probability and quantity with impact. Probability means the chance this risk has of occurring, and quantification of the risks means judging each risk on its potential impact on the project if and when it occurs. Use a scale of risk from 0 to 100 percent of relative judgments within such a scale.

Then sort the matrix of risk by relative scale. Highest risks go at the top. Then assign the risks to individual owners, making them responsible for managing that particular risk. Be certain to assign many of the risks to yourself as the producer because that is your main role, but a lot of the risks (such as technical risks) are better suited to leads with an expertise in a specific discipline.

DRAFT - RISK MANAGEMENT PLAN					
Updated: 8/21/04					

PROBABILITY (P)		IMPACT (I)				
		20%	40%	60%	80%	100%
20%		4%	8%	12%	16%	20%
40%		8%	16%	24%	32%	40%
60%		12%	24%	36%	48%	60%
80%		16%	32%	48%	64%	80%
100%		20%	40%	60%	80%	100%

RISK	OWNER	(P) FACTOR	(I) FACTOR	(PI) FACTOR
Right talent on the Team	Producer	90%	90%	81%
Depth of Gameplay	Lead Designer	60%	80%	48%
Other competitive products in same timeframe	Marketing Mgr	40%	90%	36%
Proprietary Tool Development	Lead Programmer	50%	40%	20%
Clear Gameplay Message & Essence	Lead Designer	20%	40%	8%

Figure 8.3
Risk management worksheet

In Figure 8.3, you can see that having the right talent on the team is the producer's responsibility, and it is the highest risk in the project. So after the risks have been assigned within this matrix, the next step is to develop a specific course of action for each owner of the risk. After that course of action has been established, write it down in the risk management plan. But writing it down and devising a plan doesn't mean that the risks are eliminated or addressed. The following sections look at what else a producer can do to manage risk on a project.

note

An example of the risk management plan, assessment matrix, and procedures are available at the Web site accompanying this book, at http://www.courseptr.com/downloads.

Other Risk Management Tricks

Risk is known to sneak into and blanket any development project, even those with the most experienced and seasoned personnel. But as a producer, you can master a few other tricks to defend your project against this silent ghost accompanying those who tread into the technical, creative, or highly imaginative unknowns and frontiers.

The path of least resistance to this ghost is to do nothing and then work the team to death through overtime and late schedules. Another way is to create a fake schedule, adding buffers whenever and wherever possible to milestone due dates. But because more and more publishers are requiring due diligence during the pre-production phases of new projects, you, as a good producer, should account for those risks at that time. Then identify where those risks are in the production schedule along with your risk assessment report.

Yikes! You mean a producer should actually show and address risks when dealing with the publisher and/or management? The answer is yes! Even though you've worked hard to establish that you have the right team and all of the right stuff to hit this project out of the ballpark, most seasoned publishers know and expect a certain amount of risk from their projects. Although every risk that's identified might not be clearly outlined on the schedule, it does influence the way in which you complete tasks throughout the development process. Who does the work, when it is done (highest risks should always be scheduled first), and the solutions (licensable technology or new tools) are required to minimize the risk. This also lays the foundation for a good relationship with the publisher's producer. If you're an experienced third-party producer for a publisher, you're probably already aware of many of these risks because they're addressed and challenged with your other games in development. But accounting for risk, you're buying the added insurance that makes it more likely the product ships on schedule.

Assessing risk is a tough process. As described previously, there's a method to doing that. But you do have a few things to consider. Risks are not tasks, so don't confuse the need to create more tools with more functionality as a risk. It is work that needs to be done to support a new rendering engine. A risk might be whether the gameplay concept is fully realized and unique enough to differentiate itself in the market. External dependencies might mean risk, especially if there's no way to discern a way to minimize the risk. If you're thinking of using a third-party software, DivX for example, you might not know if it is fully compatible with your rendering engine until you test it. Or the risk may be in creating a new piece of content—such as the recording of a symphony orchestra for the soundtrack, which has never been done before with your team.

Account for things such as certain features that are complex or experimental, as opposed to an asteroid falling on the building where you work. Accounting for more reasonable risks makes you seem reasonable. Include inexperience with a particular genre or platform if the team has only one or two people who've worked on the type of game that you're creating.

Working to Minimize the Risk

You can minimize risk on a video game development project in a few ways. This is the next step after identifying the risks. Some risks can't be mitigated and the schedule simply must account for them. But you, as a producer, can work to minimize a project's risk; for example:

- Don't start developing the game until there's a relatively complete design. You need a functional design; this doesn't need to include every single detail, but it does need to include use case scenarios that are clearly outlined prior to starting production.

- Eliminate the unknowns. Do the research to determine what you don't know. Use the pre-production phase to get a good handle on the entire project and eliminate the unknown factors.

- Create a backup plan for when things go wrong. Always have a draft of Plan B ready to go.

- Invest in creating a prototype or proof of concept project. Your team will waste a lot less time on one small project, and it is a lot less expensive than adding 30 people to your team and then having to redesign major parts of the game.

- Put the best talent on the highest risks first. Get them out of the way and then the worst should be over.

- Use third-party tools or other solutions for anything that requires expertise not offered by someone on the team.

- Provide flexibility in the schedule so that you can reprioritize when things change. They always change.

- Redesign when required. Eliminate and cut features early and often.

A Production Methodology That Minimizes Risk

Now look at an alternative production method called the Front Loaded Development Model.

The goals remain the same as with the standard model: to create a great game that's commercially successful. The Front Loaded Development Model ensures that the game concepts are proven through a prototyping and tuning sequence before committing to a full production. This allows a small development team to review what's been developed, determine how fun they are, and then tune the prototype and modify the game design to minimize the weaknesses of the experience while exploiting the strengths of the proven concepts. However, not all concepts that are prototyped and tested go into the game. Furthermore, it is generally wise not to include things in the prototype that have fully quantified risks, such as video playback for in-game movies. That's a standard feature for most game developers and doesn't really add risk to the development process, so don't waste time at an early stage proving something that can be implemented. Focus on the concepts that haven't been decided and refined.

The Standard Development model is a commonly used methodology. After the concept is approved and a prototype completed, the game is approved for full production. But as the game moves along through the development process, costs are mounting at the same time risks are increasing. It becomes difficult to cancel a project that has such a significant resource commitment to it, especially late in the development process because it is viewed as a waste of millions of dollars and years of time.

However, when this is compared to the Front Loaded Game Development Model, it is clear why the FLD method is used by some of the most successful game developers, including Naughty Dog, Blizzard Entertainment, Nintendo, and Insomniac. By using this model, the developer and the publisher work to reduce risk in the project and the overall portfolio of game development projects by starting several projects and nurturing them to the pre-production phase, testing and refining many concepts and gameplay design iterations until a promising prototype emerges. By this time, the creative and technical risks have been reduced and it is a matter of actually creating the game. But the risks decline as costs are going up.

note

Mark Cerny discussed this method and why it is important for publishers to follow this method to ensure that publishers have the "will to kill" some of the projects using this process.

"If adequate progress isn't occurring, or if the team has reached first playable but the gameplay doesn't appear sufficiently compelling, [it is] time to kill the project. There's no point following this process if you're not going to hold the output of pre-production up to a very high standard. The team has to be the best and the brightest. And the team has to be committed to shooting for the stars—the first playable will end up being compared to the dominant released products in its category, so it won't do to have anything but the highest standards."

By canceling some projects at this early stage, game developers and publishers can minimize the chance that they won't invest millions of dollars in an unproven gameplay concept and the millions more it takes to market the product.

Because game development is such a big financial commitment, with hundreds or thousands of man hours, it is important for the producer to ensure that their project has the best chance of being a winner. By minimizing the risks early in the project, you limit the downside risk. When the downside risk is limited, the upside reward usually takes care of itself.

Using Microsoft Project, Microsoft Excel, and the Overly Complex Scheduling Process

The nightmare of every producer includes visions of updating the project status using multiple tools, procedures, or arcane processes that might not relate to each other in any way. Because Microsoft Project is a very powerful scheduling tool, it can also be very complex and challenging to use efficiently. The following sections cover a few ways to create a flex-ible scheduling method that's easy to update and maintain. Although it isn't perfect, it is about the best hybrid I've found. It seems that there's no unifying theory for scheduling in the game industry.

Start with an Excel Worksheet

Scheduling is really started in earnest at the end of the pre-production phase, but before production. Remember the Programmer Task list and the Feature list discussed earlier? Let's go back to those lists of tasks. Pick them apart. Are they small enough that each indi-vidual task can be estimated with certainty? If not, then you've not picked the tasks apart enough. This process is called the *Work Breakdown System* and the worksheet is often referred to as a WBS sheet. Each task needs to be broken down into finite segments.

For example, a three-week task on getting the animation pipeline working is probably not as effective as "Identify the export data format, compare with game engine data require-ments, modify the art exporters to match game engine data requirements, create inter-mediary data format, and test the pipeline." Those are all finite tasks that might make up an animation pipeline. Therefore, the WBS would look like this:

1. Get the animation pipeline working
   a. Identify export data format
   b. Compare data with game engine data requirements
   c. Modify art exporters to match game engine data requirements
   d. Create an intermediary data format (if required)
   e. Test the pipeline

Using the WBS process, work with your leads and start allocating resources to tasks. Following the same process, create an entire listing of all of the art assets needed for this game, including art, sound, and music. Then double-check this against the game design documentation (after following a similar process with the lead designer), and review the proposed use case scenarios. After you've done a complete audit, you're ready to schedule in detail.

Create an Excel worksheet (there's a template on the Web site that accompanies this book) that mirrors the feature list, the programmer task annotations, and the art status sheet. This is easy to do by linking directly to the sheet on which that data is stored. Include three columns for each task labeled Best, Worst, and Most Likely, with each value being a con-sistent day value or portion of a day. Don't schedule in any other granularity than one-half days.

In each column, fill out the three scenarios given the input from the programmer, artist, or designer who is responsible for the task. Separate the project into three worksheets— one for programming, one for design, and one for art production.

To make a huge schedule manageable, I break the tasks down to a single resource sheet that's digestible by the team member. Use this worksheet approach to get them to think about the case scenarios for each task. Then, they should fill out the worksheet, also noting if there are any tasks (especially dependent tasks) that aren't listed on the sheet.

Use this data-gathering process to audit your work and ensure that each task and feature has been accounted for. For the tasks and features that are still unassigned, don't just leave them blank, but work with your lead to develop reasonable data on which to schedule. Above all, put placeholder tasks in where you think there might be work to do, but it is unconfirmed or requires more research. When in doubt, put it in, even in placeholder format. Check out Figure 8.4 as an example.

Project Estimate (Internal)

Project X for the X-box

Platform Xbox & PC
Ship Date: Fall 2005

Game System	Task Description	Resource	Best	Worst	Most Likely	Result
Technical Design			20	70	55	57
Game Engine	Outline Specifications for Game Engine	DI	5	15	12	12
Rendering	Rendering Engine DivX Support	RT	5	7	5	6
Direct X Implementation	Implement Direct X and XNA	IX	25	75	60	62
Game Logic	Review Design Specification	DI	15	25	19	20
Commands	Define Commands for all units	RC	17	55	25	34
User Inteface	Review UI Design	LM	21	45	25	31
UI Tools Defined	Create UI tools to specifications	GI	15	31	20	23
Artificial Intelligence	Review AI Design	GT	1	2	1	1
Computer Player	Implement Computer Player as designed	ER	45	70	55	58

Figure 8.4
Here's an example of a fictitious project worksheet used to gather the data about how long it would take to complete a new feature. This worksheet would be filled out by one resource (electronic versions only).

Using the Formula

There's a little formula that's used to weight the estimations into a slightly more accurate schedule. The principle is this: One time out of six times does the best-case scenario happen. Three times out of six does the worst-case scenario happen, and two times out of six does the most-likely case happen.

Therefore, the formula looks like this:

(B+3W+2M)/6= duration.

That's the figure to include in the schedule. It is flexible and provides a quick, simple, and defendable way to account for slack in the schedule. It also takes the emotion out of estimating, as this formula does well at quantifying normally unquantifiable issues. It also helps people estimate tasks correctly because emotion is taken out of the process. No longer do team members need to say "Oh, that will take about two weeks" when they know it will only take 1.5 weeks and they want to give themselves some flexibility. It allows people to be objective without fear of what reaction their answer might provoke.

note

Be certain that you have the worksheet checked into source control so that you can control versions and keep track of revision history. Also ensure that each team member fills it out electronically!

Linking to Microsoft Project

After you've completed the worksheet for the identified tasks, sort them into game system, art assets, and design tasks, grouping the similar and dependent tasks as close as possible in the rows of tasks. Then create a link between the Result column and the Microsoft Project file. See Figure 8.5.

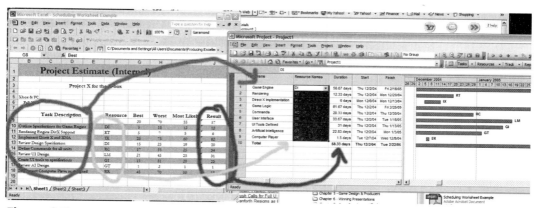

Figure 8.5
Creating the link

If you want to get really fancy, you can link the spreadsheet to the Microsoft Project file to update the durations automatically, but this is sometimes too much trouble because it is common for new tasks to be inserted.

After getting the base project set up and the estimate data on all of the programmer, designer, and art production tasks, you need to complete the process of building a full schedule and start finding the dependencies. After the project file is set up, you need to maintain and update it on a daily basis. You can refer to the Excel worksheets as estimates; if the project goes through a major overhaul or change of direction and, therefore, requires an entirely new schedule, you can go back to the worksheets. You can track the estimates for accuracy, noting how far off the estimates are and then adjusting the Microsoft Project schedule accordingly. For example, if an entire set of programming tasks was off by 50 percent from the estimates provided in the worksheets, you might adjust the remaining programming tasks by 40–50 percent to be consistent and allow for error. Otherwise, you can note a problem and then spring into action to find the solution.

The worksheet process provides the producer with a margin of error, one that is flexible, defendable, and relatively scientific, not just related purely to arbitrary values. Over time, you might develop your own formula based upon the accuracy of your team's estimating skill.

Scheduling for Risk

Another way to schedule for risk is a bit more advanced. Timothy Ryan from Gamasutra talks about it in his article from February 3, 2003 titled "Risk Management With Development Schedules." The article makes a few good suggestions that have been adapted here. Now, think back to your risk assessment work noted earlier.

Group the risks with their area of impact, such as the programming risks to the technical/programming schedule. Then organize them by feature, with the risk to that particular feature or game system being added in as the last item in that task group. By doing this, the producer is associating preceding (dependent) tasks with the feature task group (such as a feature that's due for a particular milestone). It is easier to associate the risk with the feature and the milestone this way. When using this method, complete the following steps:

1. Right-click the Predecessor column, and select Insert Column.
2. Line the Column using the Column Definition box and select the field Flag 1 with the title "Risk."
3. Then click OK and the column is inserted into your Gantt chart. This is shown in Figures 8.6 to 8.8.

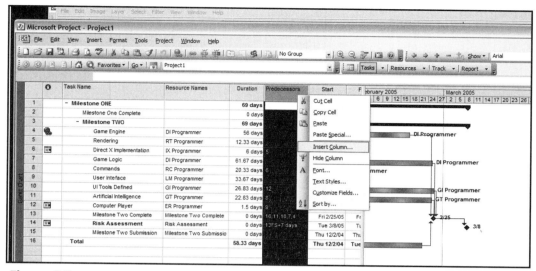

Figure 8.6
Right-click and insert a new column. Then define the column.

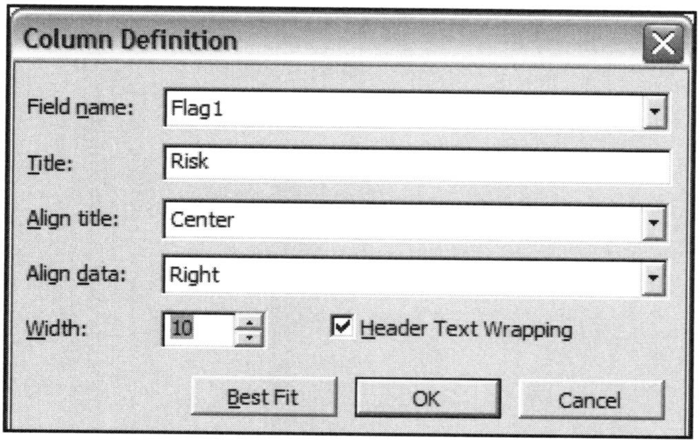

Figure 8.7
Define the column with Field Name Flag 1 and Title as Risk.

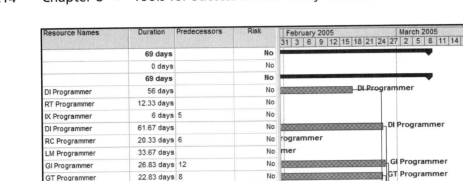

Resource Names	Duration	Predecessors	Risk	February 2005	March 2005
	69 days		No		
	0 days		No		
	69 days		No		
DI Programmer	56 days		No	DI Programmer	
RT Programmer	12.33 days		No		
IX Programmer	6 days	5	No		
DI Programmer	61.67 days		No		DI Programmer
RC Programmer	20.33 days	6	No	rogrammer	
LM Programmer	33.67 days		No	mer	
GI Programmer	26.83 days	12	No		GI Programmer
GT Programmer	22.83 days	8	No		GT Programmer
ER Programmer	1.5 days	9	No	nmer	
Milestone Two Complete	0 days	16,11,10,7,4	No	2/25	
Risk Assessment	0 days	13FS+7 days	No ▼		3/8
Milestone Two Submissio	0 days		Yes		
	58.33 days		No		

Figure 8.8
Be certain to set the Risk column to YES.

4. Select Bar Styles from the Format menu.

5. Scroll to the blank row for Risk. Then set the Show for Tasks field to Flag 1.

6. Make the bar pattern solid and then choose Blue or Red (or any other appropriate color) for the Risk tasks. Then click on OK to close the menu. This is shown in Figures 8.9 and 8.10.

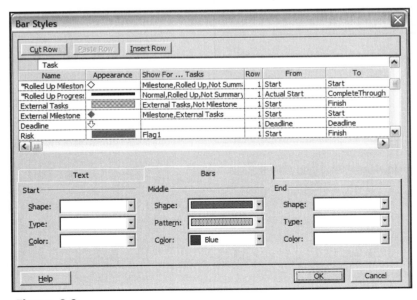

Figure 8.9
Select Bar Styles that make the risk stand out from the rest of the tasks.

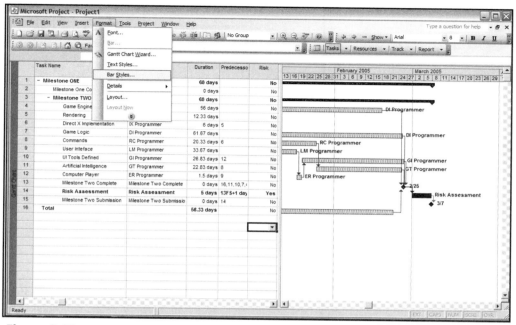

Figure 8.10
Now the risks are scheduled and easily identified.

7. Now, your risk task is easily spotted. You can modify the risk assessment to follow its predecessor by entering the formula in the Predecessor column: 13FS + 1 day (13FS being the predecessor task and 1 day being the buffer or unknown nature of risk; I often vary this number between 1 and 7, depending on the risk).

8. Lastly, as an added precaution to ensure that the risk is managed, I have two separate milestones in the schedule. The first is the Milestone Complete date. This is the date when all tasks should be completed by the team working on the feature. Then, there's time for the risk assessment and reviewing the work. After that has happened, then the milestone is "submitted." as shown in the "Milestone Submitted" milestone in Figure 8.11. This gives you time as the producer to review the work on the feature with the leads prior to the submission of that milestone to the publisher.

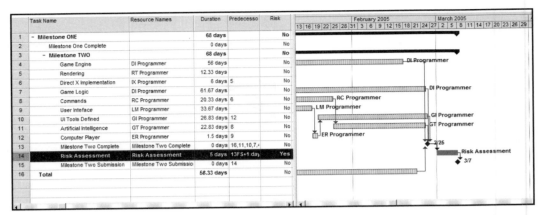

Figure 8.11
Risk assessment comes before the milestone is submitted, but after the milestone is "complete."

note

Linking subprojects with the master Microsoft Project file is often done to separate areas of disciplines on the game. This also provides flexibility for the lead programmers to review and update the schedule (with an added dependency, for example) without having to wait for you to update the artist schedule. Try separating each area of the game's production into different subproject files and then link them into a master schedule for the weekly (high-level) reviews.

Using Slack in the Schedule

Another way exists to include slack in the schedule so that you have some flexibility when the time comes: Only schedule certain resources at 80 percent, or even 50 percent. This is done by right-clicking a task or even a single resource and then entering whatever percentage is appropriate for their role in the Units field, as shown in Figure 8.12. This particular feature of Microsoft Project is extremely helpful to use when trying to schedule work for the leads (if they have actual game development work to do). This allows them 50 percent of their time to complete other tasks (administrative, problem solving, management, and so on) because you don't want to have a few hours here and there called "administrative," or "performance reviews," or something like that.

My rule of thumb is that any lead should not be scheduled at more than 80 percent. Slack is also introduced into the schedule through the use of the formula, as discussed previously, but when used with this method, you're sure to have enough slack to be comfortable and confident.

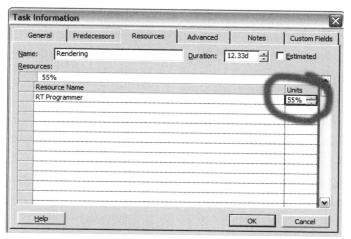

Figure 8.12
Adjust the efficiency of your resources here. If only it were that easy!

Free Form Approach

Although I don't recommend this approach, this situation is generally inevitable in most software projects. Naturally, there are going to be some people (resources) who just don't fit the pattern or go outside the normal rules and can't tell you when certain features or tasks will be done, especially if they're working on multiple features or tasks at a time. If it is not an operational problem for the team, this section focuses on how to schedule for that.

First, you can mark their tasks as zero duration and just have a fixed date by when they have to have the work completed, especially if it has dependencies attached to it. Or, you can use the "slack" method noted previously and divide three tasks to the same resource at the same time, using the allocation discussed. In such a case, the resource would be assigned as 33 percent to three tasks simultaneously, or 25 percent to four tasks, and so on. But, try to have resources focus on specific tasks one or two at a time. It is hard to do any one thing well when you're doing other things at the same time, which is why I caution against using this approach and urge a producer to emphasize the value of the WBS sheets.

note

Be certain to include some slack in any schedule in this way or by using a combination of the methods outlined here; otherwise, there's no room to maneuver or respond to changing circumstances, which is the last thing that should ever happen if the producer is doing a good job.

The Dreaded Overtime

Even if you're the best producer in the universe, overtime will be required of your team at some point during the project. Try to reserve overtime for when it is really needed and then only use it sparingly. Ensure that everyone is aware that "on these certain days, we're working overtime so we can accomplish [set out goal here]." This avoids the situation in which some people are always working overtime and others never do, or in which people don't know why they're working the overtime. Allow the team some advance notice so that they can arrange their personal lives. Avoid making overtime a common occurrence, and focus your time on making the team's normal working hours more efficient and effective.

Overtime is great to use when taking advantage of an additional opportunity or really cool feature. If you can get everyone excited and implement a new feature that makes the game really great, no one will remember the extra weekend or few late nights when the game is showing well.

note

Even during overtime, send people home after they've been working for 11 hours (10 hours of working and one hour of lunch). Most programmers, after working a 10-hour day, will start making mistakes that take longer to correct than if they'd just waited until they were fresh in the morning. Yes, I know that programmers often love to work late into the nights, but don't encourage it and if you see the mistakes starting to happen, actively discourage it.

Dependencies and Placeholders

"The more involved game development gets, the more we need rigorous processes to prevent screwups." —Jamie Fristom on Gamasutra, in "Dependencies"

Now that risk management has been covered, let's review a bit about dependencies and how they factor into a producer's job. Dependencies are things that can't be done until another task is done. For example, characters cannot be imported into a world until the world has been created (modeled and textured). Animations can't be tested until the character is in the world. Sound effects can't be placed until most of the art assets are completed and imported into the world. The characters won't be complete until they're modeled, textured, and at least some of the animations are finished. Cutscenes can't be animated until at least placeholder voice-over work has been recorded. Voice-over work can't be recorded until the script is completed, and a script can't be completed until a writer is hired!

For the producer, this means that unless you determine all of the dependencies in your project, there are going to be some people sitting by waiting for others to finish their tasks. And even if you have reviewed all of the dependencies and accounted for them in the schedule, this *still* might happen. But what is important is minimizing when this does happen and ensuring that there is some flexibility to get some other work done while the critical path is being worked on.

One way to keep the project moving forward and to not get hung up on dependencies is to create placeholders for nearly everything. This means textures, characters, levels, sound effects, voice-over, music, backgrounds, and objects in a world. But there's a trick to using placeholders. You have to ensure that using placeholders doesn't create more dependencies.

When creating placeholder assets for the game, you need to ensure that the file naming conventions are set up. This means that all sound effects files follow localization guidelines and are easily identified. The designers implement the sound effect "bigbang01.wav" and the script function that calls for this data goes to the sound effects folder and plays this file. When you're ready to implement the final sound, simply replace the old data with the final data, by copying it into the right source directory.

This example shows that this process can be done almost anytime and for most parts of a game's development. Simply create placeholder textures that say "placeholder" on them so that at least you can get something in the game quickly to see if it works as expected. It also allows time for iteration as well as innovation. If everyone waited until everyone else was absolutely 100 percent done with their work before implementing it in the game, the entire process would slow down tremendously. Encourage the types of process and procedures that encourage using placeholder artwork and assets, even individual game levels.

Using the placeholder method eliminates the need, for example, for the artist to wait for the final version of the background tool before he starts working on backgrounds, world lighting, or individual scene lighting. At least he can start working with the placeholder backgrounds and get things in the game to see how they look and how they can be improved.

Postmortems

Postmortems are really quite simple. At the end of every milestone, have the team create a short, one-paragraph description or summary of how the milestone went, outlining what is working right and what is not working. Review the data and compile the relevant and meaningful suggestions into a plan to make the remaining milestones easier and more efficient. By the time you get to the end of the project, the process should be honed, and be working a lot more smoothly and efficiently.

I've used postmortems at the end of almost everything—a big project, a small prototype, and milestones. Feedback is valuable, and postmortem reports (and articles in *Game Developer*) are an easy way to prevent mistakes in the future by knowing and understanding the mistakes of the past.

Postmortems follow the following simple format:

- What went right?
- What went wrong?
- Suggested improvements

Get the postmortem on e-mail or use a word-processing template. Either way, read it, heed the valuable bit, discard the not-so valuable bits (such as subjective opinions formed without 100 percent of the facts), and put a plan into action.

Milestone Acceptance Tests

One of the simplest and most flexible ways I've found to structure a game development project is through the use of milestone acceptance tests (MATs). The process and procedure reads something like what appears in the list below, but I'll explain why a producer should implement this process even if it is not formalized in the development agreement.

The goal of the MAT is to plan and allow for the dynamic aspects of entertainment software development. This procedure allows the publisher and the developer to respond to changes in the product focus, market, or specific gameplay direction without sacrificing time renegotiating contract specifics or milestone deliverable definitions.

The MAT procedure:

1. Milestone X (usually an early milestone at the end of pre-production) defines the overall goals for the project. The final creative and technical designs are submitted and approved.

2. Subsequent milestone deliverables definitions include basic templates and some general criteria as well as an outline of a specific number of features to be completed by a certain date.

3. The specific details of which game or engine features, art assets, and other deliverables due in the next milestone are submitted prior to the contractual due date. This is called the *Milestone Acceptance Test Criteria*. This clearly describes what will be delivered in the next milestone and what is agreed upon by the parties.

4. When the milestone is submitted to the publisher, the Milestone Acceptance Test Criteria is used as a checklist or test plan to confirm that the game features, art assets, and specific details of the deliverables are delivered as agreed.

5. The procedure allows the publisher to accurately compare the described list of total deliverables, including art assets, game features, and other deliverables to what is actually delivered. This type of checklist procedure is extremely effective in measuring the value of work compared to costs.

If you can get this language included in your development agreement, that's the best thing to do. But barring that circumstance, I highly recommend developing these procedures on an informal basis between the developer and the publisher. If each party can agree to specific criteria by which a milestone is accepted and complete, then there should rarely be cause for disagreement or dispute. It ensures clear goals are defined by the leads on the development teams and solidifies the challenges for the month into a list that's one page long. As a producer at a developer, you should never submit a milestone that you think is going to fail. And, if you're using the MAT procedure listed previously, you should be able to tell if it is going to fail before you submit it.

Looking In from the Outside

In completing the research for this book, I talked to a lot of people in the video game industry. And, naturally, everyone had their opinions about good producers and some not-so-good producers. The following list describes some of the common themes that came up when discussing this book with industry professionals:

- Be a good risk manager. Understand the risks and find ways to the solutions when required.
- Integrity is key. The team must believe in you and what you say.
- Cut features early and often. More features equals more overtime.
- Shield the team from the external flak (management, marketing, and administrative issues that don't concern the game).
- Never lie. But if they don't ask, don't always offer an answer.
- Don't sacrifice team morale for achievement.
- Work to keep proprietary tools to a minimum.
- Reuse tools and technology whenever possible, but don't make that a gating criterion for whether you'll be working on a great game.
- Treat people well. Small amounts of beer and go-cart racing can go a long way!
- Take time to get to know everyone's name on the team. Know something about that person. That's the most important knowledge a producer can hold.
- Producers buy the drinks.

Those are just the general guidelines that you should consider adopting for a successful and less stressful daily habit. An interview with a strong and reasonable programmer is included here so that you can read for yourself some of the indications provided by the team and so that mistakes of the past are not repeated in future projects.

Interview with Nick Waanders, Programmer

Nick Waanders is an industry professional having worked at several game developers in Europe and in North America. He provided some valuable feedback on producers.

Q: If you could convey to the industry (especially producers of video games), what is the one set of tools or knowledge that you value most highly in a producer?

A: Be there to help the team, not to drive the team. If people respect you, and you respect your people, it will be good for your product. There is no bigger de-motivator than thinking your boss is an idiot. It's all about the integrity again. Don't be a wiseass; you're probably working with really clever people, and they will figure you out in no time.

Q: What is the most important trait a producer can display in their interactions with programmers?

A: Buckets of money! No, seriously though, I think it's important to pose the problem to the programmer, and let him figure out what the options are. The programmer will know what will fit in the current code base, and will also have a better idea of how long it will take to put in. Make sure that you risk-manage each request. For example, in Europe the producer at one point insisted that we needed extra mini-games. We told him that it would take a lot of time and effort to create those mini-games, but he insisted that they should be made. In the end, the games played a minor part in the game, but they took about 40 percent of the total creation time spent on the (unpublished, I wonder why) product. This was a bad investment of the team's time.

Q: Can you give an example of when you worked with a producer who was committed to excellence and how that positively impacted their product? Why did this event stand out in your mind?

A: The producer (Jonathan Dowdeswell) is one of the reasons why the team worked really well on Dawn of War. He was always committed to catch the biggest problems/risks first. The closer we came to the finish date, the smaller the tolerance for risk was. So when some new feature request popped up, he would sit down with all the leads and assess the risk involved. If it was too big, it would simply get cut. There was no emotional attachment to the [cut] feature, there was just emotional attachment to the total product. I think this really made it a goal-driven process, and that really projected on the team.

Q: What are some of the common mistakes producers make, based upon your experience and how might others learn from this observation?

A: I think the biggest break of trust is speaking directly for the publisher, without making clear that you put the team first. Do this one too many times, and the team will think that you haven't done all you can to prevent something big to impact on the team.

If there are vastly different ideas about a subject, the best way to approach a lead programmer about this is by having logical arguments. This may sound obvious, but programmers think mostly purely logically. What this also means though is that you have to be able to formulate all your reasons into logical "speak."

If the subject is about how to implement a certain piece of code, then you should trust the lead programmer. For example, on my previous roles a producer would come by and say: "We want this and that in the game, and I think it shouldn't take too much time. So when can you have it done?" More often than not, the simplest thing in a producer's mind is insanely difficult to program. Any "insert magic here" in your examples will most likely prove to be incredibly difficult. What I think I am saying is that instead of saying how long you think it will take, it would be better to let the programmer come up with possible solutions and estimated times.

Q: What tools do you think that producers underutilize or should do more research about, which would make the lead programmer's job easier?

A: Just have a basic understanding of what the tools do that your team uses. Even if you've never seen a program that your people use, just ask what it's for and what it does. When tracking accomplished tasks, I personally prefer tracking of tasks just by e-mail or a weekly meeting. This way, everybody talks to everybody else at least once a week. Every producer should read *Debugging the Development Process*, published by Microsoft Press. It's about programming items, but it's relevant to any process, and it has a plethora of really interesting statements and views. Any producer who has read that book earns points of respect from programmers.

The Final Word

This chapter outlined the key tools and procedures that make the daily life of a producer easier and more manageable. It is not possible to include everything that a producer could possibly use, but some of the best methods that are found around the industry are included. Pick and choose what works for you and your project. There is rarely a one-size-fits-all solution for anything in game development.

CHAPTER 9

GAME DEVELOPMENT FINANCIALS

The game industry is a huge business. In 2002, it was a $16.9 billion (USD) industry worldwide. Today, it is fast approaching $20 billion annually and climbing. It is important to remember that no matter how fun it is to work in the video game industry, or what artistic and creative drive is required to be successful, it is about making money. That's why it is called a business. To reach a commercial success, a video game project must follow a budget that corresponds to the development. This section discusses how to prepare a budget, as well as how to create and review financial statements, including a P&L (Profit and Loss) statement for each product. A producer must think of each product as its own business and the brand as the larger business. To be successful, a producer must also be a good businessman and financial manager.

Creating a Budget

Often the easiest part of a game to create, the budget is actually one of the most important parts to keep updated and revised as the project progresses. The budget tracks all of the expenses related to or charged against the project. This includes wages, benefits, external expenses, employee benefits, travel, advance royalty payments, licensing fees, and many other charges. So, how does a producer create a budget in the first place? The following steps go into creating a budget that's reasonable, accurate, and flexible.

First consider that the rules for creating a proposed budget are somewhat ill-defined in some businesses, although most publicly traded publishers have a very clean and time-tested process. Understand that after the proposed budget is approved, that's the actual budget that your performance is measured against. Because the major part of the budget is the salary and wage costs associated with the team working on the game, you must complete the scheduling process first, as that is the biggest influence in your budget. Although scheduling is an ongoing process, the critical issue is being able to predict when the game will be done.

In the Ideal World

The ideal scenario is for the game to be fully designed first—then you'd have all of the information necessary to understand the resource and staffing requirements for your product. But in the real world, especially when following the Front Loaded Development Model (discussed in Chapter 8), it is very hard to predict what resources are needed until after the proof of concept phase and the prototype has been completed. Therefore, it is recommended that a budget be revisited at several key points during the product's development process.

Naturally, the budget is first considered at the proposal and high-concept stage, when the idea has sparked enough enthusiasm to consider moving the concept forward. The second occasion for the budget revision is when the proof of concept (POC) is functioning and the design iteration process is under way. Use this process as a valuable gauge as to whether you're even close to the right numbers included in the budget. Throughout the iteration process, re-evaluate the budget and schedule. After the POC and the prototype are completed, update the budget for the greenlight meeting with every item that you think you'll need to complete the game and a bit more for safety's sake.

While development continues, constantly manage the budget to ensure that the financial resources are properly invested. The budget might need to be revisited and changed midway through development depending on any approved feature change orders and testing requirements. When the game is complete and commercially released, review the proposed budget and compare it to the actual costs to complete the game. This should be part of any producer's postmortem process. Although it might seem straightforward, it is a difficult process to manage.

At the High-Concept Stage

Regardless of whether you're a producer at a publisher or a developer, you have a big influence on the budget of any game. You can take a few steps to ensure that this influence is positive and results in allocating sufficient financial resources to accomplish the goals of the essence statement.

At the high-concept stage, discuss the scope of the high concept with experienced people and get estimates from those who are expected to complete the project. At this stage, estimates are all that are possible to gather. Determine whether this project schedule will take

18 months, 24 months, or even 30 months, along with how many people are required to work on the necessary systems. Team sizes of 25, 50, or even 75 make a huge difference in project budgets. So, the goal of the producer is to target these two metrics to get an idea of the project size being considered.

Talking to experienced producers, team members, and other industry professionals who have managed a similar project in size and scope is one of the fundamental steps at this stage of the budget evaluation process. Use their feedback and experience to gauge where the project you're considering should be. Review the design concept and form an intimate familiarity with the goals of the project. Then consider the recommended technology, third-party software licenses, and any new production processes that might be required for the project. As an educated guess, that's about the best that can be done at the high-concept stage unless you're working on a sequel project or within an established brand, using an established technology with a proven team that's worked together before.

The goal at the high-concept stage is to determine whether this is a $3, $5, $10, or $15 million project. Then work to reduce the scope as required by your financial guidelines. Reducing scope and focusing a concept is easy to do at the early stages. The goal of budget preparation at this point is to get a commitment to fund the project through pre-production and to the greenlight meeting. Commonly, proof of concepts and first playable prototypes are funded for a period of two to three months at a cost of several hundred thousand dollars.

note

A good rule of thumb in the video game industry is that a project costs approximately $10,000 (USD) per month per person on the team. Although the actual value might be more or less depending on the team, where they're based, and what technology they're using, it is a reasonable metric to use for estimating purposes. For example, if a project is 24 months long and requires 24 people, that would be approximately 24x24 = 480x$10,000 = $4.8 million. Although most people realize that they won't need 24 people on a project at the beginning, toward the end of the project, there might be a lot more than 24 people; it is a good average to use for estimating purposes.

The Buckshot Approach

One of the approaches used by publishers and game developers alike is to start three or even five projects with the expectation that two will be canceled after the pre-production phase. This allows the publisher to spread the financial risk between three projects under the guise that the last remaining project will pay for the expense of the other projects in pre-production. For example, it is common to invest $500,000 in taking a proof of concept to a first playable prototype. If this is done three times, the total cost is $1.5 million. But if two of the three projects are canceled, the surviving project should be successful enough to earn back the $1 million invested in the other two canceled projects. This approach is used to manage risk across a large portfolio of games, so that millions of dollars and time is not invested in anything but the strongest titles that have the best chance of success in the market.

Establish a Foundation During Pre-Production

During pre-production, work closely with the development team to plan for the ideal scenario. Outline the highest goals for the project. Use this time to push the envelope of what is possible and producible. Outline everything that you think you'll need and more. Fill in the details on the budget as ideas start to converge around a producible and exciting game concept. *Agile Project Management* refers to this as the Speculate phase, followed closely by the Explore phase, and that's exactly what happens. Worry about the compromises later, in both the game design and the financial resources. By focusing on the ideal scenario, the possibility of achieving goals that might have been assumed to be improbable or impossible opens up. In encouraging the team to aim high, you're setting a high standard as a leader. Although the team might not reach all of the goals set out in the pre-production phase, if an ideal goal is never explored, it can never be achieved.

The important part is to start putting ideas down on paper, estimations of when certain features can be completed, what type of experience would be very valuable to have on the team, and how many people are going to be needed and when. If you recall, the WBS process mentioned in Chapter 8 is an important part of this estimation and helps bring together a complete, defendable, and comprehensive budget. By putting these things down on paper, the process creates thousands of unanswered questions as the team considers all of the possibilities and problems that were previously transparent.

note

While you're putting the budget and schedule on paper, don't forget to include such things as allocating time for benefits, holidays, vacations, trade shows, E3, the Game Developer's Conference, and PR trips and other travel expenses, as well as time away from managing the project.

Take the comprehensive WBS sheets and the overall schedule and determine the resources required to complete the project. For right now, just consider the staffing requirements for this project. You'll discover some of the other costs that go into a budget later on.

The human resources considered should be categorized into man months (the number of people required multiplied by the number of months on the project) as follows:

- Designers
- Programmers
- Producers
- Artists
- Sound
- Music
- Quality assurance

After you have man-month estimates for each of these fields, you can move onto the next step, estimating costs.

The goal of the budget developed in the pre-production phase is to determine as accurately as possible how much money is required to complete the project on schedule and still have it be a great game that is commercially feasible. The budget that's prepared and approved at the end of this process is usually the one that is used as a measurement for the performance of a development team and their producer. Table 9.1 shows some various monthly costs. (These are examples only.)

Table 9.1 Sample Estimate Budget (Beginning of Pre-production)

Cost Center	Monthly Cost	Man Months	Total
Design			
Designer (Level 1)	$5000	24.00	$120,000.00
Designer (Level 2)	$4000	20.00	$80,000.00
Designer (Level 3)	$3000	20.00	$60,000.00
Designer (Level 4)	$2500	18.00	$45,000.00
Art			
Artist (Level 1)	$5000	24.00	$120,000.00
Artist (Level 2)	$4000	20.00	$80,000.00
Artist (Level 1)	$3000	20.00	$60,000.00
Artist (Level 2)	$2500	18.00	$45,000.00
Programming			
Programmer (Level 1)	$5000	24.00	$120,000.00
Programmer (Level 2)	$4000	20.00	$80,000.00
Programmer (Level 1)	$3000	20.00	$60,000.00
Programmer (Level 2)	$2500	18.00	$45,000.00
Sound and Music			
Sound Effect Supervisor	$3500	18.00	$63,000.00
Composer	See Fixed Costs		
Integration	$3000	8.00	$24,000.00
Quality Assurance			
Lead QA	$3250	12	$39,000.00
QA Personnel	$2500	5	$12,500.00
QA Personnel	$2500	5	$12,500.00
QA Personnel	$2500	5	$12,500.00
QA Personnel	$2500	4	$10,000.00
QA Personnel	$2500	4	$10,000.00
QA Personnel	$2500	4	$10,000.00
QA Personnel	$2500	3	$7,500.00
QA Personnel	$2500	3	$7,500.00
QA Personnel	$2500	3	$7,500.00
GRAND TOTAL			**$1,131,000.00**

Estimating Costs

If you've completed the pre-production estimating process and you're confident that you have a solid game concept and the workings of a hit title, the rest of the process should be easy, right? Well, there's a lot more work to do in creating a budget that is approved so that the development team can realize a dream concept and bring it to market. In as much detail as the WBS provides for the game's development schedule, that level of detail is required for the budget.

A Microsoft Excel financial template comes in handy at this stage of the process. That template includes several sheets, but the budget itself consists of only a few sheets: Salary and Wages, Fixed and Incidental Costs, and Capital Expenses.

An example of the template is shown here as Figure 9.1 Break down the costs on a monthly basis because almost every business's financial situation is set up to be reconciled on a monthly basis.

Salaries and Wages

One of the easiest ways to set up a budget that includes relatively accurate costs for salaries and wages is to use pay grade scales. Although this is not 100% accurate, it can get fairly close to reasonable and accurate numbers. Work with your Finance department to determine some average pay grades within your organization. This eliminates the need to disclose specific salary figures for the entire team.

Second, I recommend against including benefits and vacation accrual directly in the salaries and wages cost because it causes the budget to reflect inaccurate costs. Benefits and vacation accrual is different for everyone and there's no way for the producer to influence this amount. Therefore, the benefits and vacation accrual should be reflected on the Fixed and Incidental Cost sheet (discussed later).

note

Be certain to include an allocation and adjustment for performance review salary increases as well as merit increases. You definitely want to be able to justify those types of increases to your executive team when the right team member(s) warrant it.

The salary and wage sheet of your budget should look similar to that in Figure 9.1 as the team completes the pre-production phase and has a first playable prototype ready to demonstrate.

Happy Games Corp
Projected Wages (Excludes Benefits)
Last Updated: 11-Dec-04

Category	Role	1 Jan-04	2 Feb-04	3 Mar-04	4 Apr-04	5 May-04	6 Jun-04	7 Jul-04	8 Aug-04	9 Sep-04	10 Oct-04	11 Nov-04	12 Dec-04	13 Jan-05	14 Feb-05	15 Mar-05	16 Apr-05	17 May-05	18 Jun-05
Artists	Art Director	6,523	6,523	6,523	6,523	6,523	6,523	6,523	6,523	6,523	6,523	6,523	6,523	6,523	7,023	6,786	6,785	6,785	6,785
Artists	Artist (Level 1)	5,000	3,817	3,817	3,817	3,817	3,817	3,817	3,817	3,817	3,817	3,817	3,817	3,817	3,817	3,817	3,817	3,817	3,817
Artists	Artist (Level 2)	4,000	3,500	3,500	3,500	3,500	3,500	3,500	3,500	3,500	3,500	3,500	3,500	3,500	3,500	3,500	3,500	3,500	3,500
Artists	Artist (Level 2)	4,000	2,583	2,583	2,583	2,583	2,583	2,583	2,583	2,583	2,583	2,583	2,583	2,583	2,583	2,583	2,583	2,583	2,583
Artists	Artist (Level 2)	4,000	5,400	5,400	5,400	5,400	5,400	5,400	5,400	5,400	5,400	5,400	5,400	5,400	5,400	5,400	5,400	5,400	5,400
Artists	Artist (Level 3)	3,000	3,425	3,425	3,425	3,425	3,425	3,425	3,425	3,425	3,425	3,425	3,425	3,425	3,425	3,425	3,425	3,425	3,425
Artists	Artist (Level 3)	3,000	4,367	4,367	4,367	4,367	4,367	4,367	4,367	4,367	4,367	4,367	4,367	4,367	4,367	4,367	4,367	4,367	4,367
Artists	Artist (Level 3)	3,000	5,208	5,208	5,208	5,208	5,208	5,208	5,208	5,208	5,208	5,208	5,208	5,208	5,208	5,208	5,208	5,208	5,208
Artists	Open - Texturer	2,500	5,200	5,200	5,200	5,200	5,200	5,200	5,200	5,200	5,200	5,200	5,200	5,200	5,200	5,200	5,200	5,200	5,200
Artists	Internship																		
Artists	Subtotal	35,023	40,023	40,023	40,023	40,023	40,023	40,023	40,023	40,023	40,023	40,023	40,023	40,023	40,523	40,285	40,285	40,285	40,285
Designer	Lead Designer	7,000	9,000	9,000	9,000	9,000	9,000	9,000	9,000	9,000	9,000	9,000	9,000	9,000	9,000	9,000	9,000	9,000	9,000
Designer	Designer (Level 1)	5,000	5,167	5,167	5,167	5,167	5,167	5,167	5,167	5,167	5,167	5,167	5,684	5,684	5,684	5,684	5,684	5,684	5,684
Designer	Designer (Level 2)	4,000	5,167	5,167	5,167	5,167	5,167	5,167	5,167	5,167	5,167	5,167	5,684	5,684	5,684	5,684	5,684	5,684	5,684
Designer	Designer (Level 3)	3,000	5,167	5,167	5,167	5,167	5,167	5,167	5,167	5,167	5,167	5,167	5,684	5,684	5,684	5,684	5,684	5,684	5,684
Designer	Designer (Level 4)	2,500	5,167	5,167	5,167	5,167	5,167	5,167	5,167	5,167	5,167	5,167	5,684	5,684	5,684	5,684	5,684	5,684	5,684
Designer/Script Wr	Contract Writer	5,000	5,000	7,500															
Designer	Subtotal	26,500	34,668	37,168	29,668	29,668	29,668	29,668	29,668	29,668	29,668	29,668	31,736	34,235	34,235	34,235	34,235	34,235	34,235
Programmer	Lead Programmer	8,772	8,772	8,772	8,772	8,772	8,772	8,772	8,772	8,772	8,772	8,772	8,772	8,772	8,772	8,772	8,772	8,772	8,772
Programmer	Programmer (Level 1)	6,417	6,417	6,417	6,417	6,417	6,417	6,417	6,417	6,417	6,417	6,417	6,417	6,417	6,417	6,417	6,417	6,417	6,417
Programmer	Programmer (Level 2)	7,417	7,417	7,417	7,417	7,417	7,417	7,417	7,417	7,417	7,417	7,417	7,417	7,417	7,417	7,417	7,417	7,417	7,417
Programmer	Programmer (Level 3)	7,417	7,417	7,417	7,417	7,417	7,417	7,417	7,417	7,417	7,417	7,417	7,417	7,417	7,417	7,417	7,417	7,417	7,417
Programmer	Programmer (Level 3)	7,417	7,417	7,417	7,417	7,417	7,417	7,417	7,417	7,417	7,417	7,417	7,417	7,417	7,417	7,417	7,417	7,417	7,417
Programmer	Programmer (Level 4)	5,308	5,308	5,308	5,308	5,308	5,308	5,308	5,308	5,308	5,308	5,308	5,308	5,308	5,308	5,308	5,308	5,308	5,308
Programmer	Programmer (Level 4)	8,558	8,558	8,558	8,558	8,558	8,558	8,558	8,558	8,558	8,558	8,558	8,558	8,558	8,558	8,558	8,558	8,558	8,558
Programmer	Programmer (Level 4)	5,500	5,500	5,500	5,500	5,500	5,500	5,500	5,500	5,500	5,500	5,500	5,500	5,500	5,500	5,500	5,500	5,500	5,500
Programmer	Open	5,500	5,500	5,500	5,500	5,500	5,500	5,500	5,500	5,500	5,500	5,500	5,500	5,500	5,500	5,500	5,500	5,500	5,500
Programmer	Open	5,500	5,500	5,500	5,500	5,500	5,500	5,500	5,500	5,500	5,500	5,500	5,500	5,500	5,500	5,500	5,500	5,500	5,500
Programmer	Internship																		
Programmer	Subtotal	67,806	67,806	67,806	67,806	67,806	67,806	67,806	67,806	67,806	67,806	67,806	67,806	67,806	67,806	67,806	67,806	67,806	67,806
Sound	In-Game Sound FX								5,000	5,000	5,000	5,000	5,000	5,000	5,000	5,000	5,000	5,000	5,000
Sound	Placeholder VO								500	500	500	500	500	500	500	500	500	500	500
Sound	Other SFX								500	500	500	500	500	500	500	500	500	500	500
Sound	Localization Mgmt								1,000	1,000	1,000	1,000	1,000	1,000	1,000	1,000	1,000	1,000	1,000
Sound	Studio Rental/Talent								2,000	2,000	2,000	2,000	2,000	2,000	2,000	2,000	2,000	2,000	2,000
Sound	Subtotal								9,000	9,000	9,000	9,000	9,000	9,000	9,000	9,000	9,000	9,000	9,000
Producer	Producer (Internal Level 1)	30,833	13,333	13,333	13,333	13,333	13,333	14,667	13,333	13,333	13,333	13,333	13,333	14,667	13,333	13,333	13,333	13,333	14,667
Ast. Producer	Assistant Producer (Internal Lev)	3,685	3,685	3,685	3,685	3,685	3,685	3,685	3,685	3,685	3,685	3,685	3,685	3,685	3,685	3,685	3,685	3,685	3,685
Producer	Subtotal	34,518	17,018	17,018	17,018	17,018	17,018	18,352	17,018	17,018	17,018	17,018	17,018	18,352	17,018	17,018	17,018	17,018	18,352
Quality Assurance	Lead Quality Assurance Engine	3,500	3,500	3,500	3,500	3,500	3,500	3,500	3,500	3,500	3,500	3,500	3,500	3,500	3,500	3,500	3,500	3,500	3,500
Quality Assurance	Open	2,500	2,500	2,500	2,500	2,500	2,500	2,500	2,500	2,500	2,500	2,500	2,500	2,500	2,500	2,500	2,500	2,500	2,500
Quality Assurance	Subtotal	6,000	6,000	6,000	6,000	6,000	6,000	6,000	6,000	6,000	6,000	6,000	6,000	6,000	6,000	6,000	6,000	6,000	6,000
	Total	134,924	125,492	127,992	120,492	120,492	120,492	121,826	129,492	129,492	129,492	131,569	131,569	135,392	134,069	134,069	134,069	134,069	135,392
		26	26	26	26	26	26	26	26	26	26	26	26	26	26	26	26	26	26
		26	52	78	104	130	156	182	208	234	260	286	312	338	364	390	416	442	468
Outside Contractors		7,500	5,000	7,500	20,000	20,000	20,000						20,000	22,500	22,500	2,500	2,500	2,500	2,500
Composer Music	Composer	7,500	6,000	7,500	20,000	20,000	20,000						20,000	2,500	2,500	2,500	2,500	2,500	2,500
Contract Writer	Composer													2,500	20,000	2,500	2,500	2,500	2,500

Figure 9.1
Salary and Wage template in Microsoft Excel.

As shown in Figure 9.1, the costs are forecast by month. Also, the level of each team member is denoted in the budget. Open positions are noted as Open. Also included on the salary and wages sheet are external costs to contractors (such as art production houses, sound contractors, composers, contract writers, and voice-over actors) and any other costs over which the producer has direct control or influence.

Fixed and Incidental Costs

Fixed and incidental costs include everything else to run a company. Examples of these costs include everything from the lease payments on the building to the benefits for employees to the cost of paper, electricity, and everything else. Work with your finance person to get an allocation of overhead in all of these areas, but be as specific as possible. This helps prevent hidden costs from suddenly showing up as charged against your project. Relocation and recruiting fees are ones that I scrutinize closely when reviewing the costs charged against my brand.

This sheet is shown on the overall budget sheet in Figure 9.2. The costs subtotal from the Salary and Wages sheet rolls over and is linked directly to this sheet.

Regarding the fixed and incidental costs, the producer needs to be mainly concerned with any costs that are specific to the team (such as required third-party software licenses) as well as required travel, trade shows, Game Developer's Conference fees, Siggraph, and other related industry events. Be certain your budget includes the allocations necessary so you can send your team members to the industry events that count. As shown in Figure 9.2, the Fixed and Incidental costs are forecasted by month.

note

Most large companies (like publishers) do not provide "exact" figures for overhead or fixed costs. Generally, there are financial guidelines that a producer must account for. For example, one programmer may be allocated at a $75,000 wage, plus 32 percent for overhead and benefits. However, at a smaller company (like game developers) it is important to clearly examine the financial details.

OVERHEAD								
Advertising	-	125	125	125	125	125	125	125
Amortization & Depreciation		6,600	6,600	6,600	6,600	6,600	6,600	6,600
Consultancy		18,748	12,536	13,342	12,870	13,454	12,870	12,353
Lease Payments		375	375	375	375	375	375	375
Books & Subscriptions		100	100	100	100	100	100	100
Courses and Training		500	500	500	500	500	500	500
Internet Service		4,333	4,333	4,333	4,333	4,333	4,333	4,333
Network		.	.	.	.	.	.	.
Biz Travel, Trade Shows & Conferences		.	.	15,000	.	15,000	.	5,000
Fees, Dues, Courses & Training		100	100	100	100	100	100	100
Delivery, Freight, Express		250	250	250	250	250	250	250
Fuel Costs		200	200	200	200	200	200	200
Insurance		1,100	1,100	1,100	1,100	1,100	1,100	1,100
Interest, Bank Charges		3,300	3,300	3,300	3,300	3,300	3,300	3,300
Tempary Housing		1,250	1,250	1,250	1,250	1,250	1,250	1,250
Employee goodwill		937	937	937	937	937	937	937
Maintenance & Repairs		945	945	945	945	945	945	945
Management, Administration Fees		.	.	.	.	.	.	.
Meals & Entertainment		2,500	2,500	2,500	2,500	2,500	2,500	2,500
Motor Vehicle Expense		225	225	225	225	225	225	225
Relocation/Recruitment		26,585	16,000	16,000	16,000	16,000	16,000	16,000
Office Expenses		900	900	900	900	900	900	900
Supplies		1,333	1,333	1,333	1,333	1,333	1,333	1,333
Legal, Accounting, Professional		5,200	5,200	5,200	5,200	5,200	5,200	5,200
Rent		17,000	17,000	17,000	17,000	17,000	17,000	17,000
Travel		3,100	3,100	3,100	3,100	3,100	3,100	3,100
Telephone, Utilities		500	500	500	500	500	500	500
Miscellaneous		300	300	300	300	300	300	300
Carry Forward Existing Leases		.	.	.	.	.	.	.
OVERHEAD	-	96,506	79,709	95,515	80,043	95,627	80,043	84,526
% Overhead		20.1%	23.8%	26.8%	23.3%	26.6%	23.3%	25.6%
PROJECT COSTS (USD)	-	480,520	334,754	356,268	343,671	359,255	343,671	329,865
NET INCOME		(480,520)	(334,754)	(356,268)	(343,671)	(359,255)	(343,671)	(329,865)
# of Developers (Includes Contractors)	26.0	26.0	26.0	26.0	26.0	26.0	26.0	26.0

POC Estimation \ **Game_Budget** \ S&W \ Capital Plan /

Figure 9.2
Fixed and Incidental template in Microsoft Excel

Capital Costs

Capital costs include items that are one-time purchases for the team, and can be things such as the following:

- Team workstations
- PC upgrades (RAM, video cards, hard drives, and motherboards)
- Software for artists/programmers: 3D Studio Max 4.0
- Other software applications: Photoshop, Premiere, and third-party software tools
- Server
- Communications: Phone system expansion
- Communications: Incremental phone sets
- Furniture: Desks/chairs
- Source (Version) control software
- Additional software: Microsoft Office, ACDSee, and so on

The key rule that producers should remember about capital equipment is that the better equipment that the team has, the more efficiently they can work. Systems that take longer to compile, render animation, or crash often do so because they're overtaxed and can cost a lot more in the long run.

Rolling It All Together

When the Salary and Wages and Fixed and Incidental sheets are complete, roll both sheets together to form the overall game development budget. It should total by month. Then, you can gain a relatively accurate understanding of how much the project costs on a monthly basis, by contribution area (art, design, programming, music and sound) and as a total. By examining this data using different metrics, such as time versus work completed, or by external costs versus internal costs, or even by internal art production costs versus external art production costs, a producer can find the most efficient allocation of the financial resources (see Figure 9.3).

Happy Games Corp
Full Production
Last Updated: **11-Dec-04**

Month	Dec-04	Jan-05	Feb-05	Mar-05	Apr-05	May-05	Jun-05	Jul-05	Aug-05	Sep-05	Oct-05	Nov-05	Dec-05	Jan-06	Feb-06
Month #		1	2	3	4	5	6	7	8	9	10	11	12	13	14
DIRECT LABOR COSTS															
Artists		35,023	40,023	40,023	40,023	40,023	40,023	40,023	40,023	40,023	40,023	40,023	40,023	40,023	40,523
Designer		26,500	34,688	37,168	29,688	29,688	29,688	29,688	29,688	29,688	29,688	31,735	31,735	34,235	34,235
Programmers		67,806	67,806	67,806	67,806	67,806	67,806	67,806	67,806	67,806	67,806	67,806	67,806	67,806	67,806
Sound (Excluding Contractors)									9,000	9,000	9,000	9,000	9,000	9,000	9,000
Producer		34,518	17,018	17,018	17,018	17,018	17,018	18,352	17,018	17,018	17,018	17,018	17,018	18,352	17,018
Quality Assurance		6,000	6,000	6,000	6,000	6,000	6,000	6,000	6,000	6,000	6,000	6,000	6,000	6,000	6,000
Admin		29,330	29,330	29,330	29,330	29,330	29,330	29,330	29,330	29,330	29,330	29,330	29,330	29,330	29,330
Benefits & Vacation (28.33%)		56,427	55,200	55,908	53,783	53,783	53,783	54,161	56,333	56,333	56,333	56,918	56,918	58,004	57,768
Voice Talent															
User Manual - Contractor															
Outside Services		7,500	5,000	7,500	20,000	20,000	20,000						20,000	22,500	22,500
Capital		120,911													
3rd Party Software Licenses															
DIRECT COSTS		384,014	255,044	260,753	263,628	263,628	263,628	245,339	255,178	255,178	255,178	257,830	277,930	285,249	284,180
OVERHEAD															
Advertising		125	125	125	125	125	125	125	125	125	125	125	125	125	125
Amortization & Depreciation		6,600	6,600	6,600	6,600	6,600	6,600	6,600	6,600	6,600	6,600	6,600	6,600	6,600	6,600
Consultancy		18,748	12,536	13,342	12,870	13,454	12,870	12,353	12,541	12,113	11,919	12,217	12,800	13,089	13,047
Lease Payments		375	375	375	375	375	375	375	375	375	375	375	375	375	375
Books & Subscriptions		100	100	100	100	100	100	100	100	100	100	100	100	100	100
Courses and Training		500	500	500	500	500	500	500	500	500	500	500	500	500	500
Internet Service		4,333	4,333	4,333	4,333	4,333	4,333	4,333	4,333	4,333	4,333	4,333	4,333	4,333	4,333
Network															
Biz Travel, Trade Shows & Conferences				15,000		15,000		5,000		5,000		5,000			
Fees, Dues, Courses & Training		100	100	100	100	100	100	100	100	100	100	100	100	100	100
Delivery, Freight, Express		250	250	250	250	250	250	250	250	250	250	250	250	250	250
Fuel Costs		200	200	200	200	200	200	200	200	200	200	200	200	200	200
Insurance		1,100	1,100	1,100	1,100	1,100	1,100	1,100	1,100	1,100	1,100	1,100	1,100	1,100	1,100
Interest, Bank Charges		3,300	3,300	3,300	3,300	3,300	3,300	3,300	3,300	3,300	3,300	3,300	3,300	3,300	3,300
Tempory Housing		1,250	1,250	1,250	1,250	1,250	1,250	1,250	1,250	1,250	1,250	1,250	1,250	1,250	1,250
Employee goodwill		937	937	937	937	937	937	937	937	937	937	937	937	937	937
Maintenance & Repairs		945	945	945	945	945	945	945	945	945	945	945	945	945	945
Management, Administration Fees															
Meals & Entertainment		2,500	2,500	2,500	2,500	2,500	2,500	2,500	2,500	2,500	2,500	2,500	2,500	2,500	2,500
Motor Vehicle Expense		225	225	225	225	225	225	225	225	225	225	225	225	225	225
Relocation/Recruitment		26,585	16,000	16,000	16,000	16,000	16,000	16,000	16,000						
Office Expenses		900	900	900	900	900	900	900	900	900	900	900	900	900	900
Supplies		1,333	1,333	1,333	1,333	1,333	1,333	1,333	1,333	1,333	1,333	1,333	1,333	1,333	1,333
Legal, Accounting, Professional		5,200	5,200	5,200	5,200	5,200	5,200	5,200	5,200	5,200	5,200	5,200	5,200	5,200	5,200
Rent		17,000	17,000	17,000	17,000	17,000	17,000	17,000	17,000	17,000	17,000	17,000	17,000	17,000	17,000
Travel		3,100	3,100	3,100	3,100	3,100	3,100	3,100	3,100	3,100	3,100	3,100	3,100	3,100	3,100
Telephone, Utilities		500	500	500	500	500	500	500	500	500	500	500	500	500	500
Miscellaneous		300	300	300	300	300	300	300	300	300	300	300	300	300	300
Carry Forward Existing Leases															
OVERHEAD		96,506	79,709	95,515	80,043	95,627	80,043	84,526	79,714	68,287	63,092	68,390	63,973	64,262	64,220
% Overhead		*20.1%*	*23.8%*	*26.8%*	*23.3%*	*26.6%*	*23.3%*	*25.6%*	*23.8%*	*21.1%*	*19.8%*	*21.0%*	*18.7%*	*18.4%*	*18.4%*
PROJECT COSTS (USD)		480,520	334,754	356,268	343,671	359,255	343,671	329,865	334,892	323,464	318,270	326,220	341,803	343,511	348,400
NET INCOME		(480,520)	(334,754)	(356,268)	(343,671)	(359,255)	(343,671)	(329,865)	(334,892)	(323,464)	(318,270)	(326,220)	(341,803)	(343,511)	(348,400)
# of Developers (Includes Contractors)	26.0	26.0	26.0	26.0	26.0	26.0	26.0	26.0	26.0	26.0	26.0	26.0	26.0	26.0	26.0

Figure 9.3
The overall project budget by month. Notice the subtotals by department

Finding the Right Solution

The important parts of a producer's role when it comes to managing the budget for the project are the efficient allocation of resources and finding the right solution. Scheduling is really a by-product of that effort. An effective producer allocates the right tool for the right job. In game development, there isn't any such thing as a crescent wrench to use on all of the loose joints.

One recent example of finding the effective solution is the use of the Sprint engine technology in *Myst III: Exile* and then a similar technology in *Myst IV: Revelation*. This technology allowed the familiar and photorealistic look of the previous *Myst* and *Riven* games, while requiring a relatively low system specification. This allowed a wide range of consumers to be able to enjoy the next chapters of the *Myst* saga. Many developers and industry professionals at the time recommended a new 3D engine that would use the latest technology, but by using an existing engine that was upgraded with a few new features and a rotatable camera, the games were kept accessible to the largest audience and market segment. This was a lot less expensive than developing a real-time, 3D engine from scratch that was specific to adventure games without the speed required by an FPS.

In finding the right solution, a producer must balance the Immutable Law of Time, Resources, and Quality (as discussed in Chapter 3). The right solution is not always more expensive, although it sometimes is. In balancing the financial investment in a video game's development, the producer must keep in mind that if the project takes too long (for example, four years because it has a small team), technology and the market is going to change over that time and the team momentum will be hard to sustain. However, a team that's twice the size might not finish the game in half the time, which would add cost to the project through overtime, bonuses, or other premium pay. Although these are just examples, they are examples of real considerations that a producer must bring to the project.

In actuality, finding the right solution is more like finding the right place on a bell curve (the peak) at which the maximum effectiveness is obtained. A move in either direction decreases effectiveness.

This is the opportunity for a producer to truly demonstrate their talent and find the right solution that is the perfect compromise between cost and effectiveness.

Stopping Feature Creep

One of the primary reasons that video game projects take too long to develop and cost more than was budgeted is feature creep. If you're a producer dealing with an overly ambitious team, one who is driven by perfection, consider establishing ground rules for inclusion of additional features and how feature requests are approved. Establishing a process early in the development cycle for this type of a situation can ensure that you're perceived as being flexible and are relying upon the expertise of others to reach the right decision.

Here's a quick checklist on how to ensure there's the right process in place to minimize feature creep.

- Start a feature request list.
- Categorize the list into art, programming, or gameplay design elements.
- Review the list with the team leads.
- Determine cost, difficulty, benefits, risks, and effects on the schedule.
- Generate options and propose alternatives.
- Make a decision, accepting or rejecting each change, and communicate this decision to everyone.
- Ensure that any accepted changes are documented properly.

Now that the budget has been established into a defendable format, it is time to plug it into a financial model and see how it looks.

Financial Modeling

It is not often that a financial model is not created until the budget is finalized and approved. The reality is that the financial model gets drafted as soon as the POC budget estimate is established. The financial model gets updated as the budget gets updated, just as the game progresses from concept to pre-production to full production to gold master. This section discusses the basics of a financial model, although each publisher has their own model and individual guidelines for each model, depending on genre, platform, and territory.

Components of the Financial Model

Many components make up a video game project's financial model. For example, some financial models have included up to 50 different Excel worksheets that print out 75 pages. The best resources for accurate financial modeling are the finance department and the marketing team. This is their area of expertise, but a producer who knows what's discussed here makes the process easier, complete, and more accurate.

Profit and Loss

The profit and loss (P&L) statement encompasses the units sold, the average sales price, any deductions from sales, the costs of goods and distribution, the profit margins, and many other financial metrics important to evaluating the business opportunity of a video game proposal. To determine these figures, review data from competitive products to determine the unit's sales price and volume as well as previous products in the same genre.

The following is a list of the components of the P&L statement that need to be estimated:

- **Units sales by territory.** The total units sold in the territory.
- **Average selling price (wholesale).** The average selling price from all territories.
- **Unit-based gross revenue.** The total units multiplied by the average selling price.
- **OEM license revenue.** Any revenue from OEM deals.
- **Dilution rate.** The market development funds, bad debt, markdowns and price protection, returns, and stock balances that comprise the dilution rate
- **Net revenue.** The product of the average sales price multiplied by the unit.
- **Cost of goods per unit.** The cost of manufacturing the media, box, manual, and everything else that goes into the game box.
- **Royalty and licensing fees.** The fees due the licensor and developer for working on the product.
- **Total cost of goods.** The total of COGs, royalties, and license fee subtracted from the net revenue.
- **Gross profit.** The total of net revenue minus the total COGs.
- **Gross margin.** The ratio of gross profit to net revenue.
- **Localization.** Any costs associated with localizing the product.
- **Fixed S and M expenses.** The product box, sell sheets, and other fixed marketing costs.
- **Rebate and other variable costs.** The rebates to the consumers.
- **Contribution predevelopment.** The total amount of money contributed toward the company prior to accounting for the development costs.
- **Contribution Gross margin.** The ratio of contribution predevelopment funds to net revenue.
- **Internal development costs.** The internal costs for a publisher associated with the production (such as external producer salaries, QA, manual creation, and so on).
- **External development costs.** The costs of any external development contractors or third parties related to the game's development.
- **Net profit.** The profit that's left when all other costs are subtracted.
- **Contribution Net margin.** The ratio of net profit to net revenue.
- **ROI (CP/total direct costs).** The return on investment expected for the product.

An example of what this P&L statement might look like is shown in Figure 9.4.

SUPER GREAT RACING

	Domestic	UK/ROE	France	Germany	Australia	Holland
Est. Unit Sales (w/o OEM)	620,000	70,000	35,000	35,000	25,000	
Local Street Price (1st Year)	$ 49.95	£ 24.99	F 249	DM 69	$ 69.95	
Avg. Selling Price (Wholesale)	$38.64	$16.49	$16.84	$12.52	$16.31	
Unit Based Gross Revenue	$23,959,580	$1,154,306	$589,427	$438,247	$407,801	
OEM License Revenue						
Dilution Rate	16.0%	12.0%	12.0%	20.0%	10.0%	
Dilution ($s)	$3,833,533	$138,517	$70,731	$87,649	$40,780	
NET REVENUE	$20,126,047	$1,015,789	$518,695	$350,597	$367,021	
ost of Goods						
Matl Per Unit	$3.68	$2.85	$2.85	$2.85	$2.85	
Total Material	$2,281,600	$199,360	$99,680	$99,680	$71,200	
% of Net Revenue	11%	20%	19%	28%	19%	
Freight In/Out Per Unit	$1.46	$1.46	$1.46	$1.46	$1.46	
Total Freight/BMG	$905,200	$102,200	$51,100	$51,100	$36,500	
% of Net Revenue	4%	10%	10%	15%	10%	
Development Roy/Lic Fees	$4,097,138	$189,079	$96,970	$60,942	$68,162	
Design Roy/Lic Fees						
Content Roy/Lic Fees						
Other Roy/Lic Fees						
Total Royalty/License	$4,097,138	$189,079	$96,970	$60,942	$68,162	
% of Net Revenue	20%	19%	19%	17%	19%	
TOTAL COST OF GOODS	$7,283,938	$490,639	$247,750	$211,722	$175,862	
GROSS PROFIT	$12,842,109	$525,150	$270,946	$138,875	$191,159	
GROSS MARGIN	64%	52%	52%	40%	52%	
Localization	$60,000					
% of Net Revenue	0%					
Fixed S&M Expenses	$1,815,000					
Rebate & Other Variable	$2,515,756	$116,816	$49,276	$15,777	$34,867	
Total Dir S&M Expenses	$4,330,756	$116,816	$49,276	$15,777	$34,867	
% of Net Revenue	22%	12%	10%	5%	10%	
CONTRIBUTION Pre R&D	$8,451,353	$408,334	$221,670	$123,098	$156,292	
CONTRIBUTION MARGIN	42%	40%	43%	35%	43%	
Internal Development	$540,825					
External Development						
Total Software Development	$540,825					
% of Net Revenue	3%					
CONTRIBUTION Profit	$7,910,528	$408,334	$221,670	$123,098	$156,292	
CONTRIBUTION MARGIN	39%	40%	43%	35%	43%	
ROI (CP/Total Direct Costs)	65%	67%	75%	54%	74%	

Figure 9.4
A sample P&L statement for a proposed product.

Each company has their own targets for each of these components, but commonly the two major benchmarks are 50 percent gross margin and 28 percent contribution (net profit) margin.

Competitive Analysis and Market Assessment

Two of the key factors that are included in any financial model is an assessment of the market and a competitive analysis. The market assessment is a function of the producer working with the marketing team to determine the demand for the product being proposed and establishing clear data points on which to base their conclusion. This generally comes from market data reports like the TRST report.

NPD Funworld (http://www.npdfunworld.com/) also provides subscribers to their services, market data reports and even a top 10 list by month and territory on their Web site. Draw corollaries between the market and the proposed product. A type of product that is successful in the United States is not necessarily going to be successful in Asia, and vice versa.

Risk Analysis

One critical part of the financial model for any proposed product is a financial risk analysis. This analysis quantifies the risk into three different scenarios and shows how they relate to each other. You should evaluate four different metrics when running a risk analysis.

First comes the proposed scenario and how much money is at risk for this investment. Second is the low-case scenario. (How much money would be lost if this product didn't sell as well as the proposed scenario?) The third is the best scenario (known as high), which sells more than the product is anticipated to sell. The remaining two metrics are break-even units and break-even price. These metrics determine how many units are required to earn the invested money back and the price to which the product can be dropped and not lose money.

- **Proposed scenario.** This is the data directly from the P&L statement.
- **Low scenario.** This is some factor less than the proposed scenario, perhaps 50 percent of the proposed scenario.
- **High scenario.** The high scenario is some factor more than the proposed scenario, perhaps 25 percent higher than the proposed scenario.
- **Break-even units.** Use Excel Goal Seek (found on the Tools menu, then on the Goal Seek submenu) to get contribution profit to zero by changing the total units sold.
- **Break-even price.** Use Excel Goal Seek to change the contribution profit to zero by changing the price value.

An example of this sheet is shown in Figure 9.5.

RISK ASSESSMENT   **SUPER GREAT RACING**

	Proposed	High Scenario	Low Scenario	Breakeven Units	Breakeven Price
Avg. Selling Price (Wholesale)	$40.51	$40.51	$40.51	$40.51	$19.10
Gross Unit Sales	1,715,000	2,572,500	857,500	465,506	1,715,000
Net Revenue	$58,558,981	$87,838,471	$29,279,490	$15,894,784	$27,603,754
COGS:					
Material	$12,051,520	$18,077,280	$6,025,760	$3,271,169	$12,051,520
Royalty/Lic Fees	$10,173,857	$15,260,786	$5,669,000	$5,669,000	$5,669,000
Freight In/Out	$2,503,900	$3,755,850	$1,251,950	$679,639	$2,503,900
Total COGS	$24,729,277	$37,093,916	$12,946,710	$9,619,807	$20,224,420
Gross Profit ($s)	$33,829,704	$50,744,555	$16,332,780	$6,274,977	$7,379,334
Gross Profit %	58%	58%	56%	39%	27%
Other Expenses:					
Int. Development	$540,825	$540,825	$540,825	$540,825	$540,825
Ext. Development	$0	$0	$0	$0	$0
Fixed Selling & Marketing	$4,115,000	$4,115,000	$4,115,000	$4,115,000	$4,115,000
Other	$5,643,120	$8,404,680	$2,881,560	$1,619,152	$2,723,509
Total Other Expenses	$10,298,945	$13,060,505	$7,537,385	$6,274,977	$7,379,334
Contribution Profit ($s)	$23,530,759	$37,684,051	$8,795,396	$0	$0
Contribution Profit (%)	40%	43%	30%	0%	0%

Proposed Scenario Risks and Assumptions:

Assumes 50% of Silent Hill sales

High Scenario Risks and Assumptions:

50% higher than proposed

Low Scenario Risks and Assumptions:

50% of Proposed

Figure 9.5
Sample risk analysis sheet.

Revenue Projection

You should note a few things about revenue projections. First, not every title is going to sell as well as *Tony Hawk*, *Grand Theft Auto*, *StarCraft*, or the *Myst* series. Second, the top titles in each genre take more than 60 percent of the revenue for that market segment. Therefore, any competitive product needs to be positioned as a top-product contender. Focus the revenue projection on just enough units that can be reasonably justified without setting the expectations too high for this proposed game. It is always easier to raise projections later as the product comes together and looks very solid.

Financial Commitment (by Milestone)

If you're working in a situation with a third-party product development relationship, it is necessary to establish a payment schedule by milestone. Because every situation is different, some publishers prefer close milestones on a monthly basis, whereas others prefer milestone payments only every three months. This is always negotiable, and you should establish a milestone payment schedule that works for your particular situation in balancing work performed for money paid and minimize the financial risks of the project at each turn. A clearly defined milestone payment schedule is critical to any third-party development relationship as it reflects the cash flow commitment to the development team.

The Final Word

Although the producer's job is focused on producing a great game on time and on schedule, the financial components of any software development product are part of the management process. Efficient allocation of resources is the name of the game and because money is directly related to the time invested in the product, it is important the producer understand how to manage both. Although there's a lot more than could be covered here involved in managing a budget for a multimillion-dollar game development project, the most important aspects and metrics are included in this chapter.

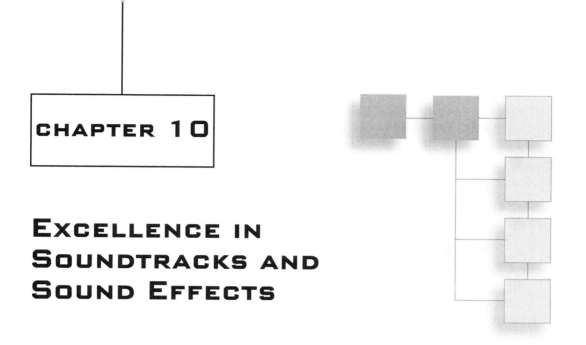

CHAPTER 10

EXCELLENCE IN SOUNDTRACKS AND SOUND EFFECTS

A   *s with film, television, and other primarily visual mediums, sound and music are often the forgotten elements in video game design. That may be because sound affects you more subtly than do splashy visuals or hyperspeedy gameplay. In fact, oftentimes the mark of superior sound design is that you don't consciously notice it at all. Instead, it goes to work on you subconsciously—heightening tension, manipulating the mood, and drawing you into the gameworld faintly but inexorably.*

— Glenn McDonald, GameSpot

There is a belief that the audio component accounts for one-third of the interactive experience, while the gameplay and visual components account for the other two-thirds. I say that audio comprises *at least* 33.3 percent of the interactive experience! Have you ever played a video game without sound? It's dull and uninviting, isn't it? But with a bad audio treatment, the experience can be really awful. This chapter discusses how to ensure that your game has an excellent soundtrack and stunning sound effects.

note

Music conveys emotion and dramatic themes to the user, while sound effects aurally describe the "reality" of the game. The term *licensed music* in this chapter includes the licensed pre-recorded tracks and licensed original tracks (songs that a company commissions a known artist to write specifically for the game). *Original music* in this chapter refers to musical themes with an underscore, main themes, stingers and any dynamic music content that is created specifically for the game as an original musical composition.

Just as in film, the audio post-production on a game is left until the very end of the project, when all of the pieces of the game finally come together. The implementation can rushed, leaving little time to polish the implementation. Although this is common in game development, it can certainly be avoided. Interactive entertainment requires a high degree of polish in its audio treatment since it is interactive and requires a response from the user to continue.

Today, video game soundtracks are introducing new artists just as movie soundtracks do. They're starting a new revolution in how the world listens to new music. Products like *Def Jam*, *Need for Speed*, and *FIFA* incorporate licensed music in a groundbreaking way by breaking new acts into an international market. Other products, like the *Myst* series, create breathtaking soundtracks and involve celebrity artists (like Peter Gabriel) in the creation of their soundtracks.

Looking forward, there seems to be no way for a video game project to succeed without a heavy investment in the sound and musical treatment. Developers of any new product cannot afford to undervalue its soundtrack or the sound effects treatment and remain in this media revolution. The importance of music and how to create a great soundtrack cannot be overstated.

Why Music Is as Important as Visuals

So, are video games the new rock and roll? I say absolutely yes: Video games are the new rock and roll. Video games are the new hip-hop. They are the new house, heavy metal, R&B, and punk. They are our culture. They are us. Within the next two years, video games will become the new radio, the new MTV, and the new record store all in one. The next level is in the code you write, the riff you play, the beat you mix. The future is—literally—in your hands. Today I invite you to seize the opportunity. Paint it black. Fight the power. And most of all, challenge everything.

—Steve Schnur, VP of Worldwide Music, Electronic Arts

Music is one of the oldest forms of expression. Its inclusion with a new visual media, one of the newest forms of expression, is a perfect marriage of the new and old. Epic movies like *The Godfather* aren't complete without *The Godfather Theme*. *Star Wars* wouldn't be the generation-defining series that it is without the stunningly memorable musical score. Similarly, epic games like *Donkey Kong*, *PacMan*, *Super Mario*, and *Metroid* included equally iconic music, helping to define video game music for a new generation. Their accelerating rhythms and persistent tones quickened pulses and still work today.

Music from a film derives its strength from passion and the emotion it evokes; it is the same with video game music. To quote composer Jack Wall, "It's about how to make the music, and therefore the game and its characters, come alive!"

Planning for the Production

The first and most important step that a producer can take is to plan the production of the soundtrack. The soundtrack should be part of the experience. Work with those who hold the creative vision for the game with the goal of providing some guidelines how the soundtrack will complement gameplay as well as story. Ask yourself some questions before starting work on the music with anyone. What should the music convey? Should it convey drama, action, and conflict; should it be melancholy or even dark and haunting? Define the tone, mood, and direction in which the music should take the user. Don't worry about how to implement or create the music, but define it so that you can provide guidelines for the talent hired to create the music.

If you don't know what you want in terms of music, involve someone on the team who knows and loves music. Find music that you like (from movies, TV, or other games) and play it with that music as a reference point. Get a conversation going about what the music can and should do for the user. I've often used temp tracks from other composers, such as John Williams, Ion Zur, Jack Wall, Hans Zimmer, and Ennio Moricone, to prove a point or just to give some indication of the emotion the music should evoke in the player. Playing music that evokes emotion is the way to ensure an audience stays motivated and excited.

Consider the following questions before recording a single note of music with anyone: Is music fully orchestrated and recorded with a live orchestra, or is it okay to use MIDI samples from existing libraries? Or is the music a mix of MIDI and live orchestra? Or does it include a band with vocals and drums? Clarify this direction first, and then work on defining the budget for this type of musical production.

Discuss how many minutes of music you're going to need for the game. Game music usually falls into just a few categories.

- Ambient or background underscore
- Battle, combat, or action score
- Musical stingers (to highlight victory, defeat, and so on)
- Scored cinematics or interstitial movies
- Licensed songs with lyrics

If the game has eight levels and each level has six minutes of ambient underscore, two minutes of battle track, four- to five-second stingers, and one cutscene, that's about one minute long, that's about 5.5 minutes of music per level, for a total of 76 minutes of music. While some cutscenes can be longer than others, following this method can help you define the scope of the work. In this case, the answer is 76 minutes of total finished music. But other projects may only have 30 minutes of music or even less.

Finding the Right Talent

In finding the right talent, a producer should not limit himself to only the resources he has available (such as an in-house Sound department). Of course, if the talent in the in-house sound department is the best talent for the job, then certainly, give them the job. The other route is to hire an outside composer.

Just as with contracting a writer or outsourcing art production, outsourcing of music generally has several distinct advantages. The first advantage is that composers who work freelance are extremely motivated to satisfy their clients and the gaming audience. Secondly, they generally can work for a fixed fee, provided some guidelines are included in their contract as to what the fee includes and doesn't include. Another advantage of using freelance composers is that there's a much broader range of talent. Many of the top composers in the industry work freelance, and they enjoy the freedom of working on only the projects they choose.

So, how do you find outside talent? Of course, there are agents you can use to find the right talent for your project. There is also an organization called the Game Audio Network Guild (GANG), where producers can network to find the most appropriate composer for their project. And don't forget the Number One way producers find talent for their project: other producers and word of mouth. If there's a game whose music you like, check out the credits (listed on the GANG Web site, at http://www.audiogang.org, or at http://www.mobygames.com) and then call the producer of the title. Ask him if he was happy with the work provided by the composer and whether he would recommend that person again.

If you're still not sure whom to hire, read on to find out about the audition process.

Hiring the Right Composer

Hiring the right composer is not an easy task. Music is a highly subjective component of any entertainment medium, and the best music has tons of hours and money invested in making it sound great. So, how do you tell if you have the right talent for your really big project? If you're still not sure whom to hire, I suggest holding an audition.

First, shortlist the composers who you think have the right appeal and talent for the job. Ask them if they're willing to audition for this project. Be clear that someone will get the job as the result of this audition. The audition should comprise three parts.

The first part is an original composition that distinguishes the composer's talent from the rest, yet is appropriate to the theme of the game.

The second part is a composition scored to a visual, as scoring music to in-game cutscenes or pre-rendered animation is generally a big part of the job. It is pretty easy to compile about 90 seconds of gameplay footage (from the prototype or POC) and string it together into a QuickTime movie or other linear media form. Send it to the composers on your shortlist. What you get back from the composers should definitely help make the decision of who to hire easier.

Lastly, ask for a specific proposal outlining the composer's plan for how the music will complement the game in a way that's totally new and beyond expectations. They should also include a budget and a schedule clarifying how they are going to create the total minutes of music needed for the game that has been outlined to them.

note

This process of outlining the scope of the work (mostly called a "pitch" these days) is the producer's job. Take this one step further when holding an audition. Before the audition, specifically define the tonality and cite some reference music that's appropriate; also define how original of a musical piece is appropriate as well as how the music will be graded, accepted, and integrated into the game. Specify any other criteria on which the project will be judged. If it's a project that's really exciting and there's a chance that a few good composers are interested, consider paying for the pitch.

caution

Composers hate doing auditions. They are never sure if it's a cattle call or a shortlist call. Secondly, you're asking a lot if you follow this audition process. In the case of a top-of-the-line, AAA job, you are justified in asking the composer to follow all of these rules. But on most games, many talented composers will (a) walk away, (b) not do their best. The reason? Composers are generally team players, and hiring them is a lot like the honor system. If you have faith in their abilities, they will kill themselves for you. If you are constantly questioning their abilities (cattle calls, enormous work in the audition, constantly re-working schedules) they lose passion for the project.

The Composer's Contract

The contract is to be worked out usually between the producer, composer, and the composer's agent. The first step is to find out what's been done at your company before regarding hiring outside composers. If there's a template or a standard for doing so, then start with that. If not, consider downloading the sample contract on the GANG Web site.

99.9 percent of all contracts include a buyout of all rights to the music for the game. However, all ancillary-product royalties should be split with the composer; this is what's stipulated in most film score and music composition agreements. I also recommend working with composers who have agents, so that you and the composer can focus on the creative issues while the agent handles the business and contractual issues. This is a very clean, clear way of doing business.

Discuss the points of the contract with the composer's agent. Consider the contract as if it were a development agreement (as discussed in Chapter 4), as many of the same principals apply. When considering a contract with a composer, be sure to mention also the ancillary products that can be very helpful in promotion of the game, such as soundtracks and online distribution of the soundtrack via iTunes.com.

note

The composer's contract and the rights gained through that agreement are as important as the technology license to the game engine, so be sure that you've clarified who has what rights to the music and for what purpose.

A case in point is when the *Myst III: Exile Main Theme* was used in the promotion of a recently released *Peter Pan* movie trailer. This re-use of the music earned a considerable financial reward for both the composer and UbiSoft, the publisher of *Myst III: Exile.*

One of the considerations in negotiating a contract with a composer (as well as other audio talent) is the difference between a limited license for the work and a total buyout. There's always a difference in price between a license and a buyout of all rights for a composition.

Ancillary Use

While music publishing is indeed a complex subject, and beyond the scope of this book, it should be explained that there are several facets of income that come from ancillary uses of music. Mechanical royalties are generated from physical copies of a musical work and performance royalties are generated from public performance of a musical work. There is the licensing income for "uses" of a musical work. Licensing generally has two sides to it—Master use and the Synchronization use. The Master use and the Sync use are generally equal in amount in most cases. The Master use traditionally goes to the record label (or in this case, the game publisher), who then splits it with the label's artist, according to the artist's deal. The Sync license goes to the publisher who then splits 50/50 with the composer. So, if a total license revenue for a piece of game music going into a movie trailer is $10,000, then $5,000 would go to the owner of the music (game publisher who then may or may not split with their developer according to their development contract) and $5,000 would go to the game publisher who would then split this amount with the composer.

Some game publishers, like EA, are now doing "sub-publishing" deals or joint ventures with actual music publishers. This is an ideal way for a publisher to exploit their growing catalogue of original music and generate further profits for themselves and the composers that wrote the music.

Live Musician Recording

The most important part of a live musician recording, whether it is of a small ensemble of brass players or a full orchestra, is that the producer *must* hire the right composer, music producers, and audio professionals to handle this job. Recording live musicians requires a lot of preparation to get it right and to ensure that the financial commitment is invested as wisely as possible.

Recording live musicians requires the coordination of efforts on multiple levels. The composer creates the score using MIDI samples and synth music. This is called a *temp score.* Then he or she must provide those examples to the development team for feedback and approval. Then the MIDI file is sent to the orchestrator, who converts the MIDI score into a fully orchestrated score. Then, the full orchestration is provided to the copyist. The copyist's job is to have the piece separated into individual sheet music for each instrument in the orchestra. This is done at least several weeks before any recording session.

Work with the person responsible for the PR of the game and organize time for the press to cover the recording of a soundtrack. Footage of a studio recording session is always useful to promote the game and any added publicity that indicates a commitment to quality sets the game apart from the rest of the market.

All of this must be done before even the first note of music is recorded. This is why the producer must hire the right person to be responsible for making the recording session happen—it's generally beyond the scope of most producers' expertise and responsibility.

Depending on the size of the music production, the amount of personnel required to make this work can reach the numbers of a small army—seventy or more players, perhaps a choir, one or more orchestrators, a music copyist to print parts, a librarian to make sure all parts end up on the right stand on the stage, a music contractor to put all the players in place, and so on. Don't forget assistants to make sure everyone is where they are supposed to be, an engineer and his or her assistants, someone to run the computers at the session, and finally, a music coordinator (if not the contractor) to oversee and make sure that all runs smoothly. It pays to have an experienced composer with all the right contacts and people to make all this happen. Proven entities can save enormous amounts of time and money in the musical life of a project.

note

Using music in place of sound effects is another trick to discuss with the audio professional charged with putting the audio into your game. Often, a simple strum of a few random guitar chords can give depth to an event in a game that a sound effect cannot.

When recording using an orchestra, a good rule of thumb to use for a non-union orchestra is about $1,000 per minute, especially if you're recording in some far-off place like Budapest or Prague. Up to $2,500 per minute is not unheard of for top-rated orchestras such as the London Symphony Orchestra or the Hollywood Studio Orchestra. Another guideline to remember is that for every hour of an orchestra's time in the studio a reasonable expectation is about three to five minutes of finished music depending such things as degree of difficulty and how well prepared the music is. A producer needs to consider the contract for the musicians as well as the composer. Ensure that a buyout is obtained for all rights related to the game and its promotion. Above all, make sure that the buyout includes unlimited quantities of the game sold.

As with every maturing entertainment medium, there will be the stars of the industry or other industries that can command higher fees and certain restrictions on how many games are sold before they receive a further payment. However, these things should be taken on a case-by-case basis.

note

In 2001 The American Federation of Musicians recognized that video games are a growing industry that has traditionally under-utilized union talent in recording soundtracks. The major reason for this under-utilization was that the rate structure required for interactive entertainment was the same rate structure used by big-budget films that could invest millions of dollars in their soundtracks—video games can often only invest a few thousand. Today, the AFM has a new agreement for interactive entertainment. It provides for a three-hour session, including an all-rights buyout for all platforms at $190 per musician. For more information on how to use the AFM contract in your soundtrack recording, see http://www.audiogang.org or go through the AFM directly, at http://www.afm.org.

Reasons to Do an Orchestral or Live Musician Soundtrack

There are a few good reasons for using live instruments in your next game soundtrack. First, they are excellent components of a wide marketing campaign that can add tremendous quality to any game trailers, TV spots, or downloadable cutscenes. Ensuring that there's press on hand to cover the session is worthwhile, as a live orchestra recording is news, and more publicity generally helps sales. I've even seen a "Behind the Scenes" video of an orchestral session on a United Airlines in-flight movie.

The game soundtrack creates another SKU for the publisher to sell at little incremental risk (inventory risk only). Soundtrack sales via direct marketing or through online distribution can easily recoup the costs of an orchestral session. After two weeks, the sales of the *Halo2* soundtrack exceeded 120,000 in North America. That could be an additional $400,000 in revenue for the brand. Creating an additional SKU for sale opens up all sorts of additional bundling opportunities, as well as collector's editions and pre-sales support.

Sound Effects Production and Management

This section continues the discussion of excellence in audio treatment by describing an excellent sound-effect production. Sound effects (and music) require a specialized production management so that the right sound effects are matched up in the game with the right visuals, gameplay, and cues. An efficient production management of both non-linear music and sound effects is one of the most important processes of finalization in any video game development cycle.

Often, sound designers cannot create the exact sounds they need using samples from a library, so they must go in search of a new sample library or create the sound themselves. For instance, whirling pipes around to capture the "whir" effect with the microphone is quite a common technique. Then, the captured effect is adjusted by slowing down the playback and changing the tones, pitch, or duration to make it appropriate for the game. And that's just the easy sound effects!

Naming Conventions

When it comes to sound effects and music management a logical, yet flexible naming convention that is compatible with the localization guidelines is crucial. It is the producer's job to decide on and put in place an effective naming convention. Without this naming convention in place, the team risks spending a lot of extra time fixing and sorting out possibly thousands of sound files, or worse yet, risks copying over data that is misnamed. One suggestion is to use a numbering scheme that can be easily renamed, automated, and sorted. This also allows the naming convention to be compatible with many languages and their various incarnations of Windows or console region OS.

One of the ways to ensure the audio is easily trackable is to create a sound effects list in Excel, using pivot tables, to help identify the type of sound effects. Once in Excel, the data can be sorted and manipulated quite easily. It can also be tracked as to its current status, and its filename can be decoded as appropriate. I also recommend that you have the filename of the sound effect programmatically updated to conform to the localization guides, rather than doing it by hand, which can be a tedious and time-consuming process. Check with your audio professional on the most efficient way to do this if you're unsure or unclear as establishing a clear process on audio production and integration is critical to any game.

Start Using Temp Sounds Early

The successful teams that have I met with during past projects always mention using temporary sound effects as early as possible. This allows testing and sorting out of problems with the sound effects integration process, as well as the setting of the game's audio palette as early as possible. By implementing sound effects early and updating them often, it is much easier to get an idea of which sound effects are annoying, inappropriate, or otherwise wrong for how they are implemented in the game.

It is very easy to simply copy new data over an entire set of directories, replacing and updating the quality of the sound effects as the game reaches alpha. But if that directory structure doesn't even exist and there's little idea of what sound effects work and which ones don't, there's no reason to invest money in creating the final version of any sound or music. Figure out what works and what doesn't using cheap, temporary sound effects and then work to improve the quality of the sound, as well as its implementation.

The Step Approval Method

Here's a three-step, or three-stage, approval method that I've used in the past with outside sound effects contractors.

1. **Temporary Sound Effects**. Straight from a library or other existing data source. Sometimes these work and are 100 percent appropriate and don't need any further revision, but that doesn't happen too often. Once you and the rest of the team hear these sound effects, you can provide feedback to the sound designer on how to improve the appropriateness of the sound effect. The sound designer updates the sound status sheet (sound effects list) and is paid one-third of the fee due for the work performed and accepted. Get these sounds into the game to see whether they're appropriate.

2. **Revised Sound Effects**. These sound effects are the second generation of sound effects, which are often implemented into the game. Typically, 50 percent of these second revision effects are appropriate for the game and can be implemented as-is. They can go to the Final and Approved stage immediately. The sound effects list is revised and updated at this time. More sounds effects may be added, while others discarded if they don't fit the bill. The sound designer is paid the second third of the payment due for this work performed.

3. **Final and Approved**. This stage is the final in-game tuning of the sound effects and final delivery and implementation in the game of any outstanding sound effects that may have required further revision. The sound status sheet is updated, and the sound designer is paid in full.

By using this method, the producer avoids paying full price for sound effects that are never used, as the required sound effect list is updated as the game's development progresses and temp sounds are implemented. This allows both the producer and the sound designer to reach a fair compromise on used and unused sound effects, ensuring that the best sound effects are included in the game—not just those listed on a spreadsheet 24 months before the product reached its final testing phase.

Match Sounds Effects to Art Assets

In every game that I've been involved with, the art assets generally had a direct connection to the sound and music assets. Although it didn't match up 100 percent of the time, the large majority of the sound work correlated to some art asset. Given this direct relationship, I recommend including the Sound Effect Status sheet in the same format and as a linked file (either as a sheet in the same workbook or in a different workbook) in MS Excel to track the status of the art assets and the sound assets. Often, the art asset list is revised to accommodate design changes, including new objects, animations, special effects, and interface or menu items. By linking the art asset status sheet to the sound effects status sheet, you can be assured that any changes in the art assets are reflected in the sound effects list. This way, you minimize the risk that a sound effect will be forgotten and left out of the production requirements.

note

There are a ton of resources available to a producers on how to create quality sound effects. These resources include *Game Developer Magazine*, *Gamasutra*, and the GANG Web site, at http://www.audiogang.org.

Voiceover Work and Direction

Voice is yet another area of the video game development process where I recommend that the producer hire an industry professional (such as a casting agent, director, or a one-stop-shopping voiceover work production house). There are many outside sound production houses that can assist the producer with casting, hiring, and recording the right voiceover (VO) talent. Unless you've done it before, it can be a lot of work to sort out the paperwork, find the right talent, provide direction, contract a studio, and arrange delivery of the sessions to the sound engineer for editing and conversion to the proper data format for the game.

Before considering going into the studio and recording anything, the producer must be assured that the script is finalized. Proper annotation of the script is required. This ensures that the session editor can edit the recordings and save the right recordings with the right file names (which work within the localization guidelines). If you're not sure whether the script is final, do *not* go into the studio. It will be a waste of time and money and create a lot more work than would delaying the recording session.

Once the script is finalized and organized by character, consider hiring a director. Hiring a director ensures that the right talent is cast in the right roles and that the session, from beginning to end, is as efficient as possible. The producer should not have to intervene much, and will only have to act as the tie-breaker during the casting if he has hired the right people to make the right creative decisions regarding the acting talent.

Once the talent has been auditioned and cast, work with the talent's agent to negotiate a fair agreement for their participation in the video game. If you're using SAG/AFTRA talent, you'll need to use the standard rate sheet for the SAG/AFTRA Interactive category and follow a few other steps that are required to hire union talent.

note

Provide an outline of the character for the talent to reference before the recording session. This is called a *character brief*. By preparing the character brief and providing it to the talent before the session, you give the talent an opportunity to memorize his or her lines before getting to the studio, and you ensure that he or she understands the motivations and background of the character without having to read the entire script.

Creating a budget is the final preparation required for the VO work—ensure that it is done before you start casting actors or any other work on the VO session. Remember that more characters = more money. Does a game really need 99,999 lines of dialog when 25,000 will do?

The budget governs who you can cast in which role and whether celebrities will be used; it should also reflect how many characters are required, when and where the recording is going to happen, and whether the recording meets the game designer's objectives. The budget is the primary gating item to a successful voiceover recording session, so be sure to have this figured out to the penny before starting any work.

Using SAG/AFTRA Talent and Navigating through Union Requirements

Another problem that the producer faces that relates directly to the budget for the VO session is whether to use union talent. I've found that there's a reason why it is called "talent" and there's a union. Hiring non-union actors or actresses can save money on the actor's fee, but it can cost money in the long run because of time that it takes to edit, rehearse, re-take, and do pickups with non-union talent. Non-union talent is often just not as talented or professional—at least in my experience.

If you're still stuck on using non-union talent, consider the additional fees for the additional editor and director time in the studio. If you get to this point, you may wish you'd hired the union talent in the first place. At first, I was not a big believer in unionized talent for actors and actresses, but after a few hard lessons, it became clear that paying for talent is a worthwhile investment.

Once in a while, you will be obliged to use a non-union actor or actress while the rest of your talent is union. With the Taft-Hartley waiver, you can include any non-union talent in a union production—a one-time exclusion for the talent. Contact SAG/AFTRA for more information on the Taft-Hartley waiver and the necessary forms. The non-union talent should join the union immediately after receiving a Taft-Hartley waiver, as he or she would not be eligible for another.

Signatory Obligations

A few requirements apply to the signatory (the producer signing the timesheets, paychecks, or otherwise dealing with the contractual arrangements with the union) to any union interactive production. These requirements are one of the reasons why I recommend hiring a production company to handle union VO productions on behalf of the game. One of the requirements is that all SAG session fees must be paid within a certain period of time and include proper deductions, just like a normal W-2 payroll check. Secondly, the production must submit a fair percentage (about 13 percent) to the union for the talent's retirement fund. Additionally, the production may be required to pay for the talent's agent fee, which is often another 10 percent.

Lastly, the production may be responsible for the buyout rights associated with the session. Generally, a producer wants to acquire all rights to the VO session so that it can be used without further restriction in unlimited copies of the game and its derivative works. This generally means paying double-scale or scale plus a certain percentage. Check with SAG/AFTRA to find out the exact requirements for acquiring the rights your game needs.

note

Currently SAG/AFTRA is working on developing a production agreement specifically for interactive media, as they realize that the movie production model and fee scale doesn't always work for interactive media and video games. Check http://www.audiogang.org for more information on the SAG/AFTRA interactive contract template.

Sound Engine

As discussed in Chapter 7, there are numerous sound engine technology solutions, including creating your own proprietary sound engine technology. The most important thing pertaining to the sound engine that a producer needs to ensure is that it includes the right features required for the game. If your game requires Doppler shifting because it is an FPS and the player needs to hear the bullets flying by and ricocheting, be sure that your solution has that feature.

Compression speed and ratio is yet another concern for the producer. Consider how much dialog, music, and sound effects you'll need for the game and at what ratio it can be compressed (8 to 1 ratio or a 10 to 1 ratio.). Then run a few tests to make sure the team is satisfied with the speed of decompression, CPU intensity required, and how big the files need to be in order to achieve the minimum quality level.

There's a lot more to consider about the sound engine, but leave that to the sound programmer and the other audio professionals you've hired to take care of that part of the game. Ask the right questions, but trust professionals to do a professional job.

Integration

Integration of sound effects (both ambient and triggered), dynamic music, speech events, and the whole host of other audio requirements is a lot of work. On my past projects, a single person has been responsible for integrating the sound effects. There's a risk having a single person be responsible, as it can cause a bottleneck at a critical time. However, one of the advantages of this approach is that you have is a go-to resource who knows how the effects are integrated and triggered by the game, as well as how many times certain things play.

Alternatively, if you have a number of level designers on your team, make each of them responsible for "hooking up" all of the sound effects on their level. This spreads the risk.

A lot of tuning is required to achieve the right level of randomization of sound effects, VO cues, and dynamic music, so be sure to have someone in this role who is a bit of a perfectionist and who is passionate about music. Integrating sound effects is a challenging role that requires a lot of attention to detail. But in the end, the last step is just as important as the music recording and every other piece of the game. If the final integration of sound doesn't come together right, there's a big risk that the game won't meet critical or consumer expectations.

The Final Word

The final word here is to always remember that the audio portion of the interactive gaming experience is at least 50 percent of the experience that the user is paying for. It may not seem like 50 percent, until you try playing a game without sound, with a poor sound implementation, or with just plain bad-quality sound. Don't neglect this part of the production and focus only on great gameplay and graphics. The experience won't be all that it needs to be without an excellent soundtrack and sound-effect folio. Ensuring that your game has the best sound possible is an inexpensive way to lend the final polish and quality to the gaming experience.

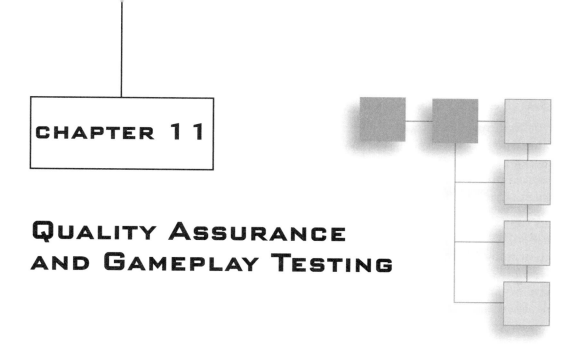

CHAPTER 11

QUALITY ASSURANCE AND GAMEPLAY TESTING

Quality assurance and gameplay testing are two very important steps in bringing a video game to completion before its commercial release. In fact, I'd go so far as to say that they are the two *most* important steps to consider before releasing any software product. Quality assurance and gameplay testing ensure that the product works as designed and that it provides sufficient functionality, usability, and fun to be attractive to critics and end users alike. If these steps are skipped or rushed, the product may be released with bugs that affect its functionality and playability.

These steps allow the producer to confirm that the team's work over the past many months has been on target and has resulted in a worthwhile interactive experience for the user. The risks of rushing the QA process are many, from crash bugs to the game's having conflicts with other software and hardware.

This chapter describes some of the commonly used and useful testing procedures and methodology a producer should employ. Often, excellent producers have backgrounds in QA and this chapter explains why that sort of background is useful for a producer to understand. It also explains how to clearly delineate responsibilities for testing the game and how to provide feedback on the game that is meaningful and valued.

Lastly, this chapter discusses some of the key risks of insufficient QA and gameplay testing procedures. There's no real way to skip over these steps without risk, so the most that a producer can do is ensure efficient methods.

QA Team Procedures

What is the producer's relationship with the QA team, exactly? Well, the best way to test a game is to play it every day and know every single part of it. In the latter portion of the development cycle a working game must be a top priority for the team. Playing the game on a daily basis also enables a producer to start working with the QA team as early as possible to develop effective procedures for testing the game.

QA procedures include an establishment of a test plan and methods for reporting, correction, tracking, verifying, and closing bugs. In researching this book, I found that different studios have different methods and that there's no one way to adopt a best practice that works for every situation. But, in this section I will offer some recommendations that have worked well in the past when writing a test plan and assigning responsibilities for managing the bug-fixing process.

What's in a Test Plan

The writing of a test plan is generally the responsibility of the QA team. However, the producer can ensure that this job is started early and that the test plan is as complete as possible by delivering updated versions of the game's design documentation to the QA team lead as early as possible (generally six to eight months prior to gold master). The purpose of the Quality Assurance test phase is to test the game to see if it meets the criteria specified by the design.

The written test plan must describe what to test in each of the following phases or testing procedures:

- **Gameplay functionality**. This section of the test plan ensures that the game provides the gameplay user experience as specified in the design documentation.
- **Unit/Character functionality**. This section covers the functionality of units or characters and how they behave in the game environment.
- **Story progression**. Story progression testing ensures that the game progresses as designed and the story and levels of the game are coherent and include all necessary cutscenes and movies.
- **User interface**. User interface testing is required to confirm that the user interface as designed is effective, intuitive and complementary to gameplay.
- **Sound and music**. Sound and music testing confirms that all required sound and music events are triggered as designed.
- **Compatibility**. Compatibility testing ensures that the game meets the minimum system specifications, as well as functionality on the widest possible set of hardware (if it's a PC game).

- **Gold Master/Final Checklist**. This is the final testing procedure used to confirm that the game is ready for manufacturing or submission to the console manufacturer for approval. These final procedures are critical to ensuring that the work of the last many months is not jeopardized by a careless error or omission.

At each one of these phases of gameplay testing, having the finalized and updated design documentation to provide to the test team is critical. Without this documentation, it is nearly impossible for the QA lead to develop a test plan that adequately reflects the intent of the designers while balancing the responsibilities to the usability of the product.

Assignment of Responsibilities

The process of testing a video game is divided into several areas of responsibility. The roles in the QA process are as follows:

- **Lead QA**. This role focuses on creating the test plan and supervising the QA staff. The lead QA role has a direct contact with the assistant producer who assigns bugs for fixing. The lead QA also works closely with the QA test manager (the department manager), ensuring that the game is completely tested. It is the responsibility of the lead QA person to include in the test plan the test case and use case scenarios from the design documentation.

- **Assistant Lead QA**. The assistant lead QA person works with the QA team whenever the Lead QA person is absent and otherwise works as a second-in-command in the hierarchy of QA personnel.

- **QA Personnel (Testers)**. The testers find the bugs and write the bug reports for the game. By testing the code written by the programming team against the functionality specified in the design documentation, the testers can find all the problems with implementation of that design. They are instructed to play the game, follow all possible paths and to try to break the game.

- **Producer (bug resolver)**. The producer's role when it comes to the QA process is to listen, learn, and provide help provide resolutions for the bugs reported on his project. The role is not to "defend" the project.

- **Assistant Producer (bug assigner)**. The role of the assistant producer when it comes to working with QA is to establish a good working relationship with the lead QA person and to assign the bugs that are reported to the right team member or team lead.

- **Compatibility Tester(s)**. Compatibility testing is often done by outside companies and managed by the lead QA person. The producer and the assistant producer also need to work in concert with the lead QA to ensure that a build is ready for compatibility testing on schedule and that it includes all of the hardware-specific features that the game promises. They also need to arrange to provide the required hardware to the programmers to fix bugs found during compatibility testing. In order to fix a "compatibility bug," the programmers often need to have the hardware that is reporting the bug provided to them for examination.

- **Playtester**. The playtesters can be anyone, from team members, designers, programmers, artists, or the producer to outsiders hired specifically to play through the game and provide an evaluation. Toward the middle—and certainly during the final stages of the project—play testing is very valuable and requires a dedicated playtester to check work as it is implemented.

The value the producer can add to each of these assigned roles and responsibilities is to understand and respect their importance in completing the project. The producer should foster efficient teamwork between the different departments and the development team.

Teamwork

Teamwork is, as in every stage of a game's development, critical during the QA process. Remember that most testers love to play games and have a passion for what they're doing—they often go home and play games until late into the night. As a producer, you should encourage them to share their opinions and ideas. Create an atmosphere where comments and criticism are delivered constructively. Share what knowledge you can about being a producer with the testers, as they generally want to learn more about how they can grow in their careers. An environment that is honest and open is the ideal one in which to test a game. If you can work effectively with the QA team, it will help your game ship on time, under budget, and as a quality product.

Here are a few suggestions for developing healthy teamwork.

- **Reward testers**. Free dinner, gift certificates, or public recognition can go a long way.
- **Analyze the competition**. Testers should be aware of how the product stacks up to others in the market. Encourage competition with a few gameplay challenges or playfests during launch of the latest competitive product.
- **Observe and listen**. A producer gets the most out of watching how people play the game. They can see what works and doesn't work about how the user interacts with the product.
- **Discourage bad legacies**. This means that testers should enter bugs on everything that they see that's wrong. Bugs that can't be fixed because of some technological or work versus time hurtle, or that's the way the engine works should never be excluded. Legacy problems develop when testers fail to report a problem because they're told, "That's the way it works."

- **Keep things fresh**. Often a test team will get bored with playing the same game over and over again. In their haste to get the job done, defects get overlooked. Keep things fresh by rotating in a few pinch hitters on the test teams during a test cycle. Also, humor and laughter make it more fun to be at work, so allow team members to "let their hair down;" maybe take everyone out of the office for drinks every now and then.

- **Respect people's opinion**. It is easy for producers to get defensive about the game they've worked so long and hard on, but remember that testers' opinions are invaluable. Respect their opinions, even if you don't agree with them. You may learn something.

- **Put your sword away**. Producers often feel they must "unsheath their swords" to protect and defend the team and the game during QA. But when critical feedback comes in from the QA department, listen to what the QA is saying. Most likely, there's a solution, so take what information you can from their comments. Of course, if the comment is "rework the entire game," then that's not really helpful and you can deflect it. But when the feedback is that "This really isn't that fun," step in and figure out why.

- **Mix up the hardware**. Often, the team uses similar hardware. That means that the game will undoubtedly run on those machines, but hopefully the QA department can provide you with a variety of hardware on which to test the game. Unusual hardware configurations can expose bugs before the product is released.

Tracking and Closing Bugs

"Fix bugs as we go" should be the mantra of any team who wants to finish their project on schedule. If you're fixing bugs throughout the development process—even before the game is being tested by the QA department—a team can be relatively certain that they have a playable game and that the code is evolving with a solid foundation.

If you wait until the end of the project to fix bugs, you run the risk that fixing them will take a lot longer and cause more bugs at the critical stage of the project—just before gold master release and commercial shipment. Bugs are usually less expensive and less time-consuming to fix when the code that created them is fresh in the programmer's mind. To quote Jamie Fristom from Gamasutra.com, "It is easier to estimate how long it will take to implement a feature than to estimate how long it will take to fix a bug."

To further complicate matters, if you're working on a game that can't run for more than a few minutes or seconds before crashing, there's no way for the team to know whether the new features they're implementing are actually being implemented properly. It is harder to implement a new feature and see if it works properly when the game is crashing, as it is nearly impossible to tell whose recent implementation broke the game. By minimizing the bugs during the development of the game, there's actually more time to make and polish the gameplay.

Here are a couple of ways to ensure that the QA and gameplay testing process is started early and effective.

- **Track bugs early**. Start a process for tracking internal bugs for the team. This can be in an MS Excel sheet or a full-blown bug-tracking database. But start the process early in the development cycle.

- **Ensure that an autobuild system is in place**. This enables the producer and the team to identify bugs early and easy, as if the game breaks, you'll know as soon as another build is completed. Make sure that this process is automated. Ensure it clearly identifies who requested the build, and notifies the team. This ensures accountability when that person checks in something that breaks a game; they'll get right on fixing it. The team can get the latest data from source control, while waiting for whoever broke the build to fix it and get a new autobuild compiled.

Track and Record all Feedback

Ensure that whatever bug tracking solution and process that is in place for your project includes the flexibility to include optional feedback from the QA—and anyone else, for that matter. Tracking and logging all suggestions, comments, opinions, and bugs is an important part of a game's development, and it ensures that the valuable feedback is recorded and managed.

Alpha

The definition of *alpha* in the game development process seems to vary from place to place and situation to situation, so I've included the commonly known and referenced definition that's worked on a few projects recently. Generally, the *alpha* version of the games is feature- and asset-complete, but that there are still some bugs present. Here's a detailed description to reference, which I have used on various contracts in the game industry:

"'Alpha version'" means the features and core shall be 100 percent integrated in accordance with the Design and Technical Design Documentation, although some known bugs may still be present. The Alpha Version shall contain 100 percent of all features and functions, including front-end menus and user interface, introductory and endgame sequences, in-game cutscenes, transition screens, preliminary sound effects, and preliminary music."

Beta

The definition of *beta* in the game development cycle is the stage at which all of the assets are integrated into the game and the product is just being checked and tested for bugs. While I've often heard of this definition including the condition "no crash bugs," it is very difficult to achieve such a state. Crash bugs are rare occurrences on console games; they are much more common on PC titles. But even when developing console games, you will encounter occasions when the game causes a computer to crash.

Here is a technical definition of beta (closed and open) that has been used by top publishers in the industry:

"'Closed Beta version' means the product features and code shall be 90 percent complete in accordance with the Design and Technical Documentation. The Closed Beta Version shall continue to be fine-tuned and de-bugged, however, until it contains no known active 'A' bugs that cause the Product to crash or freeze (there are no known open severity class-A bugs). An *A bug* means (1) a repeatable phenomenon of unintended events or any action occurring during the running of the product that results in the product being rendered partially or completely nonfunctional; (2) a failure of the product to conform to the specifications in the Design and Technical Design Documentation; (3) a detriment to the visual representation, sound, or function of the version; or (4) the destruction, disruption, or corruption of a data system, storage device, or mechanism."

At this point, there are no further milestone acceptance tests for the team, as everyone should be focused on playing the game, testing it, and fixing bugs as soon as possible. Once the publisher provides the compatibility results, then it is the team's job to ensure that they fix as many of the compatibility bugs as possible. The closed beta is tested only by employees of the developer or publisher and is not available for release to the public. Next, comes the final testing phase, called *open beta*.

Open Beta

During open beta, a small part of the game data and the complete game engine is provided to a core group of individuals (in the mod community or other fans of the game) who are part of the consumer market. While the open beta is not available to everyone, they are great for helping game development teams identify weaknesses in their product before consumers actually start buying the game, finding bugs, and returning the product or calling technical support.

Be aware, though, that any time you release an unfinished product to a segment of the market, you run the risk of its being leaked to the general public, as well as drumming up bad word of mouth if the gameplay is not finished or is deemed not fun enough.

Here's a reasonable definition of open beta.

" 'Open beta version' means the product features and code shall be 100 percent feature complete in accordance with the Design and Technical Documentation, but may be lacking certain approved content related to the testing. The product may contain localized versions and accept data using the localization tool. The Open Beta Version shall continue to be fine-tuned and de-bugged, however, it shall contain no known active A bugs that cause the product to crash or freeze (there are no known open severity class-A bugs)."

Internal QA Team versus External QA Teams

With every project, there's a need to test the game early and often. Whether the development team is solely responsible for this challenge or they have the help of others on a test team, it is generally the producer's influence that improves the chance of having the right QA support. The development team should always be playing the game and testing their work, and a good producer ensures that the development team is supported by testing resources early and as required. Here's how testing resources can add value to the game's development when employed throughout the development cycle.

Development Testing

Development testing generally refers to the segment of testing when the development team has a playable game with limited feature implementation, or temporary worlds or levels. All that's being tested is the small part of the game that was just implemented.

Development testing should be considered separate from play testing.

note

Begin testing sound implementation as soon as the placeholder sound effects are implemented. Testing for sound effects and music is often done by the audio director of the team, but this process can be accelerated by involving the composer and sound designer whenever possible. Ensure that the sound designer and composer have provided documentation to the QA lead so that the test plan for the game includes a segment specific to testing the implementation of the audio portion.

Play Testing

Play testing is when the game is played to test the enjoyableness of the experience as a whole, and whether the specific elements of the game are fun. Play testing should identify which elements of the gaming experience are not fun or are inadequately realized. Play testing often and early ensures that the game is fun early in the development process, and that as development continues, choices are shaped by this solid foundation.

I recommend that producers organize several weekend "playfests" with trusted individuals not involved in the game's development and representative of the principal demographic for the game. Playfests allow the team to witness and understand firsthand what a consumer might do when they first start playing the game. Identification of bugs and design deficiencies are the fruits of this labor, along with valuable feedback or suggestions on how to improve the gaming experience. Playfests are recommended from the time when the game becomes playable until and throughout the beta stage of the QA process. This ensures that valuable feedback is received before it is too late to be included in the game and that when it is implemented, that the implementation addresses the identified problem.

The Credits List

The Credits List includes the list of names of everyone who contributed to the making of the game in small and large ways. They are, unfortunately, usually left until the game is in the final stages of testing and there are many other challenges confronting the team. Here are a couple of suggestions for making the process of giving people credit for their work easier and more effective.

- Create a draft of the credits as a text file only, with no formatting. This makes it look very standard and no one is more important than anyone else. Then, take the list around and if practical, get everyone's signature on it. This ensures that everyone on the team reviews the spelling of his name, how he is credited, and his position on the list. You can address any concerns immediately. It takes maybe two minutes per team member, but it saves about 20 hours of heartache and conflict later.

- Once the list is complete, send the text file to the artist in charge of creating the credits movie; if you're going to use onscreen anti-aliased scrolling text through the game engine, make sure you test it yourself before anyone else sees it.

The IDGA has some recommendations as to best practices on this issue. Their standards guideline document is available from the IDGA Credit Standards Committee. The Credit Standards Committee's goal is to address the issue of credit standardization—to establish generally accepted guidelines that all studios and publishers can use. The Credit Standards Committee can be e-mailed at credits@igda.org.

The Risks of Rushing through QA

The risks of rushing through the QA process on any software can be enormous. Here are a few risks to consider when you're feeling the pressure and are tempted to rush.

- **Buggy software.** The game will always be remembered for being buggy. Only a few people remember when a product was release on schedule.

- **Incompatibility.** The game may not be compatible with certain segment of the market. The broader this compatibility issue, the worse off the product is.

- **High tech support costs.** Bugs cost money, plain and simple. All of those tech support calls at five dollars per call detract quickly from the bottom line.

- **Return costs and negative impact on sales.** Products are often returned to the retailer when they're buggy or don't work, and the retailer returns the products to the publisher. Product returns of more than 20 percent of the total unit sales can make the product commercially unfeasible and cost more than not shipping an unfinished game.

- **Including a virus on the final media.** Don't laugh. Imagine shipping a product that has a virus included in it and then having to recall the product from the shelf and destroy it. If you miss the last virus check step because you're in a rush and a new virus comes out and infects your network on the day before the product is about to go gold and be sent off to manufacturing, it could happen.

- **Including unprotected source code or data on the final media.** Even console developers have failed to protect their source code or data, including it on the final media without a big file system or any sort of encryption. If you're rushing through the QA process, this is more likely to happen.

- **Pirated versions.** Products rushed through QA may be more easily pirated when they come out, as they lack adequate copy protection methods.

- **Localization issues and simultaneous worldwide release.** Rushing your product may not help the product get to market sooner if the foreign versions haven't been completed, fully integrated, and tested in their markets.

- **Manufacturer rejection.** The console manufacturers (Sony, Nintendo, and Microsoft) will often reject a product several times before it passes their final QA process and is approved for manufacturing. It is to your advantage to ensure that the QA process is not rushed and the product passes the console manufacturer's QA process on the first submission.

note

It is common practice to continue testing while a product is being reviewed by the manufacturer—and even once it has been approved for manufacturing. Do as much testing as possible between gold and release so that any bugs or playability issues can be identified and a solution found before the product reaches the market. Develop a prioritized bug list so that the team can work on fixing the highest priority bugs first, so that if the build is rejected for manufacturing, resubmission will be easier and quicker.

The Final Word

Almost every mistake in developing and testing software has already been made by someone. There is no reason to make them again. Learn the best practices of your organization with a keen eye on the mistakes of the past. Work to prioritize the bug lists and ensure that a patch sufficiently addresses any key issues with the game (if you're working on a PC title or a console title with online capability). Working to find bugs and fix them is just as important as not making the mistakes that caused the bugs in the first place.

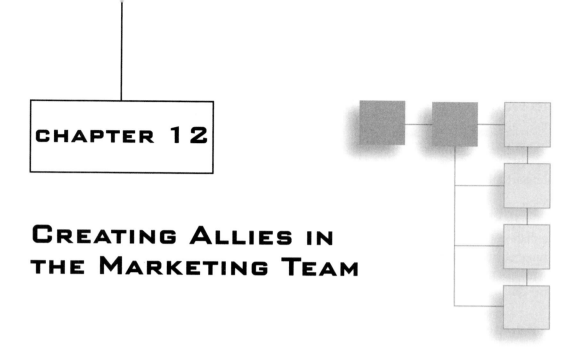

CHAPTER 12

CREATING ALLIES IN THE MARKETING TEAM

*T*he relationship between the producer and the brand manager can be powerful. Knowledge is the key to this power and it is the sharing of knowledge that fosters a strong relationship. When producers and brand managers can free-flow key data points back and forth, agree on a course of action, and then take the plan to executive management having agreed, there are very few things that can stop that relationship from being successful.

—Tabitha Hayes, Global Brand Manager for Doom 3™, Activision Publishing, Inc.

In researching this section, a common theme I heard from brand managers is that producers do not have enough faith in the brand managers' abilities, nor do they support open communication. This lack of support for the efforts to market the game can hinder their own success and that of their game. This is surprising, considering that one of the key aspects in ensuring that a game is successful is to properly market it; it is critical that the brand manager knows and understands the product, as well as how to convey the key messages to the consumer and the retail sales channel.

This chapter discusses the power of this relationship between producer and brand manager, as well as what a producer can do to ensure that he's working with the brand manager to create the biggest bang for the buck when marketing the game.

Making Life Easier for the Brand Manager

Your brand manager is your partner in bringing a successful game to market. There are many things that a producer can do to help foster this partnership and ensure that the brand manager has the tools necessary to do the right job. I've included some of the most important examples in this section.

Your mantra when working with marketing should be "Collaboration is huge!" according to Tabitha Hayes of Activision. Because marketing a game is more an art than a science, collaboration is critical to a successful outcome. If marketing were a science, data could be plugged into formulas and the output reasonably predicted. This is far from the reality when marketing games, especially original titles (meaning new intellectual property or product concepts).

Understand Marketing's Concerns

Understanding the concerns of the brand manager is critical to making this partnership work more effectively. Remember that the brand manager is concerned with the following issues—some of which may not be readily apparent to a producer:

- Price drops of competitive or complementary products.
- Pricing action, including rebates and their effectiveness (how many more products are sold at a new, lower price point).
- Media buys, which is the enormous amount of money that is spent on media prior to a game's commercial release.
- Overall profitability of a title or brand.
- Brand assessment, which includes ensuring that the assets of an existing brand— such as an engine license or an IP license—are exploited to their fullest potential.
- Market timing, including product release dates and competitive product release dates.
- Visual asset delivery schedule. It is critical for marketing to have a schedule of when the game assets can be delivered.
- Market research and analysis. Understanding the forces at work in the consumer market is a complex endeavor requiring critical and analytical thinking.
- Box cover, marketing materials, ad creation, and online promotion. These are just a few of the collateral items required to market a game.

Marketing a game is similar to making a game in that the strategic plan must involve excellent execution of many smaller, tactical elements. The following subsections will discuss some of the steps for devising a good strategic marketing plan with your brand manager.

Prepare for Marketing Early and Build It into the Schedule

At the beginning of the project, identify the key elements that are required to market the game and when they're required and build them into the schedule. Work with the brand manager to manage expectations of what type of assets can be provided and what state the game is in at certain points.

Examples of items to build into the schedule are

- Screenshots (high and low resolution)
- Conceptual artwork
- Playable demos
- Demo scripts
- Raw gameplay footage
- CG art of main characters
- Pre-release builds

For a more complete list of the potential marketing deliverables, see Appendix C, "Marketing Deliverables Checklist."

Help Define the Marketing Initiatives in the Originating Document

Most marketing organizations have a single document from which all of the other marketing materials come. This is called the *originating document*. The document specifies key points about the product, such as

- Promise
- Price
- Positioning statement
- Anticipated ship date
- Unique appeal
- Style and genre
- Product overview
- Key features
- Strengths
- Weaknesses
- Opportunities
- Threats

The purpose of the originating document is to clarify the most effective message to put forth to the consumer.

Recently, Lionhead Studios and Microsoft's Xbox shipped a product called *Fable*. The game's key feature was the ability to evolve the character in a good or evil direction, and every choice the player made contributed to the character's development. The marketing materials for the game employed a consistent positioning statement as a key part of the marketing campaign. It was "*For every choice, a consequence. Imagine a world where every choice and action determines what you become.*" The same message was communicated in the various types of ads; these helped the consumer make the connection back to the choices the player character faced throughout the game.

Ensuring the continuity of your message beginning to end is a critical part of any successful marketing campaign. By working to define the message with your brand manager at an early stage of the project, you maximize the chances of having an effective marketing campaign.

Discuss with your brand manager what each of your game's defining elements are and make sure that you're in agreement on these at an early stage of the game's development—preferably in the pre-production phase. Include the game's theme in the originating document so that it is readily accessible to anyone from Marketing who is working on a piece of the campaign.

Outline Clear Goals

Being the *best* FPS on the market is a different goal from being the *best-selling* FPS game. A game can be of great quality and get great reviews, but it still may not be the best-selling title in the genre. Be sure to identify to Marketing the goal of your game, the key points on which the product is going to go beyond what the competition has done, and the ways in which it will differ from similar games.

On the other hand, the Marketing team's goal could be to fill a revenue deficiency in a certain quarter, and if your game doesn't come out in that quarter, then their primary goal is not met. It is as important to be aware of Marketing's ultimate goal as it is to make them aware of your own.

Discuss with the brand manager other potential goals and how they impact a product. Are the goals of the product to be evolutionary or revolutionary? Is this a sequel product or an original title? These are just a few examples of the goals that need to be clearly defined.

Define Conflict Resolution Avenues

Conflict inevitably arises in business situations. The key to success is whether you resolve conflicts amicably and professionally. Your goal should be to always support your Marketing counterpart, to the extent that he can count on you to back him up in meetings with upper management or in front of his manager. But when there's a situation in which that's not possible, take the problem, as a team, to an intermediary who is objective and informed. Instead of escalating the problem up the chain of management, enlist the help of a respected peer to offer a new perspective, find a solution, and open up common ground.

Interview with Kirsten Duvall

Kirsten Duvall is former Brand Manager for EA Sports, Global Brand Manager for Activision.

Q: If you could convey to producer's everywhere, what is the one lesson or topic that you want to convey about how to be a better producer?

A: Consider your marketing counterpart as a partner. You need to understand that you both have a common goal—to develop and sell a successful game. In order to increase your chances of success, you must work together cooperatively with Marketing from the beginning of the development process. Agree on the vision for the product and understand exactly who your target market is. Continue this by working with Marketing when conducting research on a product or concept, as well as when doing competitive analyses.

Develop an understanding of the finances of your project—get acquainted with the P&L statement; make sure you understand what kind of financial impact your production decisions have. Understand how a game is sold into the channel in this industry and what is needed to create hype for a title.

Be aware of what assets Marketing may request from you and what they're used for—if you can work collaboratively with Marketing to provide the best assets for differing purposes in a timely manner, you may be able to take advantage of more marketing opportunities for your title.

Remember what your job is and what it isn't—let the Marketing department handle the Marketing of the game. For example, if you are asked for your thoughts on package design or advertising provide thoughtful, useful feedback but don't expect to be making the final decisions in these areas. Respect the expertise of others that you work with—it will be appreciated and likely reciprocated.

Q: What is the most important trait a producer can display in his or her interactions with Marketing?

A: Being a team player. Once again, a producer must understand that they are working on the same team as Marketing, working toward the same goal. There may be times when you disagree because you think you have different objectives. If that happens, then you both need to step back, take a look at the big picture and work together to get back on track to achieve the overall common objective.

(continued on next page)

Interview with Kirsten Duvall (continued)

Q: What are some common misconceptions about the role of the Marketing department at a video game publisher that you'd like to set straight?

A: One of the more common things I've seen is that Production doesn't believe that Marketing understands the production process. And in some cases, this is correct. Marketing must understand the production process and be familiar with games in order to work best with a Production team.

If a producer is in this situation (working with someone from Marketing who doesn't understand the process), I would recommend that they take it upon themselves to educate that person in order to increase effective communication. Make sure that your Marketing counterpart attends your production meetings so they can become familiar with the production process and be made aware of issues or challenges and how they must be handled by the production team. Play early builds of the game with Marketing and explain the technical or artistic terms and concepts that they may not understand—really seeing the visuals of the game and experiencing the gameplay will be much more effective than words alone.

On the other side, Marketing must work closely with the Production team in order to make sure that they understand what the process is for marketing and selling a game—how the game actually gets onto the retailer's shelves so that it can be purchased by gamers. There's a lot of work involved in getting product into retail.

Q: How have you best resolved disputes or disagreements between brand managers and producers?

A: Most disputes or disagreements are due to differing objectives. The main objective for both Marketing and Production should be the same—to develop and sell a successful game. Measurements of success (the success of the game) must be defined early in the development process and agreed to by both Marketing and Production. In addition to this, performance objectives for both Production and Marketing have to be aligned with the main objective.

For example, if Production is mainly concerned with building the highest quality game that they can build (because their performance is based on review scores of the game), they may be tempted to work on features much longer than the actual time allotted for development of those features. This can lead to the possibility of missing (or slipping) the ship date. If Marketing's performance is based on meeting forecasted sell-in numbers, meeting the original ship date is critical. Marketing may push the Production team to sacrifice quality or cut features in order to ship the game on time.

As you can imagine, this type of scenario can lead to many heated disputes because the different departments are not working toward a common goal.

Q: What overall role of importance do you place on the role of a producer with respect to marketing?

A: The producer or project manager is critical to the success of any project. First and foremost, they must be leaders, inspiring others to work together cooperatively to achieve the overall objective. They must be able to anticipate issues and roadblocks and work to overcome those challenges, while shielding the team from what they don't need to be involved in so that they can continue to work productively.

The producer must be able to build and maintain effective relationships with key partners in Marketing and with licensors, developers, and first-party publishers, to name just a few. The producer should also be the champion of the product itself, able to effectively promote the product externally and internally. And of course, an excellent producer must also be an excellent communicator.

Product Descriptions and Ad Copy

Packaging and ad creation are the responsibilities of the brand manager. However, the producer must be part of the process of developing the right packaging and forming the key messages to be conveyed in the packaging and ads. Provide concise messages regarding the features and benefits of the gameplay experience to the brand manager, so that he can include them in the advertising and packaging.

Remember that a producer does not have decision-making authority regarding packaging. The producer should review the packaging and ads at a few different points during the draft stages. Then take a look at the first pass and provide thoughtful comments. And finally, take one last look at the package or ad before it goes to film to confirm that all of the text is accurate—especially the system specifications, product ratings, licensor/licensee logos, and the requirements for shipping on a console.

By working hard to ensure that the product or brand manager has the right information from the very beginning of the process, you'll ensure that the review work will be easier and more efficient later in the process.

Public Relations and the Quest for Screenshots

Effective public relations campaigns are a critical part of an effective marketing campaign. Excellent screenshots are the backbone of the press tours, interviews, and gameplay descriptions as well as everything else. Screenshots are used in print articles, online articles, packaging, advertising, sell sheets, and various other promotional opportunities. Finding the right screenshot is every brand manager's quest, and they often can't complete their quest without the producer's help.

Why Are Screenshots So Important?

Screenshots are the Number One way to convey the status, character, and quality of a game. Be sure that the screenshots you see of your game in the marketing materials are ones that make you proud. Screenshots show to consumers, the press and the industry what the game is about and why it is fun.

Screenshots are important for promoting the product months—sometimes years—before it comes to market. Most press (with the exception of online press) requires assets well in advance of their publish or broadcast date. Screenshots for January's issue need to be provided in November or even late October. Exclusivity is also a requirement of some publications as they need a few screenshots that are exclusive content. In order to have several "exclusive" screenshots for each magazine, it is important that a wide variety of quality screenshots exist. Marketing must have a bank of screenshots that they can readily access at any point in the game's development and provide to the press.

How to Take Excellent Screenshots

The questions to ask yourself and pose to your team whenever providing screenshots to marketing are: "If you walked into a store and saw this screenshot on the back of the box, how would you feel?" and "How would you feel if you saw a cover of a magazine with that screenshot on it?"

Here are a few techniques for taking great screenshots.

- **Take them like a photographer**. Make sure they're framed with a central subject that's properly lit and framed. No one wants to see a jumbled action shot of explosions with no clearly identifiable main subject and theme. If there's an amateur photographer on the team, designate him or her to be the official screenshot taker.

- **Take them at a high resolution**. In any screenshot batch, make sure that a few of them are lossless images like TIF files at 1024×1280 resolution or higher. Magazine covers, box artwork, and full-page ads generally need to be shot at 3200×2400. Discuss the required screenshot resolution with the PR/Marketing team beforehand so that you'll know how many shots you need at the high resolutions.

- **Take 100 shots, throw out 90**. Taking screenshots is a skill, but picking screenshots is no less of a skill. A good photographer knows that out of 100 photos, only 10 will be worth publishing; apply this rule to screenshots as well.

- **Create a screenshot bank for the team**. When playing the game, each team member should be looking for cool angles, great gameplay action shots, and unique perspectives. Create a central location to which the team can copy good screenshots. By constantly taking screenshots, the team can create a virtual photo documentary of the game's progress. When the emergency PR opportunity comes up and there's a bank of screenshots to draw from, you'll be the very definition of a prepared producer.

Interviews and PR Training

There are a few rules to adhere to when it's your opportunity to talk to the press about the team's game. Don't go into the interview feeling either defensive or too confident of being well received. Reporters and other members of the press have their own opinions. By keeping your own messages in mind and preparing your statements for meeting with a reporter, you can influence the outcome of the story. The goal of any interview should be to meet the reporter's need to report on the news while getting your message across when the time comes.

If contacted by a reporter, never engage in an immediate interview. Tell the reporter you are busy at the moment, but emphasize that you want to respond as promptly as possible. Get the reporter's name, phone number, deadline, and a brief summary of what the reporter wants to know and pass that information along to your PR person.

caution

Never undertake an interview without preparation, rehearsal, and proofreading your answers. Get your PR person to go over each of these points with you before talking to any member of the media. By talking to the media without preparation you risk doing more harm than good. Imagine seeing an online article the next day that slams your product because you weren't sufficiently prepared to address a reporter's skeptical questions.

Prepare for any media contact by asking yourself "Why am I doing this interview?" Then, set a clear objective for yourself in the interview. Determine the key messages you want to get across and anticipate questions that will be difficult to answer and prepare for them.

Think about what your ideal quote on your message would be. Would you want to see it in print? This hit home for me after I was once quoted in the *San Francisco Chronicle* as saying, "There is a lot of negativity associated with *Myst*....", which was not exactly true. This was in answer to the reporter's question about the skepticism from fans at the time. A better answer would have been, "We're building on the strengths and minimizing the weaknesses with the next installment of the *Myst* series."

Practice saying quotes out loud and then memorize a few of the best quotes so that they flow naturally. Remember that the key messages on which you should be quoted must be what's most important to the reporter's readers, listeners, or viewers—not what is most important to you as the producer.

Develop good quotes by ensuring that

- They sound human, not robotic.
- There's potential to influence your audience by instilling confidence in the product.

- They are memorable.
- They are true.
- They are concise.

In order to maintain credibility, your key messages must be consistent. Here are a few good ways to ensure your answers remain credible.

- Insert your key messages as an answer to a question. If you get a question such as, "What's this game about?" you've got a great opportunity to insert all the key messages as your answer.
- You will be asked questions you don't want to answer, but don't evade them. Quickly answer the specific question, and then get back to your key messages by attaching a logical key message.
- If you don't know an answer, whatever you do, don't bluff. Respond with "I will find out," and do so quickly. And, above all, answer the tough questions truthfully. Explain why the situation got tough. Never say "No comment" without good reason—such as pending litigation or not wanting to disclose proprietary information.
- Speak in short sentences and don't use jargon the interviewer and audience aren't familiar with. Use anecdotes, comparisons, and examples. Backing up points with compelling statistics is a way to add strength to any point.
- Don't worry about repeating your key messages throughout the interview. By staying focused and repeating the key messages as often, the reporter and the audience are more likely to remember them.
- Prepare a short walkthough of the game. Reporters are busy people and if you're giving them a copy to review, make sure it is easy for them to get through the game. They just don't have time to play all the games they cover without a walkthrough.

When being interviewed, remember that the reporter's job is to tell a good story, not to damage your reputation and make you look like a fool. Nor is it to help make you or the product look good. Try not to be affected by charm, an aggressive demeanor, or apparent empathy with your point of view. Pay attention only to the content of the question and to making your points. Know that anything you say when a reporter is around is fair game to be quoted.

Production Presentation and Demo Scripts

Product presentations are critical opportunities for the presenter to establish himself as a leader committed to excellence and to demonstrate that the product is a shining example of the collective talent of the team. Every producer is called upon at some point to present the product to an internal audience or to an external audience and the media. In order to do so successfully, you should use a demo script.

Writing an Effective Demo Script

A *demo script* is the "script" of the presentation made for a product to the media. A good demo script begins with a good quote, some context, and some clear examples of the game's key features. Give the audience some perspective on what's being presented. If you don't have a good quote of your own, then quote someone else—Ansel Adams, George Patton, Aristotle, Plato, a business leader, or even a character from a film. But whatever the quote is, start off strong and follow up even stronger with an example that shows why the quote has relevance and perspective on the game. Get the audience emotionally connected to your message by establishing a familiar link and then moving in to support it. Remember that video games can and should be an emotional and passionate endeavor— we're conveying to players imagery, experience, emotion, and meaningful choices.

The demo script should address the following:

- Gameplay promise
- Key messages
- Features and benefits
- Points of opportunity

The details regarding ship date and minimum system specifications should be presented in the PR, Marketing, and Sales documents. If a producer is making this presentation, the audience wants to hear about the gameplay and the product's benefits and promise.

Presenting an Excellent Demo

There are a few tactical and practical elements required for an excellent demo presentation. Saved games and instantly loadable gameplay scenarios that show the benefits and key messages of the demo script are absolutely required. There's no way to be convincing when fumbling or struggling to show why a game is fun.

Be sure to have action, drama, and special effects ready to show the audience. Start the demo with a short gameplay or trailer clip, and then move right into the gameplay, showing each feature in action point-by-point.

Show that you're excited about what you're presenting and of course, make sure that the demo presentation has been tested on the specific hardware you'll be presenting it on!

The Downloadable Demo

The downloadable demo is another version of the game. Any time that another version of a game is created, it is important that that version is treated as if it were a separate product for release. Demos require just as much testing as the final game. Demos contain the engine on which the game is to be played, therefore, any defect that affects the security of the engine and the technology can affect the playability, security, and anti-piracy of the final game.

The downloadable demo must contain content that hooks the audience into the game in no more than one or two minutes. In other words, the demo should contain the small but very polished part of the game that is most contagious to the audience. The gameplay hook must draw the audience in and compel them to buy the game.

Previews and Strategy Guide Preparation

Almost every game these days has a strategy guide associated with its commercial release. As this ancillary product is a virtual inevitability for any game released, here are a few ways to ensure that the strategy guide for your game is complete, comprehensive, supportive, and easily completed without a headache.

- Have the design documentation ready and updated. Keep all of the design documentation in its own location in source control. Encourage updating by the design team throughout the development process. When it comes time to begin work on the strategy guide, burn the entire directory to CD and send it to the strategy guide publisher's office. They'll see to it that the author for your guide gets and reviews this information. Be sure that any such delivery includes maps of each level.

- A walkthrough needs to be done for the media and press anyway, so be sure that this walkthrough is concise and sufficient for any person who plays games for a living to get through the game in short order. They'll expand what they need to convey to the player the ancillary information.

- Each build delivered to any preview source or outside media representative should have the cheats and a build-specific readme.txt file containing the documentation relevant to that build. Updated builds are often required for the strategy guide, so be prepared to send several to the publisher while the guide is in production. If there's a screenshot feature built into the game, be sure that is included in the documentation on the build CD or DVD.

- Being available for questions is critical to ensuring that your game gets a good preview, has a complete strategy guide, and gets a fair shake at decent reviews. Whether via e-mail or telephone, be sure to respond to queries within one day.

- In the case of a derivative product, a timely review is of the essence to making that product equally successful as your game. Timely approval is the Number One reason why ancillary and derivative products don't make it to market on schedule with the game. This diminishes the value of the license fee, as well as the potential marketing cross-promotions between ancillary products. Be sure to reserve some time for reviewing and approving derivative products.

How Does a Strategy Guide Benefit a Game?

Following are some words of wisdom regarding game guides from Jill Hinkley, at Prima Publishing:

"Our guides, at 8 1/2" x 10 7/8" for console SKUs, have their box art plastered right on the front and are all over computer software stores. Plus, as people can flip through our guides but not really 'flip through' a game, our guides can help get people hyped about buying a game. The better looking and more information-packed the guides are, the better for the game.

Prima's goal is to flow with the game development process, not interrupt it. The top three things I will *always* ask for are a build, art assets (including something I can use to create a mock cover for sales), and a gameplay contact in case my author gets stuck. For the last request, we're always very careful to consolidate our questions and minimize the time we take out of our contact's day. We know game development is tough!"

The Final Word

The marketing and release of the game is the last step to ensuring that your efforts for the past many months are commercially rewarding, critically acclaimed, and industry recognized. Don't sabotage the work of a talented team by undervaluing or misunderstanding this critical process. To quote Kirsten Duvall:

By becoming familiar with the entire process of bringing a game to market—not only the production aspects, but operations, finance, sales and marketing, a producer is poised for success. The more you understand about the entire process and the more people you become good partners with in each of these disciplines, the better chances you have of becoming an excellent producer.

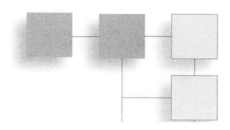

APPENDIX A

"Sample Acceptance Letter"

Milestone Checklist

Product and SKU: Skating or Dying for the PS2

Platform: PSX 2/IBM

Milestone #12   Date: September 11, 2010

Milestone Items:

Programming

- Game Build
- Music and Simple Sound effects
- Can Crash, physics in place
- AI Character in environment

Art

- 101 additional Selection Screen Animations
- 40 Object Animations
- 1 additional 3D track Layout (8 total)
- 1 Selection Screen background done (2 total)
- UI Screen Elements

Audio

- 3 additional tunes
- 101 Sound Effects

Comments Regarding Programming

Game Build   ☒ **Accepted**   ☐ **Not Accepted**

The trick package has evolved further in this build. Base scoring is now complete, not including the Groove special mode. All tricks are in with at least a placeholder animation. Each character only has four of the advanced and one of the super moves possible, as designed. (These moves are character-specific.) Our feeling with the tricks in general is that they are still too difficult to execute. Controls are touchy; we have the feeling at this stage in the build that the difficulty lies, not in the amount of time you have left in-air to execute the move, but in precise controller manipulation. We are looking for trick execution that is easier to pull off.

We also feel the air control and gravity are still set way too high. Characters can get an immense amount of air, and take a long time coming down. We would like to see lower altitudes and quicker descent. We understand these aspects of the physics part of the engine were set high to test grinding; however, we think it is time to start tuning the physics so that we may begin to look at playtest/challenges.

The challenge package is working fine. A suggestion we have on the waypoint mode is to make a messenger run out of it (for example, the user has to go to the movie house to deliver a note and from the movie house to the grocery store). The idea is to make a mission that is similar to paperboy or crazy taxi, where the player gets time extensions for dropping off packages, etc. Another variation would be to extend time for multiple combos—some of which could only be pulled off in certain areas of the levels. This would encourage exploration and experimentation.

Music and Simple Sound Effects   ☒ **Accepted**   ☐ **Not Accepted**   285

This build has some non-looping sound effects (ollie, impact, bouncing board, character saying "woo-hoo" when a successful trick is landed, etc.) Placeholder music for each playable character is in place (see note below under audio regarding music tracks).

Can Crash, Physics in Place   ☒ **Accepted**   ☐ **Not Accepted**

Skater bails when s/he lands perpendicular to surface. The crashes are closer to reality, but characters can still land successfully in particular situations. We would like to see this improved to final in two more milestones.

AI Character in Environment   ☒ **Accepted**   ☐ **Not Accepted**

The game chooses between several AI rails to run the opponent along, one of which is generated from player runs (that is, whenever you skate, your path is stored in a rail database which can be used against you by the AI during a later run).

Comments Regarding Art
101 additional Selection Screen

Animations/UI Screen Elements ☒ Accepted   ☐ Not Accepted

General: Most of these animations (including previous deliveries) show the characters as being left handed. Some of the characters should be mirrored before using them in the game in order to vary the 'handedness' of the characters.

Additionally, we would like a printout or list of the circumstances in which the following files would be used. Many of the minor comments below would be addressable during review if we had a list of what we are supposed to be looking for. Also, we would like to start seeing some of the skins on the animations.

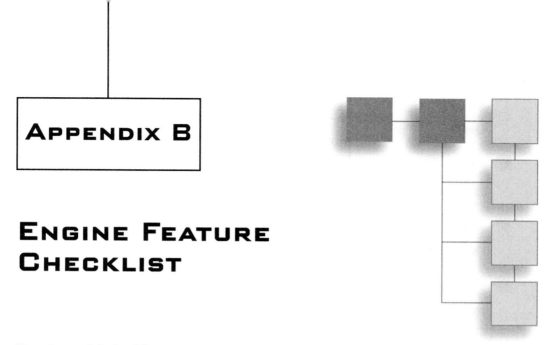

APPENDIX B

ENGINE FEATURE CHECKLIST

Here is a quick checklist to use to determine what is included in the game.

Supported APIs

- OpenGL
- DirectX

Graphics Engine

- **Geometry**. How is terrain represented? How are objects in the world represented? Are curved surfaces supported?
- **Textures**. What features beyond plain texture mapping, such as mip-mapping and environment maps, are supported?
- **Lighting**. Does the game use light maps? Does it support hardware T&L? What types of lights are possible (point lights, directional lights, or spotlights)? What special lighting effects are possible?
- **Dynamic level of detail**. Is it supported? If so, how?
- **Special effects**. Volumetric fog, particle systems, reflective surfaces, geometry deformation behind heat sources

Sound Engine

- **Sound Effects**. How many voices are supported? Of what quality?
- **Music**. How is music stored? What quality is supported?
- **3D Sound**. What (if any) formats are supported?

User Interface

- What input devices are supported? Keyboard? Mouse? Joystick? Gamepad?
- What user actions are supported? What navigation modes are possible?
- What keys correspond to each action?
- Do keys change function depending on the situation?

Dynamics (Physics) Engine

- How is collision detection handled?
- What objects are affected by physics?
- What physics effects are included? Gravity? Kinetics? Cloth dynamics?

Scripting System

- What sort of scripting system will be included?
- What sort of events will be scriptable and what must be hard-coded?
- What actions can trigger scripts? Clicking? Stepping into a certain location? More complicated conditions?
- What tools will be used to define scripts?

World Building

- What tools will be used to define world geometry?
- What tools will be used to place Non-Player Characters (NPCs) PCs and other game elements?
- Which tools are to be written in-house?

Creature Modeling and Animation

- How are creatures represented? Predefined models (like *Quake*)? Skinned skeletons (like *Half-Life*)?
- How are creatures animated? By hand? Motion capture?
- What is the format of animation sequences? Predefined routines? Procedural character actions?
- Animation Special Effects: inverse kinematics, real time speech, etc.

Object Animation

- What objects in the world can move?
- How is object movement in the world defined? Do they move on paths? Are they controlled by AI routines?
- Can users control objects (such as by dragging)?
- How do the Special Effects work? Are they objects animating relative to other objects, or objects controlled by particle systems, or even real time terrain modification? Do they use particle effects or dynamic lighting?

Artificial Intelligence

- What actions can NPCs perform?
- How does the user interact with NPCs? Special interaction devices? By clicking on them? By bumping into them?
- How are NPC actions determined? Finite state machines or more generalized AI systems?
- What game elements influence generalized AI systems?

Optimization

- **Geometry reduction**. Does the engine support frustum culling? Occlusion culling?
- **Memory handling**. Use geometry and texture caching to reduce load times? To what extent?

Menu System

On-screen, anti-aliased text? Does it conform to localization guidelines?

Game Configuration System

- What options can users set?

Other

Talk to your technical director or lead programmer.

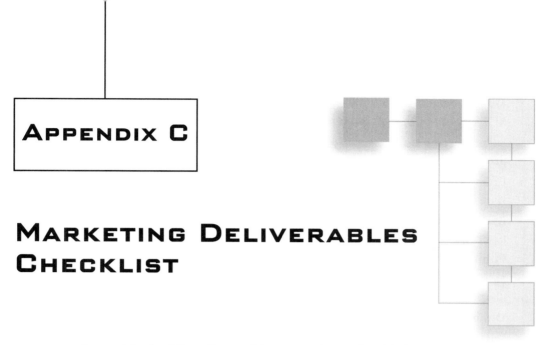

APPENDIX C

MARKETING DELIVERABLES CHECKLIST

Here's a quick checklist of everything a producer should discuss with his or her brand or product manager and work into the development schedule. Since every project is different, I've not included timelines next to each of these items. But a discussion with the brand manager about when this stuff is needed should clear that right up.

- **Final logo creation / Brand development**. Production should make sure that the logo works in the game and with the UI.
- **Monthly screenshot delivery**. Deliver a set number of screenshots to Marketing and PR every month so that they have a "bank" to work from.
- **Press release**. This announces the product to the world.
- **E3 corporate CD**. If your company creates a CD with all of their product information on it, you'll want to be sure you have something on this CD.
- **Magazine previews**. Several months prior to commercial release. Remember that magazine lead times are several months.
- **Web launch**. Web-ready art assets are always required.
- **Ad shots**. High-resolution shots for print advertising.
- **Box shots**. These are the money shots.
- **Builds**. Preview and review builds are required at a minimum, but monthly builds for Marketing to become familiar with the game are also good.
- **GDC**. What materials are you going to show at the Game Developer's Conference?
- **E3**. The annual Electronic Entertainment Expo always requires a demo if your product is announced. Be sure that you have the right PR materials available.
- **Toyfair**. Early in the year in New York City.

- **Tokyo Game Show.** Held in spring in Tokyo.
- **ECTS.** Held in the fall in London.
- **Sales Meeting Build.** The sales force has a meeting every quarter. Be sure your product gets some attention by providing a build and a demonstrator if required.
- **Press preview.** Beta, pre-release version which is released to the press so they can start on their reviews.
- **ESRB.** Not a special build for rating purposes, but nevertheless, it must be done prior to manufacturing.
- **Public "Marketing" beta.** For building community hype.
- **Non-interactive demos.** In-game movies using the engine for magazines and for downloads.
- **Design Document and Feature Lists.** Special versions or Marketing.
- **Special or custom artwork.** Such as sketches, dated and signed concept art, and renders.
- **Feature List and Product Description.** Work with Marketing to ensure that the description is accurate.
- **Character photo and/or 3D render.** This should be a central image and theme of the marketing campaign.
- **Walk-though, cheats, and/or saved games.** For editors and for the strategy guide author.
- **SoundTrack CD.** There's money to be made in music.
- **Gameplay movie captures in AVI format.** Gameplay or renders.
- **ESRB walk-through, cheats, and so on.**
- **High-res art and special renders.** For magazines.
- **Animated GIFS.** For online use.
- **Behind-the-scenes interviews, video footage, photos, and documentary-style footage.** These are all materials that can help your product gain the right exposure.
- **Editor Days.** When groups of editors, reviewers and the press come to look at the game. At the least a spokesperson and demonstrator are needed to show the game off.
- **Spokesperson and demonstrator.** For E3, international press tour, and domestic press tour.
- **Questions and Answers document.** For anyone speaking with the press.
- **Movie trailer/Promo video.** Available for download on a Web site, in theater promotions, or TV advertising.

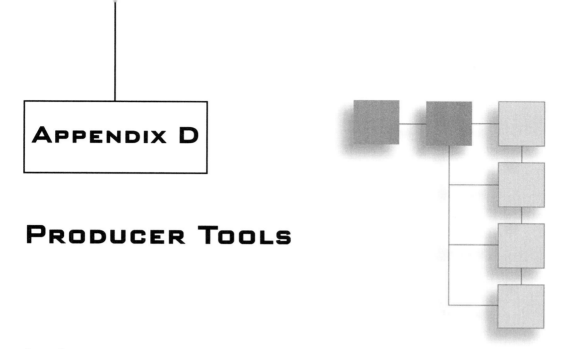

APPENDIX D

PRODUCER TOOLS

This appendix includes several tools that can help a video game producer in his or her daily routine.

- The Milestone Acceptance Test
- The Milestone Submission Checklist
- The Art Status Sheet
- The Sound Status Sheet
- Risk Management Plan

Milestone Acceptance Test
Project: Project X
Milestone Due Date: January 2006
Developer:

	Screenshot Filename	Verified by (NAME)	Required by Design Specs (Y/N)	Notes
Notes on how to use this MAT :				
Receive and review milestone submission				
Screenshot filenames are found on D:\XXX of the CD provided.				
Verified by refers to Client employee who verifies the work submitted (art asset, gameplay feature, screenshot or music/sound).				
Required by Design Specification? Refers to the asset's existence in the design spec.				Completed & Reviewed = Publisher has Approved this item
Notes is a separate section containing any additional comments required for a particular item.				Completed = It is ready for Publisher to review
Prototype Submissions Checklist tab contains a list of all required material to meet the Milestone.				Blank field = it is still being worked on.
Music & Sound tab contains a list of required audio assets for the Milestone.				
Design Production				
USER INTERFACE	Please see the following in-game.			
GENERIC				
Mouse Cursor				
FRONT-END			Y	
Intro Screen				
Icons			Y	
IN-GAME			Y	
Icons			Y	
HUD			Y	
DOCUMENTATION				
PRODUCTION				
Project File			Y	
DESIGN	Please find these documents in the Documents folder on the Assets CD provided.			
Party_Systems.doc	Documents Delivered on CD		Y	Completed
Back_Story.doc	Documents Delivered on CD		Y	Completed
Back_Story_FAQ.doc	Documents Delivered on CD		Y	Completed
Character_Development.doc	Documents Delivered on CD		Y	Completed
Character_Actions.doc	Documents Delivered on CD		Y	Completed
Character_Skills.doc	Documents Delivered on CD		Y	Completed
Combat.doc	Documents Delivered on CD		Y	Completed
Art Production				
Asset Creation (Original Specification)				
Battlements & stairway	CD/Root/Art Assets [FILENAME]		Y	
7th Century building 1	CD/Root/Art Assets [FILENAME]		Y	
7th Century building 2	CD/Root/Art Assets [FILENAME]	Publisher Rep 1	N	Unable to locate tree
Tree 1	CD/Root/Art Assets [FILENAME]		Y	
Tree 2	CD/Root/Art Assets [FILENAME]		Y	
Assorted rocks & other elements	CD/Root/Art Assets [FILENAME]		Y	
Grass & paths	CD/Root/Art Assets [FILENAME]		Y	
Ghost	CD/Root/Art Assets [FILENAME]		Y	
Male warrior	CD/Root/Art Assets [FILENAME]		Y	
Female warrior	CD/Root/Art Assets [FILENAME]		Y	

MILESTONE 1 SUBMISSION CHECKLIST
(Milestone Definition Below)

	Responsibility	Status	Filename
Build of the Game of CD-R Media, clearly labelled w/ autorun.ini	Lead Programmer		
Art Asset CD	Art Director		
Build Notes	Asst. Producer		
Instruction on how to demo the game	QA Lead, Asst. Producer	Incomplete	
Troubleshooting	QA Lead		
Executive Summary	Producer		
Project Schedule			
Part A			
Production Methodology	Producer	Complete	W:\Doc\Prc
Team Org Chart/ Roles & Responsibilities	Asst. Producer	Complete	W:\Doc\Ad
Gantt Chart	Producer	Complete	Presentati(
Risk Assessment Matrix	Producer	Complete	Risk Manaç
Post Release Services		Complete	W:\Doc\Ad
Part B			
Budget	Producer		
Change Order Proposal	Producer		
Creative Design Documentation			
High Concept	Producer, Associate Producer	Complete	W:\Doc
Background Story, including synopsis and summary	Associate Producer	Complete	W:\Doc
Gameplay Design Chapters by System	Associate Producer		
Gameplay Design Features List (by priority)	Associate Producer		
Art Production Guidelines			
Style Description	Art Director		
Art Pipeline Description	Art Director		
Comps and Special Renders	Art Director		
Music and Sound FX Treatment	Producer	Complete	
Sell Sheet	Art Director/T. Carter		
Movie Poster	Art Director		
CD Cover Artwork	Art Director		
Technical Design Documentation			
Engine Feature Summary List	Lead Programmer		
Server Side Technology Discussion	Lead Programmer		
For Milestone 2			
Engine Key Feature Description	*Lead Programmer*		
Detailed Description of Included Features	*Lead Programmer*		
Toolset Description	*Lead Programmer*		

Assets to Escrow
Be sure to send any milestone delivery to an offsite escrow service
including source code backups so that if the building burns down, the
work is not lost. This is part of a disaster recovery plan.

ART STATUS Tracking Sheet

CLASS	NAME	DES	artist (initials)	Days to complete est	3D Model MOD	3D Model artist	3D Model est	Texturing TEX	Texturing artist	Texturing est	Animation ANI	Damage Animation DAM ANI	Level of Detail LOD	Optimize RE-TEX / OPT	FINISHED! CLOSED
Bad Guys	SCOUT	X	AK	na	X	DC	1		DC	4					
Bad Guys	FIGHTER		DC	3		DC	1		DC	8					
Bad Guys	MARTIAL ARTIST1		DC	2		DC	1		DC	6					
Bad Guys	MARTIAL ARTIST2	X	AK	na	X	na	na	X	na	na					
Bad Guys	MARTIAL ARTIST3	X	AK	na	X	AD	1		AD	3					
Bad Guys	MARTIAL ARTIST4		DC	2		AD	1		AD	4					
Bad Guys	MARTIAL ARTIST5														
Bad Guys	KUNG FU GUY	X	AK	na	X	na	na	X	na	na					
Bad Guys	KUNG FU GUY	X	AK	na		DC	3		DC	8					
Bad Guys	KUNG FU GUY	X	AK	na		DC	2		DC	4					
Bad Guys	KUNG FU GUY	X	DC	na		DC	2		DC	4					
Bad Guys	SUPPORTING CHARACTE[R]	X	DC	1		DC	2		DC	4					
Bad Guys	MAGIC GUY		DC	3		DC	2		DC	4					
Bad Guys	SPECIAL MAGIC GUY														
Bad Guys			DC	5		AD	4		AD	11					
Bad Guys	Small but Deadly		AK	na		AD	2		AD	2					
Bad Guys	Big Big Bad Guy	X	AK	na		AD	2		AD	6					
Bad Guys	Big Big Bad Guy	X													
Bad Guys			DC	5		DC	2		DC	3					
Bad Guys	Other Bad Guys 1	X	AK	na	X	DC	2		DC	3					
Bad Guys	Other Bad Guys 2		RC	5		DC	5		DC	16					
Bad Guys	Other Bad Guys 3														
Bad Guys			DC	1		DC	1		DC	2	na	na			
Bad Guys	Major NPC	X	AK	na	X	DC	1		DC	2					
Bad Guys	Major NPC	X	AK	na	X	DC	1		DC	2	na	na			
Bad Guys	Major NPC	X	AK	na	X	DC	1		DC	2					
Bad Guys	Major NPC	X	AK	22		DC	2		DC	3					
Bad Guys	Major NPC	X	AK	5		DC	3		DC	4					

SOUND CONTENT CHECKLIST

ART ASSET		SOUND CONTENT				Amb + Ambient SFX					SP + Single Player Action				AN + Animation					DAM+Damage/Fighting			
Character Class	NAME	V1 SFX	V2 SFX	FINAL	Sound Effect HOOK up	Directory	AMB V1	AMB V2	AMB Final	AMB HOOK	AMB DIR	SP ACTION v1	SP ACTION v2	SP ACTION FINAL	SP ACTION HOOK	SP ACTION DIR	AN v1	AN v2	AN FINAL	AN HOOK	AN DIR	DAM AN v1	DAM AN v2	DAM AN FINAL	DAM AN HOOK

Risk Management Plan Procedures

STEPS

1	**Hold a Risk Management Identification meeting** Phase 1: Conduct a brain-storming meeting to list every possible project risk All the leads should be involved: Programming, Art, Sound, Producer, etc. During this phase of the brain-storming meeting - do not try to qualify or quantify any of the risks Finish this step by completing a list of project risks. Risks such as *technology foundation,* *scope of game, game ship date, resource requirement, expertise and experience of the team* *localization, testing, or even console development system availablility.*

2	**Phase 2 of the Risk Management Identification meeting** During this phase - qualify and quantify each risk that has been identified. Qualify = Probability: Judge for each risk what is the chance that it will occur. Quantify = Impact: Judge for each risk what is the impact to the project if the risk occurs. Use a scale from 0% through 100% with intervals of 20% Scale: Lowest 0 20 40 60 80 100 Highest Calculate the PI (Probability/Impact) factor by multiplying the two numbers *Example: P=.6 I=.6 PI=.36* *Example: P=.8 I=1 PI=.80*

3	**Determine the levels for the PI Matrix** (refer to the PI Matrix worksheet)
	You can skew the matrix to be more or less sensitive to risks by altering the scale.
	The scale can be altered may ways, such as:
	  any risk above 50% is considered high risk (red zone)
	  OR
	  multiply either the probability or impact factors by a number to increase the weight of the factor
	  example: *P=.6 I=.6 but company is very sensitive to impact factors - so weight(w)=2*
	  *PI= P * (I * W) PI= .6 * (.6 * 2) PI= .6 * 1.2 PI=.72*

4	**Build a Risk Assessment Plan** (refer to the Risk Assessment Plan worksheet) List all of the Risks, sorted by PI factors, rated by the PI Matrix

5	**Define a specific plan for each risk** (refer to the Specific Plan worksheet for an example) Who owns the risk? How will the risk be mitigated?

***This sheet courtesy of Rich Robinson*

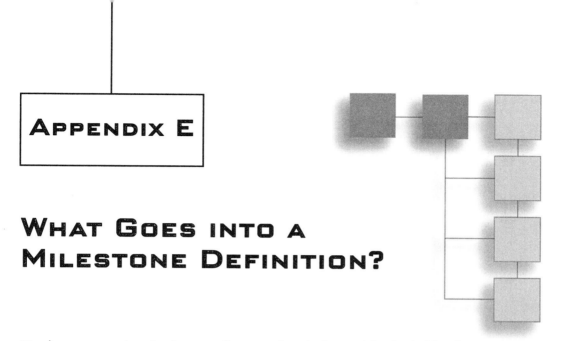

APPENDIX E

WHAT GOES INTO A MILESTONE DEFINITION?

Here's an example of what a milestone description might look like for an action-adventure game based upon a hypothetical license called *AdventureX*.

Sample Milestone List for AdventureX

COMPLETION DATE	MILESTONE DESCRIPTION
4/2111	**Proof of Concept Work for Hire**
	Contract execution
5/08/11	**XYZ Puzzle Design**

This includes the design of the main overarching game element, which depends upon elements from X-man's Prison World and included levels, the Electric World, and the Waterfall World. The deliverable includes the design of the XYZ game element using the Puzzle Template (as Defined in Schedule H), including a "golden path" section to insure all elements are complete. It describes game element mechanics in detail and includes explicit descriptions of what elements from other worlds and levels are required to solve the game element. Concept sketches are included to clarify the operation of any complex game element elements.

6/06/11   **Level 1 Textured**

This includes the geometry for the Wild Earth running in the engine for display purposes as a user controlled flyby. This will now have texturing. There will be no collisions, lighting, game elements, or gameplay. The Wild Earth Textured will not run at full speed.

7/10/11   **Puzzle Design for Waterfall and Electric Worlds**

For the Waterfall World and Electric World and included levels, this includes a written overview of the historical perspective of the World and included levels—what its purpose is in the AdventureX universe, what its basic rules are, who wrote it, why, and when. This deliverable describes the game elements that a player must solve at the same level of detail as a Strategy Guide Notes book, including identifying the game element elements and describing each in a similar Strategy Guide Notes style. It includes enough information so that readers know all the pieces of the big picture, but does not include walkthroughs or complete designs. No brainstorming notes are submitted, only recommended game element concepts. Concept sketches that give a feel for the overall theme of the World and included levels are included, as well as brief descriptions of important environmental effects of the World and included levels.

8/11/11   **First Playable and completion of remaining World and included Levels. Puzzle designs and Engine Elements List**

First Playable includes The Wild Earth running in the game engine, including lighting, collisions, and gameplay, including all age game elements completed and in, asset complete and testable. This will include one biped character walking and performing one action. The character will not have final textures, geometry, or movement. It will not run at full speed. This playable may include major bugs (e.g. crash bugs) and you may not be able to play the World and included levels from start to finish.

Remaining Puzzle Designs: For Y-Man's World, this includes a written overview of the historical perspective of the World and included levels— what its purpose is in the AdventureX universe, what its basic rules are, who wrote it, why, and when. This deliverable is specific about game element elements, describing the game elements that a player must solve at the same level of detail as a Strategy Guide Notes book, including enough information so that readers know all the pieces of the big picture, but not including walkthroughs or complete designs. No brainstorming notes are submitted, only recommended game element concepts. Concept sketches that give a feel for the overall theme of the World and levels are included, as well as brief descriptions of important environmental effects of the World and included levels. The design should also highlight any use of real-time 3D elements.

Also included will be information on any final design modifications to the Wild Earth World, as well as the following general points related to overall game story:

- A definition of story progression within the game, including a diagram of how the user progresses through the World and included levels of the game. A description of the overarching game elements of the game and specifically what elements are required from other areas of the game to solve them.

- An account of the events of the game formatted as a player discovery chart. This describes what happens, in what order, and what the user learns from each event. Where possible, character motivations and thought processes will be provided.

- In places where the game branches, acknowledgment that a branch is possible; then we will follow each branch one after the other. If necessary, include a flowchart showing all possible story and gameplay branches.

- A description of the story function of each World and included levels. This describes the plot points that players will definitely learn during the World and included levels and how they will learn them. It describes possible details and clues players may note if they are observant, final lists of which will appear in the Detailed World and included levels Designs. It refers readers to appropriate World and included levels Overviews for additional details, and considers which plot points are communicated by game elements, the XYZ game element in particular.

Engine Elements List Updated and Included

9/19/11   **X-Man's World and included levels Geometry, the Waterfall World and Included levels Detailed Design**

X-Man's World and included levels Geometry includes the geometry for the X-Man's World and included levels running in the engine for architectural purposes only as a user controlled flyby. This allows viewing the geometry of the World and included levels in the engine. It will have preliminary texturing only, and there will be no collisions, lighting, game elements, or gameplay. X-Man's World and included levels Geometry will not run at full speed.

The Waterfall World and included levels Detailed Design. This is a complete design of the Waterfall World and included levels. If the World and included levels Overview is the Strategy Guide Notes version, this is the book. Every element is described in detail and their relations to each other explained. Major game elements that significantly advance story or game play are completed using the Game Elements Template provided.

10/3/11   **Menus, Options, and Resource Prediction**

This includes a version of the engine running a sample game area and will include game menus, options screens, and resource prediction for the area. A list of all the menus and features will be included. Resource prediction is a programming technique in which the code predicts where the game player may travel soon and attempts to pre-load those areas to smooth display. All artwork for menus and options will be present. This will not run at full speed.

Electric World and included levels Detailed Design: This is the same for this World and included levels as for the Waterfall World and included levels Detailed Design, listed under the 9/19/11 Milestone: X-Man's World and included levels Geometry, the Waterfall World and included levels Detailed Design, and Engine Elements List.

10/24/11   **X-Man's World and included levels Textured; Y-Man's Prison World and X-Man's World and included levels**

Textured includes the geometry for X-Man's' World and included levels running in the engine for display purposes as a user controlled flyby. Textures are applied to all geometry. There will be no collisions, lighting, game elements, or game play. X-Man's World and included levels will not run at full speed.

Y-Man's World and included levels Detailed Design: This is the same for this World and included levels as for the Waterfall World and included levels Detailed Design, listed under the 9/19/11 Milestone: X-Man's World and included levels Geometry, the Waterfall World and included levels Detailed Design, and Engine Elements List. This is the final World and included levels to be designed.

11/08/11   **Characters (Geometry and Textured)**

All game characters and NPCs for the PC version will be completed and textured (skinned). These will be external to the game engine.

12/12/11   **X-Man's World and included levels Playable, the Waterfall World and included levels Geometry, First Playable with NPCs, Final Design Documentation**

X-Man's World and included levels Playable

This includes X-Man's' World and included levels running in the game engine, including lighting, collisions, and game play, including all age game elements which are asset complete and play testable. This will not run at full speed and will not include any NPCs or NPC interactions. X-Man's World and included levels Playable may include major bugs (*e.g.* crash bugs) and you may not be able to play the World and included levels from start to finish.

The Waterfall World and included levels Geometry

This includes the geometry for the Waterfall World and included levels running in the engine for architectural purposes only as a user-controlled flyby. This allows viewing the geometry of the World and included levels in the engine. It will have preliminary texturing only. There will be no collisions, lighting, game elements, or game play. The Waterfall World and included levels Geometry will not run at full speed.

First Playable With NPCs

The First Playable will be updated to include The Wild Earth's NPCs. NPC animations for The Wild Earth will be complete except for those dependent upon final voice.

Final Design Documentation

This includes editing of the Design Document to reflect any changes agreed upon during reviews of previous Puzzle or World and included levels submissions. Also included for review is all Game Dialog. Finally, the Final Design Documentation contains any updates necessary to the Engine Elements List as well as the full Technical Design in support of all planned game features.

1/16/11   **The Waterfall World and included levels Textured**

The Waterfall World and included levels textured, including the geometry for the Waterfall World and included levels running in the engine for display purposes as a user controlled flyby. There will be no collisions, lighting, game elements, or gameplay. The Waterfall World and included levels Textured will not run at full speed.

2/27/11   **The Waterfall World and included levels Playable; X-Man's World and included levels Playable Update**

This includes the Waterfall World and included levels running in the game engine, including lighting, collisions, and game play, including all age game elements that are asset-complete and fully play testable. It will not run at full speed. This will not include any NPCs or NPC interactions. The Waterfall World and included levels Playable may include major bugs (*e.g.* crash bugs) and you may not be able to play the World and included levels from start to finish.

The X-Man's World and included levels Playable will be updated to include its NPCs. NPC animations for X-Mans' World and included levels will be complete except for those dependant upon the final voice-over recordings.

4/17/11   **Electric World and included levels Geometry; NPC Cinematics. The Waterfall World and included levels Playable Update, Text Lock Down.**

This includes the geometry for the Electric World and included levels running in the engine for architectural purposes only as a user-controlled flyby. This allows viewing the geometry of the World and included levels in the engine. It will have preliminary texturing only. There will be no collisions, lighting, game elements, or gameplay. Electric World and included levels Geometry will not run at full speed.

The Waterfall World and included levels Playable will be updated to include its NPCs. NPC animations for the Waterfall World and included levels will be complete except for those dependant upon final voice.

All NPC cinematics will be available for viewing. Not all NPC cinematics will be in the engine, and some or all of the NPC cinematics will be available in AVI form.

Text Lock Down includes all game text finalized. All game text includes cinematic dialog, character dialog, in-game text, menus, screens, books, diaries, embedded art, and voiceovers. All final voice and text is delivered for translation.

4/30/11   **E3 Presentation**

This includes a cinematic or demo which will be used to promote the product at Electronics Entertainment Expo. The cinematic or demo will include animation sequences of a polygonal character which may or may not be used for the actual game itself. The above cinematic or demo will be provided in QuickTime format.

5/08/11   **Electric World and included levels Textured**

This includes the geometry for the Electric World and included levels running in the engine for display purposes as a user controlled flyby. This will now have texturing. There will be no collisions, lighting, game elements, or gameplay. Electric World and included levels Textured will not run at full speed.

6/12/11   **Pre-Alpha; Y-Man's World and included levels Geometry**

Pre-Alpha includes all major modules of the game running, though those modules may not run at final speed or use final data. World and included levels s playable will be all previous playables plus the Electric World and included levels running in the game engine, including lighting, collisions, and game play. This will include NPCs and NPC interactions. This will not run at full speed. The Pre Alpha may include major bugs (*e.g.* crash bugs) and you may not be able to play a World and included levels from start to finish. At this stage, the final World and included levels, Y-Man's World and included levels, will be running in the game engine for display purposes only as a user controlled flyby. This allows viewing the geometry of the World and included levels in the engine. It will have preliminary texturing only. There will be no collisions, lighting, game elements, or game play.

7/10/11	**Alpha; Final Cinematic**

All of the game's major components will be in place although not at final speed or with final data. World and included levelss playable will be all previous playables plus Y-Man's World and included levels running in the game engine, including lighting, collisions, and gameplay, including all age game elements which are asset complete and fully play testable. This will include NPCs and NPC interactions. The game will still have major bugs (e.g. crash bugs). All World and included levels will be playable, although bugs may prevent playing any particular World and included levels from start to finish without resorting to cheats. NPC cinematics will be integrated and the game interfaces will be functional. Bug testing must be fully operational at this point. Any visual or audio changes need to be made during this phase of testing.

The Final Cinematic will be available but may not be implemented in the engine. It will be available in AVI form.

8/7/11	**Beta**

Beta consists of all of the game's major components in place and running with final speed and data. The game will still have bugs, but major bugs impeding player progression in the game will have been addressed. All World and included levels are playable from start to finish on at least one game-play path. Bug testing continues focusing on play balance and final changes. All assets are frozen and will not be changed. Game will run on minimum system requirements. All controllers work. Game runs on final media. Final audio is included. A complete manual is available.

Beta includes translation, text and voice, of the game into the following foreign languages: French, German, Dutch, Italian, and Spanish. Foreign language translations, text and voice, will be supplied by the Publisher three (3) weeks prior to the milestone.

9/18/11	**Gold—Final Version of the game for manufacturing. Refer to definition of Final Acceptance.**

10/4/11	**Source Code**
	Delivery of Source Code

ON GOING   **Additional development expenses incurred by Publisher in con-
                    nection with an original musical composition, voiceover recording
                    fees, including talent and director fees**

TOTAL PAYMENT   **$Millions!**

                    Each of the foregoing milestone payments shall be payable after
                    Publisher's acceptance of an acceptable Deliverable.

INDEX

Gamedev.net

The most comprehensive game development resource

- The latest news in game development
- The most active forums and chatrooms anywhere, with insights and tips from experienced game developers
- Links to thousands of additional game development resources
- Thorough book and product reviews
- Over 1,000 game development articles!
  Game design
  Graphics
  DirectX
  OpenGL
  AI
  Art
  Music
  Physics
  Source Code
  Sound
  Assembly
  And More!

Gamedev.net